STUDENT ACTIVITIES IN THE INNOVATIVE SCHOOL

by

JERRY H. ROBBINS
STIRLING B. WILLIAMS, Jr.

School of Education
The University of Mississippi
University, Mississippi

With an introduction by R. K. Bent

Burgess Publishing Company

426 South Sixth Street • Minneapolis, Minn. 55415

Consulting Editor to the Publisher

LEO E. EASTMAN, Head
Department of Education
Illinois State University
Normal, Illinois 61761

PREFACE

As an important element of American education, student activities have undergone many changes during their development. The student activities program provides valuable educational experiences which reach far beyond the confines of the formal curriculum. By a program of student activities we mean the numerous nationally known student organizations, as well as any individual student club that has existed for any length of time.

To implement a student activities program, a number of questions must be answered:

What is a student activity?

Who is involved?

Why should there be a student activities program?

What resources must be allocated for a successful program?

These questions are not new. But the educational program of today requires new answers. Thus, we will concentrate on the innovative high school and its approaches to these answers.

Since no school should rigidly reproduce any other school's student activities program, this text is intended as a guide for further work by sponsors, administrators, and secondary school students in developing an exemplary student activities program in individual schools.

In connection with this book, a number of schools known to be innovative in some aspect of their program were surveyed. Our thanks go to the administrators, whose names and schools appear in Appendix A, for their cooperation in the survey.

We are also indebted to all those whose special interests and abilities made this book possible.

Special acknowledgment goes to Dr. R. K. Bent, a noted author himself and Robbins' former teacher, for his Introduction to this work.

In particular, we are indebted to Mrs. Roberta Ann Bowers who typed the final manuscript in the midst of the chaos of other work and responsibilities.

Jerry H. Robbins
Stirling B. Williams, Jr.

The University of Mississippi
University, Mississippi
January, 1969

ACKNOWLEDGMENTS

We are grateful to the following authors and publishers for permission to quote from the following:

Bennett, Fred A. "A Letter to New Faculty Advisers," *School Activities,* 26:13, September, 1954. Reprinted by permission of School Activities.

Boles, Harold W. *Step By Step to Better School Facilities.* New York: Holt, Rinehart, and Winston, 1965. Reprinted by permission of publisher.

Bolmeier, E. C. "Legal Aspects of the Curriculum and the Extra-curriculum," *NASSP Bulletin,* March, 1965, p. 142. Reprinted with permission of NASSP.

Carlson, Richard O., *et al. Change Processes in the Public Schools.* Eugene, Oregon: Center for the Advanced Study of Educational Administration, pp. 57-59. Reprinted by permission of the publishers.

Cubberly, Elwood P. "Editor's Introduction," in Elbert K. Fretwell, *Extra-Curricular Activities in Secondary Schools.* Boston: Houghton Mifflin Co., 1931, pp. v-vi. Used with permission of the publisher.

Cuff, William A. "Middle Schools on the March," *NASSP Bulletin,* February, 1967, p. 84. Reprinted with permission of National Association of Secondary School Principals.

Drury, Robert L., and Ray, Kenneth D. *Principles of School Law.* New York: Meredith Publishing Co., 1965. Reprinted by permission of Appleton-Century-Crofts.

Frederick, Robert W. *Student Activities in American Education.* New York: Center for Applied Research in Education, 1965. Reprinted by permission of publisher.

Frederick, Robert W. *The Third Curriculum.* New York: Appleton-Century-Crofts, 1959. Reprinted by permission of Appleton-Century-Crofts.

Fretwell, Elbert K. *Extra-Curricular Activities in Secondary Schools.* Boston: Houghton Mifflin Company, 1931, p. 302. Reprinted by the permission of the publishers.

Gores, Harold B. (ed.) "New Trends in Athletics," *Administration of High School Athletics.* Washington: American Association for Health, Physical Education, and Recreation, 1963. Reprinted with permission from American Association of Health, Physical Education and Recreation (NEA).

Graham, R. William. "A Look at Student Activities in Junior Colleges," *Junior College Journal,* September, 1962, pp. 43-45. Reprinted with permission of American Association of Junior Colleges.

Grambs, Jean D., *et al. The Junior High School We Need.* Washington: Association for Supervision & Curriculum Development, p. 8. Reprinted by permission of the publishers.

Gruber, Frederick C., and Beatty, Thomas Bayard. *Secondary School Activities.* New York: McGraw-Hill Book Co., 1954. Copyright 1954. Used by permission of McGraw-Hill Book Company.

Hand, Harold C. "Hidden Tuition Charges in Extra-Class Activities," *The Educational Forum,* November, 1949, pp. 95-96. Material used by permission of Kappa Delta Pi, an Honor Society in Education, owners of the copyright.

Imperatives in Education. Washington: American Association of School Administrators, 1966. Reprinted with permission from American Association of School Administrators (NEA).

Johnston, Edgar G., and Faunce, Roland C. *Student Activities in Secondary Schools.* New York: Ronald Press Company, 1952, pp. 37-38, 186, and 328. Reprinted by permission of the publishers.

Jordan, James W. "Non-Athletics Activities Program," *NASSP Bulletin,* October, 1963, pp. 20-21. Reprinted with permission of National Association of Secondary School Principals.

"Junior High School Activities," *School Activities,* 34:199-200, March, 1963. Reprinted by permission of School Activities.

Keim, Edwin B., and Jones, Morris C., Jr. *A Guide to Social Activities.* Washington: National Association of Secondary School Principals, 1965. Used with permission of National Association of Secondary School Principals.

Kilzer, Louis R., Stephenson, Harold H., and Nordberg, H. Orvill. *Allied Activities in the Secondary School.* New York: Harper and Brothers, 1956. Used by permission of the publisher.

Knezevich, Stephen J., and Fowlkes, John Guy. *Business Management of Local School Systems.* New York: Harper & Row, Publishers, Inc., 1960, p. 188. Reprinted by permission of the publishers.

Knowles, Laurence W. "What Schools Do About Student Marriages," *Nation's Schools,* April, 1966, p. 76. Reprinted with permission from Nation's Schools, April, 1966. Copyright 1966, McGraw-Hill, Inc., Chicago, Ill. All rights reserved.

Lewis, Sinclair. *Main Street.* New York: Harcourt, Brace & World, Inc., 1950, pp. 43-44. Reprinted by permission of the publishers.

McKown, Harry C. "Sputnik and Extracurricular Activities," *California Journal of Secondary Education,* May, 1959, p. 304. Reprinted with permission from California Association of Secondary School Administrators.

McKown, Harry C. *Extra-Curricular Activities* (Revised Edition). New York: The MacMillan Company, 1949, p. 631. Reprinted by permission of the publishers.

Matthews, David O. (ed.) *Intramurals for the Senior High School.* Chicago: The Athletic Institute, 1964. Reprinted with permission from The Athletic Institute.

Miller, Franklin A., Moyer, James H., and Patrick, Robert B. *Planning Student Activities.* Englewood Cliffs, N.J.: Prentice-Hall, Inc., 1956. © 1956, Prentice-Hall, Inc., Englewood Cliffs, New Jersey.

1967 NASC Yearbook. Washington: National Association of Student Councils, 1967. Reprinted with permission of National Association of Secondary School Principals.

Reum, Earl. "How Much Power Does the Student Council Have?" *School Activities,* 37:12, May, 1966. Reprinted by permission of School Activities.

Riechley, Robert A. "Student Publications: Are They Worth It?" *NASSP Bulletin,* October, 1964, pp. 17, 20-21, 24. Reprinted with permission of National Association of Secondary School Principals.

Schleibaum, William J. "Has the Pendulum Swung Too Far?" *Junior College Journal,* February, 1962, p. 355. Reprinted with permission of American Association of Junior Colleges.

Sells, James L. *Varsity Lettermen's Clubs.* Washington: American Association for Health, Physical Education, and Recreation, 1964. Reprinted with permission from American Association of Health, Physical Education, and Recreation (NEA).

Shepard, Jack. " 'Are You a Teenager?' 'Yeah, I'm Afraid So.' " Des Moines, Iowa: Look Magazine, Sept. 20, 1966, p. 46. Reprinted by permission of the Editors.

Spears, Harold, and Lawshe, C. H., Jr. *High School Journalism.* New York: MacMillan Company, 1949, p. 8. Reprinted by permission of the publishers.

Standards for Junior High School Athletics. Washington: American Association for Health, Physical Education, and Recreation, 1963. Reprinted with permission from American Association of Health, Physical Education, and Recreation (NEA).

Strickland, Virgil E. "The Role and Significance of the Junior High School in the Total School Program," *NASSP Bulletin,* October, 1962, pp. 70-71. Reprinted with permission of National Association of Secondary School Principals.

The Student Council in the Secondary School. Washington: National Association of Student Councils, 1962. Reprinted with permission of National Association of Secondary School Principals.

Vars, Gordon F. (ed.) *Guidelines for Junior High and Middle School Education.* Washington: National Association of Secondary School Principals, 1966. Reprinted with permission of National Association of Secondary School Principals.

Wey, Herbert W. "Desegregation and Integration," *Phi Delta Kappan,* May, 1966, pp. 513-514. Reprinted by permission of publisher.

INTRODUCTION

The aims of secondary education cannot be achieved adequately through the formal curriculum; a program of student activities is a necessary supplement.

This principle was not accepted until the present century; for, student activities had to prove themselves before they were given curricular space. Formerly, they were considered extracurricular, because they were activities engaged in outside of the school day.

As extracurricular activities, they competed with a curriculum based on a formal disciplinary philosophy which included a classical, literary, linguistic curriculum but excluded supervised activities planned and directed by the students. The entire school day was teacher-directed and planned.

A brief history of student activities, presented in this volume, is necessary for a complete understanding of the present state. In former times, when education was confined to the elite, an academic curriculum appealed to the few who pursued it. Education was a private enterprise, and those who were not interested in the classical curriculum did not have to pursue it. As middle classes emerged and education was extended to them at public expense, the curriculum planned for the elite was imposed on the students with little modification and consideration for the needs, interests, abilities, or vocational plans of the middle and lower-class students.

As school enrollments increased, the abilities and interests of students became more variable. The study of academic subjects and foreign languages appealed to a smaller percent of the students. They pursued the courses of study for lack of other more agreeable alternatives. In some schools, students had no choices; they either pursued the courses of study offered or did not attend. Even in large high schools that offered a number of electives, the majority of the curriculum was prescribed; and the electives were even more academic than the prescribed courses. These curriculums were influenced by college entrance requirements long after the time when the majority of pupils did not go on to college.

The reactions of students to this situation were varied. Some submitted to an uninteresting curriculum; many dropped out of school after failing to make passing marks; and others who remained did so because they improvised some meaningful activities which compensated for the uninteresting courses of study. Thus, student activities were developed by students to fill a need, rather than by educators.

The first activities were sports, games, and free play in which the students participated before and after school hours and during recess periods. Since they were not supervised and directed by the teachers, "free play" often resulted in the destruction of property and injury to fellow students. As a result the activities were condemned by teachers who spent so much time trying to control pupil conduct. The attitude toward them as related by a retired teacher was: "We now are taught and get credit for what we formerly were punished for doing."

Slowly teachers learned that normal, healthy youth are active, fun-loving, gregarious, and creative and that attempts to keep them confined to their seats and remain quiet period after period were futile. Even the academically oriented students got tired of conjugating verbs, balancing equations, and translating uninteresting Latin into English. To overcome boredom and psychological fatigue, students found outlets in activities as soon as formal restrictions were removed. When teachers realized this, they ceased to condemn activities and tolerated them as inevitable.

Slowly student activities were accepted and their values recognized. Rather than being condemned or tolerated, teachers considered them a vital part of the school's program — a part which should be planned as carefully as the formal curriculum.

Student activities serve the same purposes and functions as the required and elective courses in the curriculum. However, they provide experiences which are not included in formal courses of study. They permit students to make applications of knowledge acquired in various courses and to acquire concepts of democracy through democratic living.

The student activities, in addition to the regular instructional program, allow for a well-rounded, balanced program including intellectual, physical, social, and emotional experiences. Even the ancient Greeks, whose influence is still felt in the academic world, promoted such a well-balanced program of education. In one respect the student activities program is more psychologically and philosophically sound than the formal curriculum because it is based on the needs, talents, and interests of the students.

The student activities program provides experiences which approximate life in the adult community. For the student the penalties for failure in this program are not as serious as in the academic program, and he can easily obtain credit and approbation for an honest effort. This experience is an excellent preparation for the roles the student will eventually play in adult life. Youth also learns the meaning of commitment, communication, and participation in his society.

Student activities have increased the attractiveness of secondary schools. Some students have remained in school to play football or basketball or to play in the school band. Others have remained in school because of the total program, rather than some specific student activity. They like the color and excitement of athletic contests; they enjoy group singing, school cheers, parties and dances, and the fun of school elections, or participating in school plays, or holding a club office.

One characteristic of the dropout is that he is a nonparticipator. Students who finish school participate in the student activity program to a greater extent than the dropouts.

Student activities did not necessarily originate with pupils of low academic ability; those of high academic ability probably began many student activities too. However, relationships between participation in activities and scholarship or ability are not high enough to predict one from the other. Low grades are probably caused by factors other than participation in student activities. Some student activities require as much ability as academic courses such as English, science, and mathematics. Others require a high degree of performance skills as well as knowledge, such as dramatics, speech, music, art, and athletics. Some of the best students in high school hold such positions as editors of the school paper, class presidents, and membership on the student council, and also participate in dramatics, speech, and literary pursuits. Individual activities such as preparing exhibits for a science fair, writing essays, giving talks, or pursuing hobbies attract the best students. On the other hand, those low in academic ability may be successful in band, chorus, athletics, dramatics, and other activities; for the relationship between these and academic ability is not necessarily high.

Laymen as well as educators recognize the values of student activities; they support the programs financially and attend various events — athletic, dramatic, musical, artistic, and scientific. Furthermore, parents seem to enjoy observing these types of programs.

Student activities are found in all divisions of our school system, especially in secondary schools. In the approximately 25,000 public high schools of the United States, they are what students consider "school life."

Finding an appropriate balance between the various phases of the curriculum is difficult. Often there is a tendency for one phase to be stressed at the expense of others. For example, academic programs may be weakened by too much emphasis on activities. Both are essential, and those who believe that increased scholarship can be accomplished by abolishing or de-emphasizing student activities are misinformed. Student activities do not dilute scholarship; they promote it. They do not divide interests; they create them. They do not encourage misconduct; they contribute to better citizenship.

One of the innovations being introduced in many schools is independent study. This idea is based on a realization that students are capable of directing their own learning activities. The discovery was made in part by teachers who observed students in self-directed activities such as preparing science fair exhibits, writing for school papers, making community surveys, and participating in student government. Students have demonstrated that they can direct their own efforts and control their own conduct without the close supervision formerly believed to be necessary.

There is a reciprocal relationship between the student activities program and innovations. One of the major problems in planning has been finding curricular space for student activities after the idea was accepted that they should be incorporated in the daily schedule. The introduction of the short period (modules) and flexible scheduling have promoted the inclusion of student activities into the total curriculum.

The extension of the school day, the school week, and the school term have also added more time. The twelve-month school which includes a summer program makes it possible to provide additional time and an increased number of student activities.

In core programs, especially in junior high schools, student activities have been integrated into instructional units through the use of the long period in teaching integrated units.

These and other innovations and their effects on activities are described in this volume.

Student activities have finally been recognized as a valid part of the high school curriculum. They are here to stay. Whether the high school is in a large city or in a small town, students consider student activities to be a vital part of school life: the band and majorettes in parades during the half-time show at the game; the boys making a touchdown; and the excitement, songs, and cheers during the games. They delight in portraying characters on the stage, singing at assemblies, writing for school papers, preparing exhibits, running for an office on the student council, and, finally, wearing a cap and gown and receiving a diploma.

R. K. Bent

Professor of Education
University of Arkansas
Fayetteville, Arkansas

CONTENTS

Part I

BACKGROUND OF THE ACTIVITIES PROGRAM

The present student activities program is composed of two distinct facets. First, there has been a long historical background of student activities. The forerunners of the present-day program had their beginnings in early cultures. Every major period of education has added its own unique contributions to the program. In the United States the student activities program has survived both restrictions and exploitation by school personnel, and it has become an integral part of the educational program.

Presently, the student activities program is being changed from an "extracurricular" activities program into an integral part of the regular curriculum.

Chapter One gives an historical background of the student activities program. Chapter Two contains a discussion of the influence of innovative practices.

Chapter 1

THE DEVELOPMENT OF
STUDENT ACTIVITIES

What is now thought of as the student activities program has had a wide and a varied history. Recorded information about this program is difficult to obtain, since early educators did not record information about the less formal phases of the school program. Schoolmasters of the past either took the activities program as an integral part of the educational process, or looked upon the entire concept with disfavor. This was the case in modern Western culture until the twentieth century. In both cases, the historical record of student activities is small.

THE EARLY DEVELOPMENT

Primitive Cultures

In primitive cultures much, if not all, of the education was of an activity nature. Contests, music, the dance, social events, story telling, and the like were used as means of transmitting the culture. The physical skills — fighting, hunting, fishing, and others — were greatly emphasized as means of self-preservation, family support, and tribal interest. The concept of "learning by doing" is common to both early and modern times.

The Greeks

School-related activities are as old as formal education, and much of Greek education was approached through these activities. From the Homeric period there is a history of games, musical entertainments, dancing, and singing. Among the sports often found during this period were boxing, wrestling, racing, jousting, putting the weight, archery, javelin-throwing, and chariot-racing.

The famous Olympics were products of the Spartan era, and considerable emphasis was placed on sports for both males and females. Both vocal and instrumental music were taught; and competitions were common. The writing and reciting of poetry, festivals, dancing, and dramatics were also frequent. Sometimes systems of student government in the schools were used.

In the period of Platonic influence, the emphasis was on "gymnastics for the body and 'music' for the soul." This approach involved the use of wrestling, archery, javelin-throwing, slinging, marching, maneuvers, camping, riding, and hunting, as well as dancing and singing. Again, systems of student government were found in operation. The Helenistic period put emphasis on physical activities for both boys and girls. The activities included riding, gymnastics, weapon training, swimming, boat racing, various types of ball games, running, jumping, throwing the discus and the javelin, wrestling, and boxing. Music for the soul, however, was not neglected; for evidence of drawing, playing the lyre, accompanied singing, choral singing, and dancing could be found.

The Romans

The Roman emphasis was on transplanting the conquered Greek civilization and establishing it on the banks of *Mare Nostrum*. Thus, the Roman system of education was patterned after the Greek system, except for a few major differences.

Early education in Rome was passive, and mental acuity — abilities of rote memorization and broad imagination — was the highly prized quality. While competition was encouraged, punishment was often essential to maintain interest. Romans reacted against music and art, which Scipio Aemilianus was said to have termed as "unseemly and immodest for Romans." The Romans reacted even more strongly to athletics of the Greek design. Roman sport developed from youth associations, rather than from formal athletics.

By the end of the first century AD, the emphasis on schooling shifted from brutality and rigid discipline to activities. Utilitarian physical activities were highly favored in Roman education.[1]

---

[1]Additional information about Roman education is found in H. I. Marrou (trans. by George Lamb), *A History of Education in Antiquity* (New York: The New American Library, 1964), pp.309-418.

Societies, mutual benefit unions, and student guilds, usually in connection with the universities, developed during the medieval period. These student guilds often participated in the mystery and morality plays presented in the cathedrals and churches. These guilds, or "nations" as they were also called, were fraternal-type organizations; and in them hazing was common.

The universities were often governed by these student nations, an extent of student participation in institutional affairs that has seldom existed in more modern times. An early example of secondary school students' participating in the management of school affairs was at Winchester College in England in 1383. During this time many of the commencement and other academic customs originated.

The sports of this period tended to be individual: the training of the knight included riding, swimming, and the use of weapons, as well as the elements of courtesy, courtly manners, proper speech, and dancing.

DEVELOPMENT IN MODERN TIMES

Early Modern Times

The "Pleasant House" of Vittorino de Feltre in Mantua in the fifteenth century had a student government system that included an elaborate arrangement for competitive games. This school also encouraged drawing and music. Some, though by no means all, of the German humanists of this period supported the teaching of singing.

During the sixteenth century speech activities assumed greater importance in schools in Italy, Germany, and especially England. The English schools of this period encouraged dramatics, both in English and in Latin. German students often presented both original and classical plays.

Sports and games of this period were of the individual type and were often directed toward the "education of the gentlemen" — riding, running, ball playing, leaping, fencing, archery, hunting, and swimming. Hunting and fencing were often found in German schools, while dancing, wrestling, fencing, walking, running, swimming, and riding were found in the English schools.

Student participation in school control often consisted of some variant of the monitorial system. This system, in use at Eton around

1561 and in the Westminster School about 1630, was also used in France and in Germany under Trotzendorff. Various types of student senates were in use in some of the Italian and German schools during this period.

The English Schools

The Duke of Wellington's remark that "the battle of Waterloo was won on the playing fields of Eton" indicates the influence which activities had on the English public schools of the seventeenth and eighteenth centuries. The monitorial system became more common in England and India through the work of Lancaster, Bell, and Hill. By 1786 Eton and Rugby had student government systems.

The Merchant-Taylor's School had a dramatic production in 1665, and Rugby had a Speech Day in 1699. Eton had a school publication in 1786 and The Pops debating society was founded in 1811. Before 1750 Harrow had had contests in archery; Aberdeen, in golf; and Westminster, in cricket. Rowing was also among the physical activities of these schools. Clubs gradually appeared, and during the nineteenth century musical groups and certain informal study groups were added to the available activities.

Early American Schools

Student Government. Student government in American schools dates from as early as 1777. In that year "The Assembly" existed at the Public Latin School in Philadelphia. Other early schools that had some form of student participation in school control were the William Penn Charter School (1800), the English High School of Boston (1821), the Temple School in Boston (1824), the Matta-keeset (Massachusetts) School, the Duxbury (Massachusetts) School (1834), and the Hartford Public School (1852). Monitorial systems were in existence in the New York Public High School and the Boston High School for Girls in 1825 and 1852, respectively.

Literary Activities. The Concord (New Hampshire) School presented "scenes of entertainment" in 1793. Exeter Academy organized a literary society in 1812, and the Eucleia Debating Club was established about 1860 in Worcester, Massachusetts.

Early publications developed from the literary society. Many of the early works were in manuscript and were probably intended to be read orally. *The Students Gazette* of the William Penn Charter

School (1777) and the newspaper of the Public Latin School (1774-1777), both of Philadelphia, were among the earliest student newspapers. Other early papers included *The Athenian* of the Athens (Pennsylvania) Academy (1842); *The Constellation* and *The Aspirant* of the Girls' High School of Portland, Maine (1851-1863); and newspapers from the Hartford Public High School, the Boston Latin School, Worcester (Massachusetts) High School, and Central High School of Philadelphia (c. 1859).

Yearbooks for public schools are of more recent vintage. Early ones include the one at the Hopkins Grammar School of New Haven, Connecticut (1837), *The Plan* of the Phillips Exeter Academy (1880), and *The Meteor* of the Cheshire (Connecticut) School (1882).

Music. Singing schools were popular in the South in the colonial period, and secular singing societies were organized at various places along the Eastern seaboard about the time of the Revolution. The first orchestras were found in public schools around 1800, but instrumental music in the schools showed a slow growth until the beginning of the school band movement in the early years of the twentieth century.

Societies. Fraternal, social, and scholastic societies in the schools began in the early colleges. One of the early societies was Phi Beta Kappa, founded at William and Mary in 1776. A secret society, the Golden Branch, was organized at Exeter in 1818; and another, Sigma Phi, was founded at the High School in Hartford in 1859.

Sports and Games. Sports and games in the early American schools were largely copied from the English schools. However, Franklin's Academy in 1749 recommended swimming, wrestling, running, and leaping. Exeter had football and bat ball games in the early 1800's. Among the first public schools to have games and sports was Central High School in Philadelphia — their program included handball and town ball around 1840. Exeter and Andover played their first baseball game in 1859 and their first football game in 1878. Organized cheerleading dates from the 1870's in the colleges. The secondary schools apparently adopted the practice soon after that date.

STAGES OF DEVELOPMENT IN AMERICAN SCHOOLS

The history of student activities in this country may be traced through several general stages. While these stages are not well-defined — with nondiscreet starting and ending points, and a great deal of overlap — they are roughly parallel to other important developments in education. Like the chicken and the egg, it is difficult to draw any cause-and-effect relationships between broad educational movements and the increasing liberalization of attitudes toward student activities.

Stage I — Ignoring Student Activities

For many years after the establishment of schools in this country, student activities were, at best, ignored, and in many instances scorned. To a large extent this attitude was a reflection of the economic conditions of the times. Especially on the frontier and in the newly settled areas, education itself was a luxury. Six days a week men, women, and children labored from dawn to dusk; recreation usually consisted either of changing to a lighter form of work or of several people working together on the same job. During most of this period, formal education consisted of a few weeks or months of schooling during winter for those children who were too young for heavy work. Play and idleness were treated with scorn.

Under such conditions, the student activities that existed during this time were generally found on the Eastern seaboard in the earliest settled section of the country and usually in the private schools. Elsewhere, the hardships of life and the severity of the religious views of the time made any consideration of school-related activities out of the question.

During this time, education was characterized by formal discipline and expressed in the terms of "faculty psychology." Schooling was almost exclusively teacher-centered, and classwork usually consisted of recitations. Subject matter was closely related to the "3 R's" and other academic subjects as languages and history. Such views of teaching and learning left little room for the logical inclusion of student activities.

Stage II – The Toleration of Student Activities

As the country matured, a period of toleration began. School rules prohibiting the wasting of time in "frivolous" activities were relaxed, and school administrators permitted — even if they did not encourage — membership in student-organized activities. Organizations of this time were characterized by their loose connection with the schools. Little or no school time was available; membership in groups — even on athletic teams — often included nonschool youth, and it was by no means necessary for organizations to have a faculty sponsor. In many instances the school's concern with student activities ended with granting permission to participate — that is, providing there was not any interference with studies. The term "extracurricular," outside the school program, is accurately applied to student activities in this stage of development.

Among the first student activities to be tolerated were athletics and sports and debating and publications. Student activities in the public secondary schools were strongly influenced by both the activities in colleges and private schools. For some student activities, toleration came slowly in certain portions of the country. Even today in some schools certain types of activities, such as dances and other social functions, are not tolerated because of community mores.

Stage III – Acceptance of Student Activities into the Curriculum

In the past few decades, most secondary schools and colleges have grown to accept student activities as part of the curriculum. Now many schools give extensive encouragement for student activities rather than just tolerating them. Few high schools of any size are without athletic teams in several sports, student councils, musical groups, dramatic productions, honor groups, clubs, social functions, and other aspects of the curriculum that were not included in the schools of a few decades ago. It would appear that administrators and teachers have found significant educational value in these areas of the educational program.

The trend toward acceptance of student activities into the curriculum has moved at different rates in different places. On the national level, the trend may be considered to have had its origins shortly after World War I. Relatively little had been written about student activities before the War. Teachers College at Columbia

University first offered Dr. E. K. Fretwell's course, "The Organization and Administration of Extra-Curricular Activities," in 1919.

As an explanation of the movement toward acceptance, Elwood P. Cubberly, writing in 1931, held that:

> Largely within the past decade, and wholly within the past two, an entirely new interest in the extra-curricular activities of youth has been taken by the school. In part this change in attitude has been caused by the new disciplinary problems brought to the school through the recent great popularization of secondary education, in part by the marked increase in leisure time accruing to youth as a result of our increase in wealth and the application of recently enacted child-labor laws, in part by the many new temptations to which young people in the present age are subjected, and in part by the general speeding-up that all evolutionary social changes have experienced as a result of the World War.[2]

Following World War I student activities experienced a great growth, a large body of literature developed; and many public secondary schools added various activities to the school program. Galen Jones, in an oft-quoted 1935 study, found that the median year of installation for 21 of 28 types of activities included in the study was 1919 or later in the 269 secondary schools studied.[3] Only the magazine, the yearbook, basketball, football, track and field events, baseball, and assembly were typically found in these schools prior to World War I. However, the schools were selected because of their reputations as leaders in the establishment and maintainance of student activities programs.

During the 1930's, although schools were cutting programs to bare essentials, terms were reduced, "extra" teachers were dismissed, and veteran teachers were unpaid, student activities continued to be expounded upon. An already vast amount of literature expanded, and public school personnel, perhaps partly overwhelmed by the "big names" supporting student activities, partly in response to community pressures, and partly in response to "recognizing a good thing

---

[2]Elwood P. Cubberly, "Editor's Introduction," in Elbert K. Fretwell, *Extra-Curricular Activities in Secondary Schools* (Boston: Houghton Mifflin Company, 1931), pp. v-vi.

[3]Galen Jones, *Extra-Curricular Activities in Relation to the Curriculum,* Teachers College Contributions to Education No. 667 (New York: Bureau of Publications, Teachers College, Columbia University, 1935).

when they saw it," maintained most parts of the student activities program.

Very shortly after the depression many American schools had increased enrollments, antiquated facilities, few men teachers, shortages of vigorous young women teachers, and shortages of supplies and equipment — all because of the War. Still student activities thrived.

During the more stable post-World War II period, authorities and writers in the field began to notice differences in the way student activities were being handled as compared with that of the 1920's and 1930's. Many activities began to be "curricularized," that is, to be set up in the school program as an elective with credit, rather than as an extracurricular activity. Administrators became more and more concerned with the control of the activities program, not only at the local level but at regional and state levels. New activities appeared, and others gained popularity: for example, intramural athletics, service organizations, school camping, and foreign study and travel.

A number of surveys of student activity offerings were made during the early and mid-1950's. A few of these will be mentioned below to illustrate the growing diversity.

Bowden, in a study of trends in administration of activities, found that (of the 98 schools from throughout the country that he investigated) most had homerooms, football, basketball, and track; 90% had student councils; about 66% had organized recreation programs; and at least 50% had athletics, drama, homemaking, honors groups, journalism, music, a photography club, a press club, a science club, and a Spanish club.[4]

Arkansas. Walker, in a study of a sample of Arkansas schools, reported that over 50% had basketball, an agriculture organization, a home economics organization, and cheerleaders. More than 25% reported softball, football, baseball, volleyball, chorus, band, dramatics, newspapers, yearbook, and student council.[5]

California. A study of 324 secondary schools in California by Shipp revealed that administrators in that state felt that student

---

[4]E. L. Bowden, "Current Trends in Administration of Student Activities," *School Activities,* 25:27-30, September, 1953.

[5]Wanda H. Walker, "A Study of Pupil Participation Costs in the Public Secondary Schools of Arkansas" (unpublished doctoral dissertation, University of Arkansas, Fayetteville, 1953).

government was their "most outstanding" activity.[6] About the same time Tompkins found a student council, some form of student government, athletics, and athletic organizations in all of the 22 secondary schools in the San Francisco area.[7]

Colorado. School parties were the most common form of activity found by Romine in a study of secondary schools in Colorado. Other activities commonly found were cheerleaders, assemblies, school dances, dramatics, school paper, girls pep club, annual, and student council.[8]

Indiana. Jung and Fox found that about 60% of the secondary schools in Indiana had a student council and that large schools were far more likely to have a student council than small schools.[9] Christopher and Howard reported, in a study of a number of high schools in Indiana in 1953, that over 84% of all activities offered had been added within the previous thirty years and that 37% of these had been added within the previous ten years. Basketball was found in all of the schools surveyed. FFA, Hi-Y, and football were the most frequently mentioned all-boy activities; the Girls Athletic Association, FHA, and the Sunshine Society were the most frequently mentioned all-girl activities. Band, newspaper, the annual, and the student council were the most frequently mentioned activities for both boys and girls.[10]

Nebraska. Miller and Dahl studied North Central Association schools in Nebraska and found that about 75% had student government. None of these schools felt that they had "too many" subject matter clubs, although some felt that they had "too few."[11]

[6]F. T. Shipp, "Extraclass Activities in the California Secondary Schools," *California Journal of Secondary Education,* 26:346-348, October, 1951.

[7]Ellsworth P. Tompkins, "A Survey of Extraclass Activities," *School Activities,* 24:115-117, December, 1952.

[8]Stephen Romine, "Administering Pupil Activities in Secondary Schools," *Journal of Educational Research,* 45:615-621, April, 1952.

[9]Christian W. Jung and William H. Fox, *Extra-Curricular Activities in Indiana High Schools: The General Program, and Student Participation in School Government,* Bulletin of the School of Education (Bloomington: Indiana University, 1952).

[10]A. Z. Christopher and W. L. Howard, "Cocurricular Activities in 200 Indiana High Schools," *School Activities,* 25:43-45, October, 1953.

[11]Floyd A. Miller and Sam Dahl, "Survey of Student Activity Programs," *School Activities,* 23:275-277, May, 1952.

New Mexico. Heller, in a study of the secondary schools in New Mexico, found that 67% of the reporting schools had FFA and FHA, that 40% had Spanish clubs, and that 67% had music activities.[12]

Pennsylvania. Jenkins' study in Pennsylvania revealed that music, physical activities for boys, school publications, assembly, social life, and student government were found to be "most nearly adequate."[13]

Texas. A study by the Texas Committee of Ten reported that most small Texas schools have basketball for girls. All reporting districts that had a daily attendance averaging under 500 allowed senior trips. Of 220 districts, 215 published annuals. School dances were held in approximately 66% of the districts surveyed.[14]

Utah. McAllister's study in Utah revealed that all schools had a newspaper and yearbook.[15]

However, a turning point in American education was about to be reached. Schools in this country were jolted by the orbiting of Sputnik. At the time, writers disagreed on the effect that the "new emphasis on quality" would have on student activities. For example, in May, 1959, Harry C. McKown wrote:

> Sputnik has had relatively little direct effect upon extracurricular activities and upon the provisions for housing, equipping, and handling them. Its main effect is to be found in the added impetus given to a more critical evaluation of their purposes, materials, equipment, organization, promotion, handling and accomplishments. This resultant emfrasis (sic) is all to the good because evaluation is still the weakest part of the extra-curricular activity program.[16]

[12]Herbert L. Heller, "A Study of the Extracurricular Activities in New Mexico's Secondary Schools," *School Activities,* 25:157-159, January, 1954.

[13]Thomas Jay Jenkins, "The Organization and Administration of Activity Programs of Public Secondary Schools of Pennsylvania," (unpublished doctoral dissertation, Pennsylvania State University, University Park, 1956.)

[14]Texas Committee of Ten, "What Pupils Do Outside of Class," *Texas Outlook,* 42:16-17, July, 1958.

[15]Ellis S. McAllister, "The Extracurricular Activities of the Senior High Schools of Utah," *NASSP Bulletin,* 40:88-93, November, 1955.

[16]Harry C. McKown, "Sputnik and Extracurricular Activities," *California Journal of Secondary Education,* 34:304, May, 1959.

In opposition to the point of view expressed by McKown, William J. Schleibaum, with the advantage of three additional years' observation, said:

> An astute student of education today can review the past forty years and see the rapid rise of the extra-class program to an apex after the second world war only to see, during the past decade, a definite trend away from this facet of the curriculum.[17]

Little evidence is available to indicate just what, if any, major changes occurred in student activities in the late 1950's and early 1960's. One attempt to uncover this information was made by Gerald M. Van Pool, Director of Student Activities for the National Association of Secondary School Principals. In 1960 he reported the results of personal correspondence with 125 eminent educators from 39 states who described the activity in their respective areas. He found that, although there were some examples of downgrading and severe limitations of the student activities program, changes were being made as a result of careful evaluation, an attempt for better balance, and an effort to reduce the amount of time a student was away from school.[18]

Modified viewpoints over a decade of time can be seen by comparing the sections on activities in the 1950 edition and the 1960 edition of the *Evaluative Criteria,* a document used extensively for accreditation purposes. The later edition[19] put emphasis on exploitation of students, on orientation activities, on articulation, and on economic considerations that the earlier edition did not include. The 1960 edition put more emphasis on the role of school authorities in the areas of planning and evaluation. The section on "Homeroom" was omitted from the later edition, but "Worship" and "Service" activities were added. Greater emphasis was placed on interscholastic physical activities for girls in the later edition.

Surveys made during the post-Sputnik period have indicated a continued growth in student activities with refinements. Eash

[17] William J. Schleibaum, "Has the Pendulum Swung Too Far?" *Junior College Journal,* 32:355, February, 1962.

[18] Gerald M. Van Pool, "What's Happening to the Activities Program?" *NEA Journal,* 49:41, May, 1960.

[19] National Study of Secondary School Evaluation, *Evaluative Criteria* (Washington: National Study of Secondary School Evaluation, 1960), pp. 241-256.

reviewed several years research in the general area of student activities and found trends toward relating objectives of "nonclass" activities to general objectives of education, alleviating problems of participation and imbalance, broader student participation in school management, and a viewing of non-class activities as a part of the teacher's regular load.[20]

A study of the practices relating to activities in the junior high schools of Texas was made for the West Texas School Study Council by Fallon. He found that band was generally provided and that, although large schools had plays, generally the small schools did not. While most schools had school-sponsored parties, most did not have picnics. The Student council was commonly found, and a large number of special interest clubs were reported. The greater number of schools began athletics in the seventh grade. Athletics for girls was of minor importance in the large schools, but it assumed more importance in the smaller systems.[21] Fallon also surveyed the junior high schools in the school systems which were members of the West Texas School Study Council for "desirable" practices for junior high school activities. He found that band, dramatics, class parties and picnics, a newspaper, football, basketball, and a pep squad were generally considered desirable. Proms, an annual, a directory, promotion exercises, and a banquet were generally considered undesirable.[22]

Among the conclusions reached by Mullins in his study of the activity program in Oklahoma in the early 1960's were that the larger the school, the more varied and comprehensive the program of activities. Interscholastic athletics occupied a position of dominance among activities. All small schools in Oklahoma had interscholastic athletics, but only 22% of the small schools had a student council organization. A balanced program was rare in the small schools. Interscholastic athletics was the only activity found in all schools.[23]

[20]Maurice J. Eash, "The School Program: Nonclass Experience," *Review of Educational Research*, 30:57-66, February, 1960.

[21]Berlie J. Fallon, *A Study of Practices Relating to the Co-Curricular Activities of the Junior High Schools in Texas* (Lubbock: West Texas School Study Council, June, 1961).

[22]Berlie J. Fallon, *Standards for Junior High School Activity Programs* (Lubbock: West Texas School Study Council, June, 1961).

[23]J. Dale Mullins, "Activity Programs in Oklahoma – A Report to the Profession," *School Activities*, 33:197-199, March, 1962.

Stage IV — An Overbalance of Student Activities

There is a thin line between having a rich student activities program and permitting student activities to get the upperhand. Unfortunately, some schools have permitted some student activities to progress to a point where the students are taken advantage of. Critics of present-day American education have little difficulty in finding examples of schools and administrators and coaches or sponsors who permit student activities to dominate the educational program. The fact that a few schools do permit the activities program to go to extremes, and that many other schools are not far behind, casts a reflection upon those schools that have well thought out, balanced programs. Although those who point to the "fads and frills" of the educational program sometimes find much to criticize legitimately, excesses in the activities program probably do not involve a large number of students.

Sometimes students are urged to participate in an athletic contest, dramatic production, concert, or other public appearance when they are ill or when to do so will be detrimental to their academic work. Many activities involve out of town trips; and while travel is broadening, some administrators find that certain students, especially during the spring of the year, are in class infrequently.

School service groups are particularly susceptible to exploitation. Library Clubs sometimes degenerate into a corps of unpaid clerical assistants to the librarian. Much the same is also true of such other groups of students as the audiovisual club, business club, office assistants, and others who have learned or who are learning some skill useful around the school. Student council members are sometimes used as spies and monitors by unenlightened administrators. Future Teachers of America Club members are sometimes used as unpaid substitute teachers in lower grades — an act that if not illegal is certainly unprofessional. Recruitment of high school athletes and other outstanding students is sometimes accomplished, even if it has to be done in a subtle way.

How can a problem of exploitation of students through student activities be alleviated? One way of approaching the problem is by evaluation. Administrators, sponsors, coaches, and others should from time to time evaluate the program of activities in terms of the school's philosophy and educational objectives. Use of consultants would probably heighten the objectivity of such an evaluation.

Another approach is to improve the school staff. To use students for free labor, such as typing, filing, operating machines, etc., even if these activities have some educational value, is not wise. It would be far better to hire enough secretaries, library clerks, and teachers' aides to insure that the routine work of the school gets done without having to ask the students to do it.

A third approach is to have well-defined, well-publicized, generally understood, and carefully enforced policies involving participation in various phases of the student activity program. It is highly recommended that these policies be included both in the general written policies of the school district and in a student handbook.

A fourth approach would be a continuation and expansion of the work now being done by many state activities associations — that is, setting up and rigidly enforcing eligibility requirements and other rules and procedures for *all* types of interscholastic competition and interaction.

A fifth approach, and one of the most difficult to accomplish, would be to redirect community pressures. Pressures to produce winning teams, to win band contests, and even keep a high school in a small community can be very great. Various problems require various approaches. An understanding of the workings of pressure groups, knowledge of social class structure and wants, and other elements of sociology, social psychology, and political science plus first-class educational leadership will be required to effectively combat the pressures that have a detrimental effect on the student activity program.

REFERENCES

Bowden, E. L. "Current Trends in Administration of Student Activities." *School Activities*, 25:27-30, September, 1953.

Christopher, A. Z., and Howard, W. L. "Cocurricular Activities in 200 Indiana High Schools," *School Activities*, 25:43-45, October, 1953.

Churchill, Ruth, and Rothman, Phillip. "Extraclass Experiences," *Integration of Educational Experiences. Fifty-seventh Yearbook.* Chicago: National Society for the Study of Education, 1958, pp. 126-142.

Cubberly, Elwood P. "Editor's Introduction," *Extra-Curricular Activities in Secondary Schools.* Boston: Houghton Mifflin, 1936, pp. v-vi.

DeYoung, Chris A., and Wynn, Richard. "Co-curricular Activities," *American Education.* 5th ed. New York: McGraw-Hill Book Co., 1964.

Eash, Maurice J. "The School Program: Nonclass Experience," *Review of Education Research,* 30:57-66, February, 1960.

Enbreck, Robert. "Justifying the Extracurricular Program," *School Activities,* 32:178-179, February, 1961.

Fallon, Berlie J. *Standards for Junior High School Activity Programs.* Lubbock, Texas: West Texas School Study Council, 1961.

Fallon, Berlie J. *A Study of Practices Relating to the Co-Curricular Activities of the Junior High Schools in Texas.* Lubbock, Texas: West Texas School Study Council, 1961.

Faunce, R. C. "Extracurricular Activities," *Encyclopedia of Educational Research.* 3rd ed., pp. 506-511.

Frederick, Robert W. *Student Activities in American Education.* New York: Center for Applied Research in Education, 1965.

Frederick, R. W. *The Third Curriculum.* New York: Appleton-Century-Crofts, Inc., 1959.

Fretwell, Elbert K. *Extra-Curricular Activities in Secondary Schools.* Boston: Houghton Mifflin Co., 1931, pp. 1-19.

Hamilton, Homer. "The Educational Value of the Extracurriculum," *NASSP Bulletin,* 43:132-136, December, 1959.

Heller, Herbert L. "A Study of the Extracurricular Activities in New Mexico's Secondary Schools," *School Activities,* 25:157-159, January, 1954.

Hilliard, Robert L. "Are Four Walls Enough?" *Liberal Education,* 49:488-492, December, 1963.

Jenkins, Thomas J. "The Organization and Administration of Activity Programs of Public Secondary Schools of Pennsylvania." Unpublished doctoral dissertation, Pennsylvania State University, University Park, 1956.

Johnston, Edgar G., and Faunce, Roland C. *Student Activities in Secondary Schools.* New York: The Ronald Press Co., 1952, pp. 3-16.

Jones, Galen. *Extra-Curricular Activities in Relation to the Curriculum.* New York: Bureau of Publications, Teachers College, Columbia University, 1935, pp. 30-40.

Jung, Christian W., and Fox, William H. *Extra-Curricular Activities in Indiana High Schools: The General Program, and Student Participation in School Government.* Bloomington, Indiana: Indiana University, 1952.

Karner, Edwin F. "A Combined Program is Paramount," *School Activities,* 27:261-262, April, 1956.

Krug, Edward A. "The Curriculum Beyond the Classroom Studies." *Secondary School Curriculum.* New York: Harper and Brothers, 1960.

McAllister, Ellis S. "The Extracurricular Activities of the Senior High Schools of Utah," *NASSP BULLETIN,* 40:88-93, November, 1955.

McFarren, George A. "Have Student Activities Missed the Boat?" *The High School Journal,* 40:236-238, March, 1957.

McKown, Harry C. "Sputnik and Extracurricular Activities," *California Journal of Secondary Education,* 34:304, May, 1959.

Marrou, H. I. *A History of Education in Antiquity.* New York: New American Library, 1964, pp. 309-418.

Miller, Floyd A., and Dahl, Sam. "Survey of Student Activity Programs," *School Activities,* 23:275-277, May, 1952.

Mullins, J. Dale. "Activity Programs in Oklahoma — A Report to the Profession," *School Activities,* 33:197-199, March, 1962.

National Recreation Association. *The New Leisure Challenges the Schools.* Washington, D.C.: NEA, 1933.

National Study of Secondary School Evaluation. *Evaluative Criteria.* Washington: National Study of Secondary School Evaluation, 1960, pp. 241-256.

Rivlin, Harry N. "The Cocurriculum: Bringing the Activities Program into the Curriculum." *Teaching Adolescents in Secondary Schools.* 2nd ed. New York: Appleton-Century-Crofts, 1961.

Romine, Stephen. "Administering Pupil Activities in Secondary Schools," *Journal of Educational Research,* 45:615-621, April, 1952.

Rybus, Henry E. "Activities Are Education Too," *School Activities,* 33:267-269, May, 1962.

Schleibaum, William J. "Has the Pendulum Swung Too Far?" *Junior College Journal,* 32:355, February, 1962.

Shannon, J. R. "Curricular and Extracurricular," *School Activities,* 23:229-230, March, 1952.

Shipp, F. T. "Extraclass Activities in the California Secondary Schools," *California Journal of Education,* 26:346-348, October, 1951.

Stiles, Lindley J., McCleary, Lloyd E., and Turnbaugh, Roy C. "Student Activities." *Secondary Education in the United States.* New York: Harcourt, Brace and World, 1962.

Strang, Ruth, *Group Work in Education.* New York: Harper and Brothers, 1958, pp. 72-97.

Texas Committee of Ten. "What Pupils Do Outside of Class," *Texas Outlook,* 42:16-17, July, 1958.

Tompkins, Ellsworth P. "A Survey of Extraclass Activities," *School Activities,* 24:115-117, December, 1952.

Van Pool, G. M. "Cherish Your Activity Program," *Clearing House,* 29:259-263, January, 1955.

Van Pool, G. M. "What's Happening to the Activities Program?" *NEA Journal,* 49:41, May, 1960.

Walker, Wanda H. "A Study of Pupil Participation Costs in the Public Secondary Schools of Arkansas." Unpublished doctoral dissertation, University of Arkansas, Fayetteville, 1953.

Wood, Donald I. "Student Activities — A Hope or Delusion," *NASSP Bulletin,* 46:201-205, April, 1962.

Xavier, Sister Mary. "Some Educational Trends in School Activities," *Catholic Educational Review,* 55:24-34, January, 1957.

Yon, John F. "What Do Activities Contribute?" *School Activities,* 35:20-21, September, 1963.

Zimmerman, J. Richard. "Please Don't Say 'No' to the Extracurriculum," *School Activities,* 35:152, January, 1964.

Chapter 2

EDUCATIONAL INNOVATIONS
AND THE
STUDENT ACTIVITIES PROGRAM

THE NATURE OF INNOVATION

On her first encounter with the superintendent of schools in Gopher Prairie, Carol Kennicott inquired:

> Tell me, Mr. Mott: Have you ever tried any experiments with any of the new educational systems? The modern kindergarten methods or the Gary system?
>
> Oh. Those. Most of these would-be reformers are simply notoriety-seekers. I believe in manual training, but Latin and mathematics always will be the backbone of sound Americanism, no matter what these faddists advocate — heaven knows what they do want — knitting, I suppose, and classes in wiggling the ears.[1]

If only all such administrators existed only in fiction!

Our current era is as challenging as any in the history of education. Over the country, many steps to modernize curriculum organization and to otherwise update educational programs are now being taken. In every aspect of the curriculum — elementary, secondary, academic, vocational, required courses, electives, student activities — efforts are being made to select the most appropriate content from the proliferation of knowledge. Methodology is shifting away from factual accumulation to an emphasis on search, inquiry, and discovery. Many new educational tools have been put into use, and there is every indication that there will be more in the future. Research and evaluation are rapidly pointing out ways that these new tools can be put to use to improve the efficient utilization of the professional staff. The use of noncertified personnel and machines to carry out the menial tasks of record-keeping, hall duty, and the like will continue to elevate teaching to a more professional status.

---

[1] Sinclair Lewis, *Main Street* (New York: Harcourt, Brace, and Howe, 1920), pp. 43-44.

The physical environment of our schools is being rearranged to harmonize with the new ideas in methodology, content, and organization. Educational horizons are being extended for adult education, vocational education, and junior colleges. Largely on the basis of recent research, education for early childhood is receiving a new orientation and a new emphasis.

Permeating all of these changes is a new emphasis on the individual. Verbally oriented education for the few is being abandoned; and, more and more, universal education in terms of the needs of the last half of the twentieth and the twenty-first centuries is being implemented. These developments are long overdue, although many have been advocated by progressive educators for years.

A growing awareness that the pace of change in education must be stepped up sharply underlies these developments. Changing needs, on all levels from the individual to the total world community, demand a more rapid movement. While many schools are already overwhelmed by recent developments, it appears that a new and different age of education is beginning.

Until recently, the rate of change in education was slow. For example, Governor DeWitt Clinton of New York — generally considered one of our most progressive states — advocated in 1827 that every high school should have a library for the students. It was not, however, until about 1875, some 48 years later, that the *first* high school put in such a library. It was 1924 before every school in the state of New York had a library.

In the 1940's the late Paul Mort developed a theory of diffusion of educational innovations — or "lag theory" as it is commonly known — which holds that a period of about fifty years elapses between insight into an educational need and the invention of a solution which will be accepted. After an innovation which is destined to spread throughout our schools first appears, fifteen years typically elapse before the innovation is found in 3% of the school systems. However, after an innovation has reached the 3% point of diffusion, its rate of spread accelerates. An additional twenty years usually suffices for an almost complete diffusion in an average state area.

Barriers to Change

Why is it that this change has traditionally taken place so slowly? What are the barriers to educational change? Many have been identified by recent research, but the following three will be illustrative of the others.

The Absence of a Change Agent. A change agent is a person who attempts to influence decisions in a direction he feels is desirable. If there is no such person in a school, then the status quo will tend to be perpetuated.

A Weak Knowledge Base. It is rare indeed when an educational innovation is backed by solid research. It is even rarer to find an educational innovation which has been fully developed and subjected to careful trial and experimentation. At the present time there are not many effective communication channels for the dissemination of research and innovations.

The "Domestication" of Public Schools. Public schools do not compete with other organizations for clients; in fact, a steady (even excessive) flow of clients is assured. There is no struggle for survival; funds are not closely tied to the quality of performance of the public school or the teacher. The public schools are domesticated in the sense that they are protected by the society they serve — perhaps excessively so.

Development of Innovations

Changes, of course, run in cycles. The first major step in the cycle is that of innovation, the process whereby a new element or combination of elements is made available to a group. The second step is that of dissemination, the process whereby an innovation comes to be shared. The third step is that of integration, the process whereby an innovation becomes mutually adjusted to other elements in the system. At this point the system is again static, and the time is ripe for another change cycle.

Innovations can come from anywhere. Every person connected with the schools, with related fields, or with just even an interest in the schools is a potential innovator. For various reasons, the means for effecting innovations have not been readily available. However, some observers of the contemporary educational scene feel that the impetus for implementing innovations must come from agencies outside the local school district such as the state and federal governments. Hardly anyone can disagree with the statement that the actions of all three branches of the federal government in the 1950's and the 1960's have had a profound effect on the rate of change of many aspects of our educational programs.

The Nature of Innovators

Innovators, although not always popular because of their beliefs, are the first members of a social system (such as a school) to adopt new ideas. Rogers has given us a word picture in these terms:

> Innovators are venturesome individuals; they desire the hazardous, the rash, the avant-garde, and the risky. Since no other model of the innovation exists in the social system, they must also have the ability to understand and use complex technical information. An occasional debacle when one of the new ideas adopted proves to be unsuccessful does not disquiet innovators. However, in order to absorb the loss of an unprofitable innovation, they must generally have control of substantial financial resources.
>
> Their propensity to venturesomeness brings them out of their local circle of peers and into more cosmopolite social relationships. Even when the geographical distance between them may be considerable, they often have been found to form cliques. They spread new ideas as their gospel.
>
> The description of innovators is sharpened by contrast to that of laggards, who are the last to adopt an innovation . . . . Laggards are localistic; many are near-isolates. Their point of reference is the past, and they interact primarily with those peers who have traditional values like theirs. Laggards tend to be frankly suspicious of innovations, innovators, and change agents. When laggards finally adopt an innovation, it may already be superseded by another more recent idea which the innovators already are using. While innovators look to the road of change ahead, the laggards gaze at the rear view mirror . . . .[2]

[2]Everett M. Rogers, "What Are Innovators Like?" in Richard O. Carlson, *et al.*, *Change Processes In The Public Schools*, (Eugene, Oregon: CASEA, University of Oregon, 1965), pp. 57-59.

EXAMPLES OF EDUCATIONAL INNOVATIONS

Even though change has not been as rapid as many educators would like, on a national scale a great deal of educational change has taken place in the past few years. Much of this change has been in academic areas of the curriculum. Science and mathematics have, perhaps, received the greatest amount of attention; and various study groups have developed new teaching materials for K-12 levels in these areas. In many parts of the country, the change cycle for mathematics and science is virtually complete, and it probably will not be long before a new set of innovations is developed. Largely as a result of the NDEA of 1958, foreign language has received a new impetus; and while most schools have added or strengthened programs in Spanish and French, such languages as German, Russian, and Latin have had considerable growth. A few schools are now offering several years of such languages as Chinese, modern Greek, Hebrew, Italian, Norwegian, Polish, and Portuguese.

The teaching about various ideologies, including democracy and communism, has been emphasized in the past few years — either as separate courses or as units in social studies courses. Various attempts at teaching international understanding and human relations have been made by a significant number of schools.

Reading, as the preeminent intellectual tool, has received great emphasis. New materials for elementary grades, an emphasis on remedial reading, the development and use of various machines to teach reading, and formal reading instruction on the secondary level have come about.

Many subjects have been moved downward in the curriculum; and often new ones have been added at the top, or students have been encouraged to tackle what was formerly considered college-level work. To a considerable extent this has occurred in the fields of mathematics and science, and foreign language has been strongly encouraged on the elementary school level.

Standards for work, both in quantity and quality, have been raised, to the extent that many people now feel that excessive pressure to achieve is being put on the students in our schools. Various audiovisual devices, including programmed materials, computer-assisted instruction, language laboratories, educational television, the overhead projector, and so on, have come into their own.

Many elementary schools and some secondary schools have organized units cutting across several curriculum areas. The self-contained classroom in the elementary school has given way to a partially or completely departmentalized arrangement in a number of school systems, especially in the upper elementary grades. Non-graded arrangements for younger children have become common, and in some instances they are found in the upper elementary grades and, from time to time, in the secondary grades.

Ability grouping, especially in larger schools, has shown a sharp increase in the past decade, and multitrack programs are now rather common. Team teaching, especially on the secondary level, has become common within the past few years, although there are a great many forms that this instructional arrangement is taking. Various arrangements for large-group instruction, small-group instruction, and independent study, often in connection with a team-teaching arrangement, are currently found. Teacher aides, almost completely unknown a few years ago, now are often found at all grade levels, performing a great variety of nonprofessional tasks. The mosaic schedule has gone by the wayside in many secondary schools, and various approaches to modular scheduling, floating periods, staggared sessions, along with other novel arrangements, are now found.

THE EFFECTS OF INNOVATIONS ON THE STUDENT ACTIVITIES PROGRAM

By no means do the innovations mentioned above cover the range of even the major innovations that have taken place and are taking place in American education. Neither do they all have an effect on the student activities program. Some, however, have had a major influence on the student activities programs, and, as such, deserve special attention.

Scheduling. Perhaps the most important group of innovations affecting student activities pertains to scheduling. Various arrangements of modular scheduling are now found in many secondary schools. In modular scheduling, the day is divided into many more divisions than the usual six to eight periods; the divisions are usually 20-25 minutes each. This arrangement permits an unequal distribution of time for various subjects.

Some schools that are adopting this method of scheduling are incorporating the student activities schedule into the master schedule, especially in those instances where a cyclic arrangement is used. For example, the Spanish Club might be alloted one module of time on Thursdays. Students who wished to belong to the Spanish Club would incorporate this into their Thursday schedule.

Another new arrangement is that of the "floating period." In one type of this arrangement, the schedule consists of five long periods each day. Each student, however, registers for six subjects, each of which meets four times weekly, which results in the creation of an "uncommitted period" during the week. This uncommitted period is often used as an activity period, for assemblies and club meetings on a rotating basis.

Some schools have extended the school day to include an optional period either immediately before or immediately after the regular school day. In some instances, this is used as an activity period, or to permit students to participate in student activities during the day and yet take an additional academic course.

In addition to extensions of the school day, the school week and the school year are being extended in many communities. Saturdays and school holidays are sometimes used for various special-interest meetings. Field trips, regional meetings, leadership training, contests, and other competitions often take place on these occasions. Not all of these, by any means, are connected with the organized student activities program, but many or most are, and as such require special arrangements for faculty time, transportation, meals, and other considerations. Summer sessions, often formerly associated with remedial work, now often offer enrichment work as well. Talented students, interested in taking more than the usual number of courses in their high school career, may take this work during the summer and retain adequate time for participation in student activities during the regular year.

In an effort to gain greater utilization of school plants, some schools operate double sessions. Under this arrangement, students have varying times for the start and end of the school day. All are, however, at school during the middle of the day, and all student activities, band, chorus, and athletics are scheduled for this time.

At least one small school has a 90-minute period in the middle of an otherwise conventional schedule. In this school, band is scheduled for this period with the provision that students can go to an academic class for the first 45 minutes and then go to band or to band for 45 minutes and then to an academic class. Some students will, of course, have band the full 90 minutes. A similar arrangement could perhaps be made for various student activities.

In many schools, it has been common practice to excuse students from study halls for participation in such student activities as the newspaper or yearbook. Other arrangements will have to be made, of course, in those schools that are following what appears to be a general trend toward abolishing or cutting down on the number of study halls. At least some of these schools are "curricularizing" such activities as journalism, art, and dramatics, and including an activity period for other student activities.

A few schools are experimenting with having students take only a few courses, usually three, for long periods per day for a semester's time. Unless all activities are scheduled outside school hours, unless an activity period is provided for, or unless some other arrangements are made, the activity programs would suffer under such an arrangement.

Organization

Several organizational schemes are having their influence on the student activities program. One of these is ability grouping. If student activities are held during an activity period, or outside school hours, there is no particular problem of participation. If, however, some or all student activities are integrated into the master schedule, then a scheduling problem may occur which would permit students of one ability group to participate and those of another ability group not to participate in a given student activity. Heterogeneous grouping in student activities has long been recommended by authorities.

Another scheme is team teaching in its various forms. In its simplest form, team teaching is merely the correlating of efforts of two or more teachers, and as such, probably would have little influence on the student activities program. In its more complex forms, team teaching involves several teachers, a hierarchy of personnel, special facilities, and a high degree of flexibility for the use of students' time. To what extent can, and should, student activities be integrated into the team teaching organization? It is probably too early to tell what direction will be taken. It is easy to visualize arrangements which will accommodate a great deal of special interests. While this might mean the demise of many clubs and special interest groups, it is always possible that more sophisticated special interests will develop which cannot be accommodated within the regular framework. For example, those functions now performed by the Math Club might be incorporated into the planned instructional program; however, a Topology Club or a Logic Club might evolve to provide for interests which could not be accommodated in the planned instructional program.

In a few public schools (and in more non-public schools) there is a partial or total segregation of the sexes for instruction. This has, of course, been common practice for years in such courses as physical education; and voluntary segregation has occured in home economics, agriculture, industrial arts, and even in such areas as advanced mathematics and physical science. If, however, an entire school is made up of students of the same sex, or if students have only limited contact with students of the opposite sex, it will have an obvious and considerable effect on the usual student activities program.

The "house plan" or "school within a school" plan currently in use or being studied by a number of large secondary schools has implications for the student activity program. Many organizations may be duplicated among the various "houses," which will give more students an opportunity to participate and to exercise leadership. On the other hand, if students are grouped in any way — by grade level, interests, ability, or sex — the amount of heterogenity within each organization will be reduced. This may or may not be a good thing, depending on the local school's philosophy.

Schools with the house plan or with several campuses will have to determine whether or not there will be "super" organizations, such as a student council for the entire school with additional student councils in each of the houses; whether or not there will be organizations that cut across all houses, such as special interest groups in which only a few students in each house would participate; whether such functions as athletics, music, drama, and journalism (if they are considered student activities) will be conducted on a centralized basis or on a decentralized basis, and so on.

Some attention is being given to proposals that schools operate the year around, with students attending any three of four quarters or any two of three trimesters. Certainly this would create some internal problems; for example, organizations with rapidly changing memberships, student council members representing changing constituencies, some students might be deprived of participating in seasonal sports, etc.

A few schools, notably in Florida, have moved to a nongraded arrangement on the secondary level. In a sense, this "nongradedness" is a misnomer, for there are still achievement levels — only many more of them than in traditional arrangements. Obviously, such an arrangement will have some effect on the student activities program. For example, it would be difficult to have a senior play or a junior prom when there are no seniors or juniors as such. What effect would there be on interscholastic eligibility requirements, especially when most of these requirements insist on a student passing a certain number of courses? The student may be "passing" in a very satisfactory manner, but he isn't taking courses in the traditional sense. At what point may students participate in the traditional "senior activities," or are these activities to be eliminated? In theory at least, a student may spend more or less than the usual number of years in high school under such an arrangement. What effect will this have on eligibility requirements, on class organizations, and on social events? Certainly these are not insurmountable problems, nor does such an arrangement imply that certain activities will be done away with, but for many the traditional approach will have to be modified.

As more and more schools move toward worthwhile pre- and postsession planning and evaluation for faculty and staff, a corresponding movement is taking place within the student activity branch of the curriculum. Students and sponsors are taking time to plan activities for a year or more, and they are taking time at the end of the year for evaluation. Not only is evaluation taking place more and more in relatively formal sessions following the school year, but various forms of continuous evaluation during the year are being used with student activities. Certainly planning and evaluation are not innovations; they are, however, receiving much more attention now than formerly, both in quantity and quality.

Guidance Activities

Spring registration, for both classes and student activities, is taking place in more and more schools as administrators need more time and information in order to set up master schedules. This means that student activities must, among other things, be planned ahead for relatively long periods of time and many traditional organizational functions must be conducted in the spring rather than in the fall. As computerized scheduling becomes more commonplace, however, the time necessary to determine a master schedule may become quite small. In fact, one work has been done with the idea of having a new master schedule each day.

Registration in some schools involves a visit to the school by those students who will be entering. Sixth graders often have an opportunity to visit the junior high school that they will attend the next year, and ninth graders often have an opportunity to visit the senior high school that they will attend the next year. As part of the orientation and visitation procedure, the various student organizations should make arrangements to explain their organizations to students who are not familiar with them.

As counselor-student ratios approach adequacy, students entering high school are asked to plan a program of courses and activities for their entire high school career. This, of course, facilitates planning, not only by the administration, but for setting up special interest groups, abolishing archaic clubs and groups in which there is little interest, and for giving the student a "tailor-made" set of experiences, hopefully more valuable than the all too common "cafeteria" approach.

Racial Integration

While hardly an innovation, one of the greatest changes to occur in the public schools is racial integration of both student body and staff. In many schools, not all of which are in the South, students of a minority race do not, for various reasons, participate in the student activity program of the school in the degree that students of the majority race do. It is heartening to see that the situation continues to improve.

Multiracial athletic teams are now not unusual. Students of minority races are being elected to office in various student activities. When economic conditions permit, students of the minority race are participating on an equal status with others. To be sure, much remains to be improved. As *de facto* school segregation is being eliminated at an accelerated rate, student activities will continue to become increasingly desegregated. In the desegregation process, there is a point beyond which the school staff is not very effective, however. At this point strong student leadership is essential.

A current major problem area is that of social events. To cope with this somewhat delicate situation, talented administrators, interested sponsors, and students with common sense are needed. There is great need for leadership of a sound nature on the part of faculty, students, and parents. It may be relatively easy to desegregate student activities; it is more difficult to integrate them.

Honors

Many schools have moved to various types of "honor systems," such as permitting students with a certain grade point average or with unblemished disciplinary records to be excused from study hall or to have other types of special privileges. The awarding of "letters," similar to that done for years in athletics, has taken place in some schools.

Instruction

Many changes in instruction have been occurring in recent years. Some of these, such as team teaching, have been previously mentioned. Some, however, require little exertion on the part of the student. For example, the physical activity involved in working a "scrambled" textbook, a mechanical "teaching machine," a computer terminal, or other types of programmed learning is small. Educational television, for all its advantages, seldom involves much activity on the part of those watching. If we still believe in "learning by doing," and that the "doing" involves interaction among people, or the handling of materials, or the opportunity to "branch" in ways not programmed, then the student activity program may be called on to provide, through laboratory experiences and relatively unstructured arrangements, the necessary supplement to the excellent instruction being provided through use of many of the new media.

As the quantity of knowledge expands, as teachers expect more from students, and as school plant use expands, facilities will have to be made available for additional periods of time. This may indicate an increased use of student monitors and assistants to help supervise and work with expanding instructional needs. This could mean, for example, that Library Clubs would assume additional responsibilities as school libraries remain open in the late afternoons and in the evenings.[3]

Areas of the Curriculum

The history of student activities in American secondary schools notes that many have come into the curriculum "by the back door." Some, once they have obtained a foothold on respectability, have eventually become curricularized and a part of the formal instructional program. A few of the new ideas — new in the sense that more than just a few schools are taking a look at them — which might have some effect on either the formal instructional program or the student activities program are given below:

1. School camping.
2. Co-educational physical education activities (bowling, tennis, golf, badminton, social dancing, the dance, etc.)
3. Noon-hour recreation programs.
4. Elementary physical fitness and training programs.
5. Elementary school newspapers.
6. The writing, preparation, and presentation of radio and television scripts.
7. System-wide music fesitvals.
8. Publication of student original writing, art work, music, etc.
9. Column, page, or section of local newspaper devoted to the school and student activities.
10. Extension of future teachers interest groups to the junior high school (and even elementary) level.
11. Use of tutorial arrangements among students.
12. Increased use of "cadet teachers," student teachers, and teacher aides.

---

[3]Certainly if students are pressured in any way to assist with such duties as indicated, not to mention other school equipment, office work, etc., this would constitute an exploitation of the students and should be avoided at all costs. It would be far better if the school could arrange its staffing patterns so that adults were available to handle these chores. On the other hand, if the students are interested in and volunteer for such tasks as a school service (and social service is an interest of many adolescents), then we see no reason to deny them the opportunity for service in this form. There is, however, a fine line between permitting students to help with school chores and exploiting this help.

13. Use of the "buddy system" for slow learners.
14. Student-prepared codes of conduct, dress, and grooming.
15. Placing full-length mirrors at strategic places in corridors.
16. "Historical sites" and other social studies games.
17. Student exchange programs, both interregional and international.
18. Having students attend school board meetings, either as observers or as participants.
19. Placing science students in industry for short periods of time.
20. Increased use of individual science laboratories and study centers.

The increased number of programs likely to arise from new approaches to student activities is exemplified by the program offered by such innovative schools as Como Park Junior High School, St. Paul, Minnesota. The "Student Activity Program Bulletin" offers 156 different student activities for approximately 1000 students in the late 1960's. Such a program allows individual students to develop their own interests and not be forced to fit into a limited number of activities such as those generally found.

Activities Offered at Como Park

Electricity-Electronics	Boys' Bowling
Morse Code	Girls' Bowling
Radio	Boys' Swimming
Audiovisual	Girls' Swimming
Foreign Cooking	Cross Country
Boys' Cooking	Baseball
Future Nurses	Roller Skating
Future Teachers	Field-Stream
Office Careers	Fishing
Library Club	Camping
Modeling	Basketball
Choral Ensembles	Football
Girls' Glee Club	Square Dancing
Beginners' Band	Acrobatics
Band Ensembles	Social Dancing
Swing Band	Volleyball
Music Appreciation	Track
N.R.A. Rifle Club	Seasonal Sports

Baton Twirling
Boys' Golf
Girls' Golf
Archery
Badminton
Gymnastics
Hockey
Table Tennis
Wrestling
Math Enrichment
Fun With Math
Algebra Coach
Girls' Self-Improvement
Girls' Teen-Age Club
Know Yourself
Host-Hostess
Junior Red Cross
How to Study
Remedial Math
Remedial Reading
Remedial Spelling
Penmanship Club
Scrabble
Fun With Games
Cribbage
Checkers-Chess
Bridge
France and Language
Germany and Language
Latin
Spanish
Russian
Stamps and Coins
Model Building
Fun With Science
Junior Academy of Science
Needlecraft
Sewing
Future Homemakers
Auto Mechanics
Predriver Training
Bird Study
Play Production

Tennis
Our American Heritage
United Nations
Travel Club
World Wide Neighbors
Enjoyment of Books
Discussion Club
Debate
Current Events
Creative Writing
Journalism
Newspaper Staff
Public Relations Club
Creative Dramatics
Theatre
Toastmasters Club
Magic
Gardening and House Plants
Wild Flowers
Natural History
Interior Decorating
Camera and Photography
Posters
Printing
Charcoal Sketching
Painting
Oil Painting
Swedish Painting
Painting Sets and Figurines
Copper Enameling
Drawing and Sketching
Arts-Crafts
Handicraft
Leathercraft
Knitting
Crocheting
Woodworking
First Aid
Stamp Club
Lawyer's Club
Speed Reading
Coin Club
Girls' Metalwork

Audiovisual Workshop	Girls' Electricity
Speech Workshop	Officiating – Football
Free Exercise	Officiating – Basketball
Physical Education Careers	Officiating – Baseball
Ice Skating	Officiating – Girls' Sports
Ceramics	Camera, Photography, Printing
Experimental Psychology	Natural Science
Future Librarians	Slide Rule
Airplanes	Library Service Assistants
Automobiles	Precision Dancing and Marching
Art-Metal Craft	Beginning Baton Twirling
Industrial Technical Outlook	Weight Lifting
Appreciation of Comedy	Junior Great Books
Welding	Leadership
Horseback Riding	Skiing
Creative Stitchery	Competition Swimming
Rocket Building	Home Crafts

The teacher or administrator who is interested in new ideas for student activities will want to do a considerable amount of reading in a number of areas. The obvious sources – *School Activities, Student Life Highlights,* the *Student Council Yearbook,* the *NASSP Bulletin* – are invaluable as sources of descriptions of programs and ideas which can be modified for use in other schools. The creative teacher or administrator will also read newspapers, general magazines, and professional journals while asking about every article "Could this be adapted for student activities in any worthwhile way?" An idea advanced for yearbooks, for example, may be modified into an excellent student council project, or a description of some field work in science may lead to a good idea for a social studies club.

SUMMARY

This chapter has briefly presented some of the innovations now current in education which are expected to have an effect on the student activities program. Among the innovative practices are the following: lowering the grade level for various subjects, departmentalization, grouping, teacher aides, and scheduling by other than the traditional mosaic pattern. Naturally, as changes are advocated, there will be those who will oppose the proposals. Therefore, the competent administrator will necessarily have to evaluate the individual innovations for his school, while understanding the processes leading to change. The age of rapid change, innovation, and research has been in many segments of our society for decades. It has been in many segments of our school program for years. It must affect the student activities program now.

REFERENCES

Dillon, Edward M., Shellenbarger, Guy, and Shafner, Hugh M. "How Much and What Kind of Student Activities in Today's Secondary Schools?" *NASSP Bulletin,* 45:254-258, April, 1961.

Jacobson, Paul B., Reavis, William C., and Logsdon, James D. "Extracurricular Activities — Some Representative Programs." *Effective School Principal.* 2nd ed. Englewood Cliffs, N. J.: Prentice-Hall, Inc., 1963.

Johnston, Edgar G., and Faunce, Roland C. *Student Activities in Secondary Schools.* New York: The Ronald Press Co., 1952, pp. 268-289.

Jones, Galen. *Extra-Curricular Activities in Relation to the Curriculum.* New York: Bureau of Publications, Teachers College, Columbia University, 1935, pp. 12-29, 41-54.

Kilzer, Louis R., *et al. Allied Activities in the Secondary School.* New York: Harper and Brothers, 1956, pp. 272-297.

McKown, Harry C. *Extra-Curricular Activities.* Revised ed. New York: Macmillan Co., 1949, pp. 316-332.

Robbins, Jerry H. "Trends in Student Activity Offerings in the Public Secondary Schools of Arkansas." Unpublished doctoral dissertation, University of Arkansas, Fayetteville, 1965.

Rogers, Everett M. "What are Innovators Like?" *Change Processes in the Public Schools,* Eugene, Oregon: CASEA, 1965, pp. 57-59.

Tanner, Daniel. "Extraclass Activities." *Schools for Youth.* New York: Macmillan Co., 1965.

Wiles, Kimball. "Student Activities." *Changing Curriculum of the American High School.* Englewood Cliffs, N. J.: Prentice-Hall Inc., 1963.

Willman, Clyde A. "Activities at Expense of Program?" *Educational Leadership,* 18:213-216, January, 1961.

Part II
ORGANIZATION OF THE STUDENT ACTIVITIES PROGRAM BY ACADEMIC LEVEL

The student activities program in American schools includes elementary, junior high, and senior high schools, as well as junior colleges and universities. This text deals with student activities through grades 13 and 14.

Elementary schools, although having the longest historical development in America, have fewer formally organized student activities than the other levels of education. While innovative practices are definitely at work in the elementary activities field, there are certain limitations which to some extent restrict activities in the elementary schools. Age, maturity, class arrangement, and ability are some of the factors influencing elementary school activities which are discussed in Chapter 5.

The junior high school is a unique American educational creation. It is, unfortunately, a stepchild of education, and its activity program has often become a mere copy of the senior high school program. Some suggestions are given in Chapter 4 for creating an innovative junior high school student activities program.

Chapter 3 serves as an introduction for Parts III, IV, and V of this book. A brief examination of certain considerations about the high school student activities program is given.

Some school systems have expanded to include grades 13 and 14. Student activities in the junior college years often bear closer resemblance to those in colleges and universities than to those in high schools. Chapter 5 discusses the junior college student activities program and makes suggestions for creating a program unique to the junior college.

Chapter 3

ORGANIZATION OF STUDENT ACTIVITIES IN THE HIGH SCHOOL

Although student activities are found at various levels of school organization, the greatest amount of participation and the greatest variety of student activities are found at the senior high level. Historically, the college has led the senior high school in the development of student activities, just as the senior high school has led the junior high school and lower units. Nonetheless, it is likely, although statistics are not readily available, that a greater proportion of senior high school students participate in student activities than do college students, especially if membership in social fraternities and sororities is excluded. Because more and a wider variety of student activities are generally available to senior high school students than to junior high school students, there is usually greater participation among senior high school students.

The activities available at each level of organization influence the student activities available at other levels. Historically, student activities at the secondary level have imitated those at the college level. On the other hand, student activities at the secondary level have been influenced by students who have participated in activities at a lower level but are ready for activities of a more sophisticated or different nature. Thus to a very large extent student activities revolve about the activities of the senior high school.

Few, if any, student activities are peculiar to the senior high school. While there is, of course, great variation in the pattern of student activities offered among secondary schools, most nonrural American high schools will have most or all of the following types of student activities:

1. Student participation in school administration — usually the student council.
2. Athletics and physical activities — often interscholastic sports, as well as intramurals.

3. Publications — yearbook, literary magazine, and sometimes the school newspaper.
4. Subject matter and special interest clubs — math club, Spanish club, radio club, and stamp collectors club, etc.
5. Service and recognition groups — National Honor Society, Key Club, and audiovisual club.
6. Fine arts — Thespians, musical groups, and literary societies.
7. Social activities — dances, parties, and banquets.

Each of these types of student activities will be considered in detail in later chapters.

DEFINITION OF STUDENT ACTIVITIES

What is meant by a student activity varies from school to school. What is considered an activity in one school may not be so considered in another school. It is unfortunate that there is not more general agreement among educators as to the definition of the term. A great deal of the misunderstanding about student activities and a considerable amount of the criticism of student activities has a semantic origin. For example, the band in one high school may be a student activity while in another school it is not, even though the conditions are comparable. The newspaper may be under the supervision of the director of student activities in one instance and under the supervision of the journalism teacher as a class project in another instance. We have arbitrarily defined a student activity as *an aspect of the curriculum which is voluntarily engaged in by students, which is sponsored by the faculty, and which does not carry academic credit toward promotion or graduation.* As used in this book, the term student activities carries this meaning.

This definition excludes a number of worthwhile endeavors which have been considered as student activities by other writers and by many educators. It excludes such organizations as the Boy Scouts, 4-H Clubs, and DeMolay. Since they are usually sponsored and supervised by other agencies, these and other such youth groups are not ordinarily a part of the curriculum of the school.

The assembly, the home room, and the various class organizations are excluded since, as a rule, they are not voluntary as far as participation is concerned. There is no question that they are "extraclass" in nature, because they are under somewhat different organizational patterns from that of the major part of the instructional program.

Organizations unsponsored by the faculty, such as social fraternities and sororities, whatever their merits, are excluded because of the lack of sufficient connection with the school program.

In addition, credit courses, whatever their origins, are excluded. If even partial credit is given for athletics, band, the school newspaper, and similar groups, then these activities are considered in the same category with English, history, and mathematics classes and become courses of instruction rather than student activities.

PHILOSOPHY AND OBJECTIVES OF STUDENT ACTIVITIES

Part of the school philosophy is that youth have certain developmental needs which the school can help them meet successfully. In theory, if not always in practice, student activities are a part of the instructional program of the school and have a useful and valuable contribution to make toward meeting these needs.

The general objectives of a program of student activities should be much the same as those of education in general. The specific objectives of a local program of student activities should be developed by personnel at the local level and should be developed from the local school philosophy.

After the careful development of a school philosophy and the development of specific objectives for the student activities program, any necessary modification in the present program should be made. The process of developing philosophy and objectives is time consuming and expensive, but essential to the development of a sound educational program. This is a process that must involve not only the administrative staff of the local school, but the instructional staff, the students, parents, alumni, and other interested parties.

Compromises will have to be made; for the program of student activities which arises out of the school philosophy and objectives must be coordinated in at least some aspects with other schools in the system and with other school systems. Furthermore, it must be articulated with junior high school and college student activities, and it must not make unreasonable demands on available resources of time, space, money, and personnel.

Ideally, the outcome of this process will be a unique, tailor-made program of student activities for each school; the program will be flexible and will continually be revised, in the light of constant evaluation, to meet changing educational conditions and changing student needs. In practice, this ideal situation is seldom attained. Only rarely is a student activity program carefully planned, which is extremely unfortunate. Instead of being developed from the school's philosophy, well though out objectives, and student interests, the student activities program is more often influenced by such factors as tradition, imitation of other schools, community pressures, and regulations of extralegal, multischool associations. In practice, the student activities program is often relatively inflexible. Archaic student clubs are seldom dropped from the program.[1] Few administrators have had the courage to drop such functions as interscholastic contact sports, even when they are convinced that such activities are detrimental to sound educational programs.

Many writers have advanced lengthy lists of objectives for student activities. However, Robbins and Williams believe that there are few, if any, objectives that are unique to student activities, and there aren't any objectives that are appropriate for all schools. Rather, student activities should be a means to an end — a way of accomplishing the general educational objectives determined by a local school system. Thus, in some schools, a great many student activities may be necessary to accomplish objectives; in other schools, few, or perhaps none.

Even though the typical high school student body of today is considerably different from that of several decades ago, and even though, in recent years, major changes in curriculum and methods have come about, relatively few changes, except perhaps in a quantitative sense, have occurred in the student activities program.

Relatively little research has occurred in the field of student activities; and the body of writing in this field, while perhaps quantitatively adequate, is not particularly noted for its quality. Fresh ideas are few. A great volume of writing about student activities was created in the 1920's and 1930's; but in recent years the quantity has diminished. In many respects much of the material written since World War II does not differ greatly from that written prior to that time.

[1] See Donald I. Wood, "Archaic Student Clubs; Those Entrenched by Tradition May Be at Odds With Enlightened Student Activities," *Clearing House,* 39:91-93, October, 1964.

Each high school should evaluate its present program of student activities in terms of the best current thinking and practice in student activities with respect to a well-developed local philosophy of education and in line with specific objectives and goals. The educational value of student activities has, in many schools, hardly been touched.

ORGANIZATION

Multischool Relations

Americans are seldom content with mere local programs, and this is true with student activities as well as other educational endeavors. There are more and more interschool associations of student activities, including regional, state, and national organizations. Assuming that such associations are desirable — and there are many advantages — it becomes necessary for the local school to work with students, sponsors, and administrators from other schools for the broadening experiences on large geographical bases. Many states now have quasi-official, albeit extralegal, state associations of student activities to regulate interschool participation in contests, conventions, and the like. Additional states have athletic associations and state and regional organizations for other activities. In addition, most schools are affiliated with one or more national organizations such as the National Association of Student Councils, the National Honor Society, the Future Farmers of America, and the Future Homemakers of America, which have independent organizational structures. Chapter 13 examines multischool organizations in detail.

Local Organization

The principal, as the responsible head of all functions of the local school, is the person most influential in the student activities program. In smaller schools the principal usually exercises personal supervision of the student activities program; although when there is an assistant principal, these duties are often delegated to him. In larger schools, there is often a director of student activities who exercises the direct supervision of the student activities program. The organization for student activities on the building level is discussed in detail in Chapter 14.

Allocation of Resources

Every administrator must make decisions about the allocation of the resources available for education, and often these are a consequence of official policy action. As these allocations affect student activities, decisions must be made about available time, personnel to work with student activities, space for these activities to take place, and funds for equipment and supplies. Decisions must be made about which student activities, if any, will meet "on school time" in an activity period, or otherwise. Physical requirements for the Poetry Club may be quite modest, but this is not so for elaborate interscholastic football games. Funds for education are always in short supply, and often the student activities program receives the short end of tax funds for the various undertakings. This means that student clubs must often assume responsibility for raising their own funds. This, however, creates many additional problems for the sponsors and administrators. In administering the complex arrangements of personnel, funds, equipment, transportation, and facilities which are required for most student activities programs, many legal considerations are involved or are potential problems.

The person most directly responsible for the success or failure of each student activity is the sponsor of each organization. Many sponsors assume their duties willingly and enthusiastically, especially when the student activity is one closely related to the sponsor's teaching field, is one in which the sponsor has personal interest, or was active in during high school or college. Unfortunately, not all sponsors approach their duties in such a positive way. In some schools sponsors are selected in such a way that the teacher is not happy with or competent in the student activity in which he is working. Such a situation cannot help but have an undesirable effect on the student activities program. Each of these items is considered in detail in later chapters.

REFERENCES

Allen, Charles F., *et al. Extra-Curricular Activities in the Elementary Schools.* St. Louis, Mo.: Webster Publishing Co., 1937, pp. 1-16, 68-132.

Anderson, Vernon E., and Gruhn, William T. "Experiences in Extraclass Activities." *Principles and Practices of Secondary Education.* 2nd ed. New York: Ronald Press Co., 1962.

Farmer, S. "School Morale: A Fringe Benefit of the Student Activity Program," *NASSP Bulletin,* 45:134-140, September, 1961.

Foster, C. R. *Extra-Curricular Activities in the High School.* Richmond, Va.: Johnson Publishing Co., 1925.

Green, H. L. "High School Mentally Retarded and Extra-curricular Activities," *NASSP Bulletin,* 46:209-216, April, 1962.

Gruber, Frederick C., and Beatty, Thomas Bayard. *Secondary School Activities.* New York: McGraw-Hill Book Co., Inc., 1954, pp. 1-29.

Hand, Harold C. "Vitalizing the Extra-Class Activities of the Secondary School," *Principles of Public Secondary Education.* New York: Harcourt, Brace and Co., 1958.

Hansen, Kenneth H. "Extra-Class Activities." *High School Teaching.* Englewood Cliffs, N.J.: Prentice-Hall, 1957.

Jones, Galen. *Extra-Curricular Activities in Relation to the Curriculum.* New York: Bureau of Publications, Teachers College, Columbia University, 1935, pp. 54-69.

Kilzer, Louis R., *et al. Allied Activities in the Secondary School.* New York: Harper and Brothers, 1956, pp. 1-19.

Kourmadas, J. F., (ed.) "Student Activities in Today's Secondary Schools," *NASSP Bulletin,* 48:entire issue, October, 1964.

McKnown, Harry C. *Extra-Curricular Activities.* Rev. ed. New York: Macmillan Co., 1949, pp. 1-23.

Miller, Franklin, *et al. Planning Student Activities.* Englewood Cliffs, N. J.: Prentice-Hall, Inc., 1956, pp. 1-32.

Mills, Hubert H. "The Subject and the Extracurriculum." *The High School Curriculum.* 3rd ed. New York: Ronald Press Co., 1964.

Rollins, Sidney P., and Unruh, Adolph. "Extra-Class Activities in the Secondary School." *Introduction to Secondary Education.* Chicago: Rand McNally and Co., 1964.

Wood, Donald I. "Archaic Student Clubs; Those Entrenched by Tradition May Be At Odds With Enlightened Student Activities," *Clearing House,* 39:91-93, October, 1964.

Chapter 4

ORGANIZATION OF STUDENT ACTIVITIES IN THE JUNIOR HIGH SCHOOL

THE JUNIOR HIGH SCHOOL MOVEMENT

The concept of a specialized program for students in grades seven through nine is unique to the American educational system. As an intermediary position holder in the educational system between the senior high school and the elementary school, the junior high school has adopted certain elements of both of the other educational divisions. In fact, Grambs *et al.* have made the following statement about the nature of junior high schools:

> Today's junior high school is essentially a hybrid. The seventh and eighth grades, while formally restructured in the direction of secondary school patterns, retain some of the flavor, character and content of the elementary school. The ninth grade, brought into the junior high school from the senior high school, is closely tied to the forms and traditions of the latter.[1]

As first envisioned by educators, the junior high school was considered to have more specific responsibilities than to serve as a transitional period between elementary and high school education. While Grambs *et al.* reported that one of the concepts behind the junior high school movement was "to reduce the length of elementary schooling,"[2] the junior high school was considered as the proper educational medium through which vocational training could be offered to boys, so that they would be prepared for jobs at the end of the ninth grade.

Changing demands by society upon the junior high school have caused a great shift in emphasis on these schools since the first junior

---

[1]Jean D. Grambs *et al., The Junior High School We Need,* Association for Supervision and Curriculum Development (Washington, D.C.: National Education Association, 1961), p. 8.
[2]*Ibid.,* p. 7.

high school was opened in 1909. Today, over 80% of American secondary school pupils are in districts with junior high school provisions,[3] and the emphasis has shifted from a primarily vocational orientation to one of an integral part of a twelve year, or longer, educational period.

Strickland has noted the changing emphasis of the junior high school and enumerated the trends. In general, the trends which he pointed out are the following:

1. Change from vocational education to information about many vocations.
2. Change from rigid departmentalization to core curriculum and a return to some departmentalization.
3. Continued emphasis on general education with some electives in the ninth grade and fewer at the eighth grade.
4. Various approaches to grouping.
5. School-within-a-school program organization.
6. An upward extension of elementary school, not a downward development of high school.[4]

The last trend mentioned has been the most difficult to implement, for whether the junior high school is part of the 6-6, 6-3-3, or 6-2-4 organizational pattern, or the 4-4-4 organizational pattern including a "middle school," the influence of the senior high school is very great. Particularly since junior high school students are often housed in the same or similar educational facilities as senior high school students and since ninth grade academic achievements usually become part of the high school transcript, it is often difficult to separate senior high school and junior high school educational programs.

THE ACTIVITIES PROGRAM

Probably no other element of the junior high school reflects the influence of the senior high school more than does the student activities program. It has been pointed out that "in general, junior high school activities are somewhat watered down senior high activities."[5]

[3]*Ibid.*, p. 8.

[4]Virgil E. Strickland, "The Role and Significance of the Junior High School in the Total School Program," *NASSP Bulletin*, 46:70-71, October, 1962.

[5]"Junior High School Activities," *School Activities*, 34:199, March, 1963.

Certainly the junior high school in general, and its student activities program in particular, should not become only a training ground for senior high school. Educators have recognized the need for educating junior high school students in a special type of program. The activities program should also be special; for students of junior high school age are undergoing emotional, social, and physical changes that require special considerations.

The Committee on Junior High-School Education of the National Association of Secondary-School Principals has found a student activities program to be educationally valuable in the junior high school for the following reasons:

[1] One generally accepted function of the junior high school is to provide exploratory opportunities for the students. An activity program is basic to the exploratory function.

[2] Early adolescents are most interested in seeking status with their peers. Such status is often determined more by social acceptance than by academic achievement. The well-planned activity program provides a wholesome outlet for this adolescent need.

[3] The student activity program should attempt to develop desirable behavioral traits for early adolescents through individual and group involvement. Citizenship, responsibility, cooperative effort, and leadership should be inculcated in the students through the activity program.

[4] Many regular school subjects and services require additional activity time — homemaking, science, library. Students in activities adjunct to such subjects and services perform duties valuable to the total school program.

[5] The student activity program should help students develop wholesome leisure-time interests, which may well carry over into adult life.[6]

Types of Student Activities

A great variety of student activities may be utilized to carry out educationally desirable practices. The Committee on Junior High School Education listed the following general activities areas as appropriate for junior high schools:

[6]James W. Jordan, "Non-Athletic Activities Program," *NASSP Bulletin,* 47:20-21, October, 1963.

1. Service clubs
2. Scholarship or honor societies
3. Interest clubs
4. Subject connected clubs
5. Athletically-connected clubs
6. Social clubs[7]

In practice, this list of clubs and organizations may be expanded to include many special activities. Table I indicates the junior high school student activities offered in a portion of the schools of the 36-member Mississippi School Study Council.

The Colorado State Junior High School Principals' Study Group, which met in May, 1962, made the following recommendations about student activities in the junior high school:

Recommendations Strongly For:
1. Awards Assemblies
2. Science Fairs and Related Activities
3. Intramurals (for schools with 100 or more students in Grade 7)

Recommendations As Acceptable Within Limits:
1. Social Gatherings
2. Pep Assemblies
3. Fund-Raising Drives
4. Inter-school Academic Contests
5. Assemblies
6. Newspaper
7. Handbook
8. School Clubs

Recommendations Strongly Against:
1. Graduation Ceremonies
2. Continuation Ceremonies (when in building with the high school)
3. "Special Days"
4. Drill Teams
5. Yearbook
6. Hazing
7. Athletic Letters
8. Publication of Junior High School Athletic Scores by City Newspapers

[7]*Ibid.*, p. 21.

TABLE 1[a]

STUDENT ACTIVITY PROGRAMS AVAILABLE BY GRADE LEVEL IN MISSISSIPPI JUNIOR HIGH SCHOOL GRADES [b]

Activity	1-8		1-12			7-9			7-12		
	7th	8th	7th	8th	9th	7th	8th	9th	7th	8th	9th
Art Club						20	9	13			
Athletic Club					6	10					
Band			29	28	29	10	9				
Baseball	43	43	18	17	29	10	9				
Basketball	57	57	35	33	35	40	45	25	60	60	60
Beta Club	14	14	6	6	41						20
Chorus			35	39	41	10	9	13	60	60	60
Coin & Stamp Club						10			20	20	20
Conservation Club	14										
Crafts							9				
Debate Club			6	6				13			20
Dramatic Club					6	20	18	25			40
Explorers' Club								13			
FFA				17	59			13			40
FHA				33	65	10	27	38	20	40	80
Football	43	43	29	28	35	40	45	25	60	60	60
Forestry Club				6							
French Club								13			
FTA				6	6						
Future Nurses' Club					6						
4-H Club	57	57	76	78	53	30	36	13	60	60	60
Health Club						10	9				
Hi-Y	14	14	12	17	6				40	40	40
Hobby Club						10	9				
Journalism Club					6						
Jr. Historical Society									20	20	20
Jr. Red Cross	14	14	6	6	6	10	9	13	20	20	20
Library Club					12				20	20	20
Math Club						20	9	13			
Model Airplane Club							9	13			

TABLE I (continued)

Activity	1-8		1-12			7-9			7-12		
	7th	8th	7th	8th	9th	7th	8th	9th	7th	8th	9th
Music Club			6	6	12	10	9	13	20	20	20
Orchestra							9				
Pep Club							9				20
Photography Club									20	20	20
Projectionist Club									20	20	20
Public Speaking	14	14									20
Reading Club						10	9	13			
Safety					6			13			
School Newspaper	14	14	6	6	24	10	9	38	20	20	60
Science Club			6	6	29	20	27	38	40	40	80
Sportsman Club			6	11	6	10	9				
Student Council	29	29	18	22	24	30	27	38	20	20	40
Tennis									20	20	20
Track			6	6	6						20
Yearbook					12			13			40
Y-Teens	29	29	12	17	12	30	27	13	40	40	40

[a] Source: Lamar Moody, *The Junior High School: A Survey of the Faculties, Educational Programs and Student Opinions Under Four Types of Grade Organization,* Mississippi School Study Council (Hattiesburg, Mississippi: University of Southern Mississippi, 1964), p. 26.

[b] Percent of schools making activity available.

No Recommendations Except Maintenance of Rigid Control:
1. Pep Clubs and Related Activities
2. Inter-school Athletics[8]

Administrative Considerations

For the student activities program to be effective, the administrators and the teachers of a junior high school must fully understand all considerations dealing with the administration of the program. Within each school, responsibility for the program must be placed with a person or group for effective coordination. Activity sponsors and the members of the faculty who do not sponsor activities must be advised of the goals intended for the activities program. A positive attitude toward the program by all faculty members will be extremely valuable.

Considerations. The following statements stress some of the important administrative considerations of the junior high school student activity program:

[1] Time for the activity program should be provided within the daily class schedule. If the activity program extends beyond the regular school day, provision should be made for transported students.

[2] Activity sponsors should help students utilize skills and knowledge acquired in other areas of the curriculum. Conversely, teachers in the class room should encourage and help students use skills and knowledges (*sic*) acquired in the activity program.

[3] Experiences in the activity program should be designed to develop student responsibility, initiative, and self-direction.

[4] Students should share responsibility for selecting, organizing, executing, and evaluating activities. Activities should be appropriate to student age groups and should not merely imitate the senior high school. The activity program should allow for more student freedom than is exhibited in the classroom.

[5] The student activity program should be voluntary. Students should be encouraged, but not forced to participate.

[6] Care should be taken that students not over-extend themselves by trying to participate in too many activities. Leadership in the activities should be spread as widely as possible, rather than allowing it to cluster in a few students.

---

[8]Quoted in "Junior High School Activities," *op. cit.,* pp. 199-200.

[7] A faculty member or small committee should direct and be responsible for coordinating the school's activity program.

[8] Student activities should be evaluated each year by the faculty and students. The community should be kept informed regarding the philosophy of the activity program, its objectives, and purposes.[9]

An additional point which should be added to this list is: [9] "Club activities should be organized around two or three grade levels in the junior high school."[10]

Evaluation. Evaluation is of particular importance in the junior high school, where interests and talents change so rapidly, that student activities of the past may no longer be of interest. Additional evaluation is needed to determine the appropriateness of the amounts of time and funds spent and the usefulness of the program as a portion of the curriculum.

Martin researched the student activities program of one junior high school to find the transfer values of science and mathematics to the student activities program. According to the students polled, approximately 24% of the learnings in the two subject fields were applied or reinforced in the student activities. Teachers indicated that approximately 26% of the experiences of children in the two subject fields were applied or reinforced in activities sponsored by the faculty.[11]

Principles. In executing a program of student activities — after the organizational framework for the program has been developed and after all persons have been made aware of the expected and potential goals — a number of basic principles for maintaining an effective program must be formulated. This listing of principles will vary from school to school and from year to year within a school as pupils, teachers, administrators, goals, and public influence vary.

Among the principles to be considered are the following:

1. Administrators, teachers, and pupils should continue to revise objectives of the student activities program and be certain that these objectives are understood by faculty, students, parents *et al.*

[9] Jordan, *op. cit.,* pp. 21-22.

[10] William D. White, "Pupil Progress and Grade Combinations," *NASSP Bulletin,* 51:90, February, 1967.

[11] Keith F. Martin, "The Educational Process Is Assisted By the Activity Program," *School Activities,* 33:10-11, September, 1961.

2. The activities selected for inclusion in the student activities program should be geared to student interests and problems. As such, they should not be rigidly constructed, but should change or be changed as student interests change. "Enthusiasm and apathy are equally contagious."[12]

3. Regulations governing the student activities program should be permissive enough to allow a student to change his activity participation at the end of each term, but restrictive enough to prohibit continual change without thought.

4. Although participation in the student activities program — both by students and faculty — should be of a voluntary nature, all students should be encouraged to participate in as many activities as possible without negatively effecting their performance in the more formal phases of the curriculum. Teachers should be given the time and opportunity to sponsor or co-sponsor activities.

Specific Activities Often Found in Junior High Schools

Student Council. The organization within the junior high school activities program that perhaps most closely resembles student activity offerings at the senior high school level is the student council. Just as in the senior high school, the student council is extremely valuable in the junior high school, as the following statement points out:

> The junior high school student council provides a laboratory for students to learn how to make wise, moral, and informal choices, and to carry them into action. Every school needs a program for developing and training both leaders and participants in student activities, so that democratic citizenship is learned through practice.[13]

Because of the age and maturity of the students at the junior high school level, the junior high school student council is usually not given the same amount of authority that similar bodies at the senior high school level have. Commonly accepted responsibilities of the junior high school student council are as follows:

[12]Albert Kaminsky, "Principles for a Successful Program of Student Activities," *The Clearing House,* 36:41, September, 1961.

[13]Gordon F. Vars (ed.), *Guidelines for Junior High and Middle School Education,* (Washington, D.C.: National Association of Secondary School Principals, 1966), p. 11.

1. Regulation and evaluation of student activities.
2. Representation of the student body to the administration pertaining to the conduct of student affairs.
3. Organization of assembly programs.
4. Provisions allowing for student participation in the management of school affairs.

Naturally, the junior high school student council must have a constitution, some form of representative assembly, and other standard needs which are more fully discussed in Chapter 6 where student government in general is dealt with.

Athletics. Another of the activities which have come from the senior high school down to the junior high school is athletics. Particularly at a time when much emphasis is placed on physical fitness and the role of the school in providing proper physical educational training, it is extremely important to consider the place of athletics in the junior high school.

It has been suggested that the purpose of junior high school athletics is "to serve students *now* rather than to prepare them for senior high school athletic teams."[14] It is at this point that the question of organized intramurals should be considered.

Certainly if the administration were willing to provide supervision, and if the size of the school were such that sufficient numbers of students were available, a voluntary program of organized intramurals could be beneficial. Games could be played after school or during the noon break. Intramurals provide for the development of school unity and *esprit de corps* without the encumbrances of long trips, numerous games, admission charges, and overzealous Booster Clubs.

The most objectionable element of the junior high school athletics program is interscholastic competition. While intramurals are generally favored, many authorities feel that interscholastic athletics are a misuse of time, effort, and funds.

The NASSP Committee on Junior High School Education has reported that "there is much evidence that body-contact sports, such as football, are unsuited for the junior high school boy."[15] There are many educators and parents who also feel that too much

[14]Vars, *op. cit.,* p. 12.
[15]James W. Jordan, "Interscholastic Athletics – Yes or No?" *NASSP Bulletin,* 47:5, October, 1963.

anxiety is a part of interscholastic athletics. The possibility of physical injury creates further opposition to interscholastic sports on the junior high school level.

It is recognized that a program of junior high school interschool competition is well-established at some schools. Since this would indicate that the school and the community have found such an arrangement satisfactory, no suggestion will be made to terminate this program. Rather, the following guiding principles should be followed:

1. Junior high school interschool competition should in no way be considered an element of preparation for high school athletic programs.

2. The American Association for Health, Physical Education, and Recreation has suggested the following:

> The interscholastic athletics program for boys in the junior high school should supplement — rather than serve as a substitute for — an adequate program of required physical education, intramurals, and physical education for all students.[16]

3. Close supervision must be exercised over all aspects of the program. This must include competent supervision by professionally skilled coaches and physical education teachers.

4. All possible care must be taken to guard the physical and emotional well-being of the participants in the interschool competition.

5. No awards or athletic letters should be considered. On the junior high school level teamwork and cooperation should be emphasized, not intrateam competition.

6. No Booster Clubs or parent organizations should be allowed to function. Unnecessary parental influence often tends to bring pressures upon the students that are not in line with the goals of junior high school sports programs.

7. No tournaments, contests, or detailed publicity should be encouraged. Early beginnings in sports should encourage the qualities which make sports of interest and value to many persons. Anything

---

[16] American Association for Health, Physical Education, and Recreation, *Standards for Junior High School Athletics* (Washington, D.C.: National Education Association, 1963), p. 17.

which relegates the basic goals of the program to a lesser position must be removed.[17]

While lettermen's clubs and other similar organizations related to athletics should not exist in junior high schools, pep clubs and cheerleaders are excellent for the student activities program, if some type of sports program does exist.

In evaluating the entire athletics program, Jordan suggests asking the following question:

> Is this for the welfare of the students participating and the morale of the student body?[18]

Social activities. Perhaps in no other field of the junior high school student activities program do the problems of the students show themselves more than in social activities. Physical and social problems faced by the rapidly growing and rapidly maturing student must be considered and prepared for. While some students are ready for the heterosexual relationships of dances and boy-girl parties, many others still prefer group activities with their own sex. A wide range of socially oriented activities (folk dances, games, picnics, skating parties, etc.) should be planned for all, and all students should be encouraged to participate. Unfortunately, as has been pointed out, "few schools organize their social activities with sufficient attention to these physically and socially important problems."[19]

Interest clubs. The wide range of clubs on the junior high school level is correctly attributed to the changing interests of the junior high school students. These clubs should provide opportunities for

[17]For an in-depth discussion of the problem of interscholastic sports at the junior high school level, consult the following:

Gordon Vars (ed.), *Guidelines for Junior High and Middle School Education,* pp. 12-13: a booklet prepared by the National Association of Secondary School Principals.

American Association for Health, Physical Education, and Recreation, *Standards for Junior High School Athletics,* 20 pp.: a joint report of the AAHPER, NASSP, and NFSHSAA.

James E. Jordan, "Interscholastic Athletics – Yes or No?" *NASSP Bulletin,* 47:5-6, October, 1963: a report of the Junior High School Education Committee of the NASSP.

[18]Jordan, "Interscholastic Athletics – Yes or No?" p. 5.

[19]Philadelphia Suburban School Study Council, Group B, *The Junior High School Years: Growing Up – Problems and Pathways* (Philadelphia: University of Pennsylvania Educational Research and Service Bureau, 1965), p. 23.

the students to develop new interests or to pursue fields of some interest to them already. Such clubs may include subject-oriented clubs (poetry club, science club, geology club) and service clubs (audiovisual club, library club, office assistants). In the relatively few instances where school newspapers and yearbooks exist on the junior high school level, the publications club, journalism club, photography club, and other similar groups may play a large part in the publication. Many junior high schools have organizations sponsored by the Y.W.C.A., Y.M.C.A., and the Y.M.H.A. which provide fellowship as well as direction in the orientation of values.

Recognition Groups. On the junior high school level, the National Association of Secondary School Principals sponsors the National Junior Honor Society. This recognition group encourages the development of leadership, service, character, and scholarship. While there are those who feel that honor society recognition is out of place at the junior high school level, some means of recognizing achievement (honor rolls, awards, etc.) is, indeed, appropriate.

SUMMARY

The junior high school is a unique American educational creation. The student activities program unfortunately does *not* seem to be unique, as the program often imitates the program of some nearby senior high school. It is essential to remember that junior high school students have special physical and emotional problems and that neither elementary nor senior high school activities are necessarily appropriate. Academic interest, service, and recognition groups are useful in junior high schools. A variety of types of social activities should be provided, and interscholastic athletics should be discouraged.

REFERENCES

American Association for Health, Physical Education, and Recreation. *Standards for Junior High School Athletics*. Washington, D.C.: NEA, 1963.

Bossing, Nelson L., and Cramer, Roscoe V. "Student Activities." *Junior High School*. Boston: Houghton Mifflin Co., 1965.

Elicker, Paul E. "The Student Activity Program: The Activities." *Administration of Junior and Senior High Schools*. Englewood Cliffs, N.J.: Prentice-Hall, Inc., 1964.

Fallon, B. J. *Standards for Junior High School Activity Programs.* Lubbock, Texas: West Texas School Study Council, 1961.

Fallon, B. J. *A Study of Practices Relating to the Co-Curricular Activities of the Junior High Schools in Texas.* Lubbock, Texas: West Texas School Study Council, 1961.

Fretwell, Elbert K. *Extra-Curricular Activities in Secondary Schools.* Boston: Houghton Mifflin Co., 1931, pp. 118-133.

Grambs, Jean D., *et al. The Junior High School We Need.* Washington, D.C.: Association for Supervision and Curriculum Development (NEA), 1961.

Gruhn, William T., and Douglass, Harl R. "Extraclass Activities." *Modern Junior High School.* 2nd ed. New York: Ronald Press Co., 1956.

Jordan, James W. "Interscholastic Athletics — Yes or No?" *NASSP Bulletin,* 47:5, October, 1963.

Jordan, James W. "Non-Athletic Activities Program," *NASSP Bulletin,* 47:20-21, October, 1963.

"Junior High School Activities," *School Activities,* 34:199-200, March, 1963.

Kaminsky, Albert. "Principles for a Successful Program of Student Activities," *The Clearing House,* 36:41, September, 1961.

Koos, Leonard V. "The Program of Extra-Class Activities." *Junior High School Trends.* New York: Harper and Brothers, 1955.

Martin, Keith F. "The Educational Process Is Assisted by the Activity Program," *School Activities,* 33:10-11, September, 1961.

Moody, Lamar. *The Junior High School: A Survey of the Faculties, Educational Programs and Student Opinions Under Four Types of Grade Organization.* Hattiesburg, Mississippi: Mississippi School Study Council, 1964.

Philadelphia Suburban School Study Council, Group B. *The Junior High School Years: Growing Up — Problems and Pathways.* Philadelphia: University of Pennsylvania Educational Research and Service Bureau, 1965, p. 23.

Strickland, Virgil E. "The Role and Significance of the Junior High School in the Total School Program," *NASSP Bulletin,* 46: 70-71, October, 1962.

Van Til, William, Vars, Gordon F., and Lounsbury, John H. "Developing the Co-Curricular Activity Program." *Modern Education for the Junior High Years.* Indianapolis, Indiana: Bobbs-Merrill Co., 1961.

Vars, Gordon F., *et al. Guidelines for Junior High and Middle School Education.* Washington: NASSP, 1966, p. 11.

White, William D. "Pupil Progress and Grade Combinations," *NASSP Bulletin,* 51:87-90, February, 1967.

Chapter 5

ORGANIZATION OF STUDENT ACTIVITIES ABOVE AND BELOW THE SECONDARY SCHOOL

Once centered largely in the secondary schools and senior colleges, the student activities program today has broadly permeated the American educational system. The junior college, originally conceived as an extension of the high school, has taken certain types of student activities from the secondary school and developed them for its program. Following the junior college in borrowing from the student activities program of the secondary schools, the American elementary school — with its increasing orientation to activities in recent decades — has slowly developed a more formal student activities program.

The reasons for the extension of the student activities program to levels above and below the secondary school are easily understood. In a democracy it is the responsibility of the schools to prepare students to accept full participation in adult life. Student government, publications, clubs, athletics, etc., provide valuable experience not only for the present but for later life as well. It is foolish to believe that the secondary school should function as the sole educational agent to provide the valuable experiences that can come from student activities. Nevertheless, until only a few years ago, there had been no concerted effort to bring a program of student activities into the nation's elementary schools. Over a somewhat longer period of time, student activities that are more like those in the secondary school than those in universities have been brought into the junior colleges. Today programs at both levels are receiving a great deal of attention.

Any program at the high school level, student activities or otherwise, must be well-articulated with similar programs at organizational levels above and below the high school in order to be maximally effective. The following discussion is included to familiarize the reader with programs available before and after the high school years in order to put the high school student activities

program in an appropriate perspective. The student activities program in the junior high school was discussed in Chapter 3. Inasmuch as most secondary school personnel are generally familiar with student activities programs in senior colleges and universities, no discussion of this level is included.

THE JUNIOR COLLEGE

The junior college is essentially a twentieth century movement, but it can be traced to outgrowths from the German *Gymnasium* at the fourteenth grade level. The rapid growth of the institution may be traced to many items: the changing manpower needs of the nation, increased emphasis on mass education beyond the secondary level, and the growth of adult and vocational education programs.

Within recent years many communities in the United States, from the most populous metropolitan centers to sparsely settled rural regions, have set up publicly supported junior colleges. Public junior colleges now number 900, with over 1.5 million students, which is a 15% increase over last year.[1] The growth of these institutions is the result of the increased emphasis placed on both youth and adults to have some college experience.

These two-year colleges are located close to high school graduates and adults who need not only academically oriented course work but also comprehensive training for semiprofessional and technical employment. To fulfill the tasks assigned to them by the community they serve, the junior colleges strive to provide needed instructional programs, adequate student services, and a minimum of the distractions found at the four-year colleges.

A recent study by Robbins of the catalogs of 309 public junior colleges throughout the country revealed that a great variety of student activities were offered and that there was a considerable variation in the patterns of offerings among the various sections of the country.[2] Table I gives a summary of the student activities found in a majority of the junior colleges studied in each region. Some form

---

[1] "News and Trends," *NEA Journal,* 57:3, February, 1968.
[2] Jerry H. Robbins, "Student Activity Offerings in Public Junior Colleges," Faculty Research Grant No. 5654-M, The University of Mississippi, 1967.

TABLE I

Student Activities Found in a Majority of Junior Colleges in Each Region

Name of student activity	No.	%
Region I[a]		
Student government	65	82.3
Orientation or guidance activities	55	69.6
Yearbook	53	67.1
Honor society	50	63.3
Religious groups	49	62.0
Drama club	42	53.2
Region II[b]		
Student government	20	80.0
Interscholastic basketball	17	68.0
Interscholastic track and field	16	64.0
Interscholastic baseball	15	60.0
Honor society	15	60.0
Miscellaneous interscholastic sports	14	56.0
Miscellaneous intramural sports	14	56.0
Region III[c]		
Student government	85	86.7
Orientation or guidance activities	59	60.2
Honor society	56	57.1
Interscholastic basketball	54	55.1
Miscellaneous intramural sports	51	52.0
Region IV[d]		
Student government	56	96.6
Honor society	48	82.2
Orientation or guidance activities	47	81.0
Cheerleaders	33	56.9
Region V[e]		
Orientation or guidance activities	7	70.0
Student government	6	60.0

TABLE I (Continued)

Name of student activity	No.	%
Region VI[f]		
Orientation or guidance activities	35	89.7
Student government	34	87.2
Newspaper	28	71.8
Yearbook	26	66.7
Interscholastic basketball	24	61.5
Drama club	23	59.0
Interscholastic golf	21	53.8
Religious groups	21	53.8
Intramural basketball	20	51.3
Miscellaneous intramural sports	20	51.3
Total Regions[g]		
Student government	266	86.1
Orientation or guidance activities	212	68.6
Honor Society	183	58.9

[a] Region I: Alabama, Florida, Georgia, Kentucky, Louisiana, Mississippi, North Carolina, South Carolina, Tennessee, Texas, Virginia. N = 79.

[b] Region II: Alaska, Idaho, Montana, Nevada, Oregon, Utah, Washington. N = 25.

[c] Region III: Arizona, Arkansas, Colorado, Illinois, Indiana, Iowa, Kansas, Michigan, Minnesota, Missouri, Nebraska, New Mexico, North Dakota, Ohio, Oklahoma, South Dakota, West Virginia, Wisconsin, Wyoming, Puerto Rico, Canal Zone. N = 98.

[d] Region IV: California, Hawaii. N = 58.

[e] Region V: Connecticut, Maine, Massachusetts, New Hampshire, Rhode Island, Vermont. N = 10.

[f] Region VI: Delaware, Maryland, New Jersey, New York, Pennsylvania. N = 39.

[g] Total of all regions. N = 309.

of student government, orientation or guidance activities, and one or more honor societies were the only student activities found in a majority of all the junior colleges studied. However, in addition to these, the following were found to exist to some extent in all parts of the country: student newspaper, interscholastic basketball, yearbook, interscholastic baseball, a drama club, miscellaneous interscholastic sports, miscellaneous intramural sports, intramural basketball, all-school dances, a mixed chorus, a French club, and a Spanish club, in approximately that order.

Types of Activities

Student Participation in School Government. Junior college student councils are similar to those found in the secondary school in that written constitutions, assigned areas of operation, and faculty cooperation are all prerequisites. Like their secondary counterparts, they often charter clubs and supervise activities; however, much more is involved in the areas of time, money, and students. Unlike the student councils in most secondary schools, the junior college student government is given considerably more authority, often including major disciplinary functions. The rapid turnover of members of the student body in junior colleges allows fewer opportunities for developing leadership; student government activities are limited with respect to available time and to the types of activity. The junior college student body is sometimes prone to the development of cliques or "in-groups" — an unfortunate transfer of conditions from less-successful senior college organizations. Like any form of student organization, the student government in a junior college has only those powers given to it by the administration of the institution. The amount of authority given to student governments by junior college administrators has led to three descriptive categories for these organizations.

1. *Council with little or no authority.* Sometimes an organization for student government with little or no authority will be created at a junior college. This results either from student apathy or from an administration that desires only a "rubber-stamp" agreement from the student body organization.

Apathy by students in their governmental organization is, of course, not unique with the junior college. However, within its very nature the junior college possesses certain elements that foster poor student government; among these are the following:

a. *Brief student matriculation period.* Since junior colleges are designed for only a two-year educational program, there is a rapid and continued turnover of student leadership. This does not make for a continuous, effective government, which causes student disinterest.

b. *Age of students.* While the duties and responsibilities of student government are approximately the same at the junior college and senior college levels, the junior college leaders are younger. In addition, student leaders at the junior colleges have not had the added years of experience which student leaders at four-year colleges have had. Since both leaders and students lack some degree of maturity, the organization may not always be too effective.

c. *Minimum school spirit.* Particularly in the nonresidential-type community colleges undergoing widespread development at this time, student bodies have little or no opportunity to develop the school spirit necessary for successful student government organizations. Where few, if any, students live on campus and where classes are arranged to allow students to hold part-time jobs off campus, there is little opportunity or perhaps even necessity for an active student government organization.

Fortunately, few junior colleges have these "rubber-stamp" student councils.

2. *Council with complimentary authority.* This type of student government represents careful planning by the institutional leadership to find a distinct, responsible place for the student government in the administration of the junior college. Furthermore, it recognizes the students' ability to govern themselves and certain aspects of college life cooperatively with the administration of the institution. In such arrangements, student government organizations are allowed to direct student activity programs, usually with coordination by a staff member; to form and carry out a responsible government composed of executive and legislative divisions and, often, of a separate judicial division; to recommend student punishment to school authorities for certain types of cases; and to carry out such other duties as are extended to it. Most student government groups are of this type in American junior colleges.

3. *Council with sole authority.* The tendency is for student government groups in junior colleges to move toward areas of wide responsibility, as in senior colleges. Under such arrangements, the administration delegates broad authority to carry out activities

programs, to charter other campus organizations, to handle student discipline problems, to issue publications, to organize and supervise residence halls, to operate certain concessions (bookstore, grill, etc.) for additional funds, and to carry out other tasks with a minimum of administrative control.

Unfortunately, such beneficial arrangements sometimes result in the student government's becoming a scapegoat for the administration when anything unfavorable occurs involving the student body. Such an attitude toward the student government is unfortunate; for in giving authority to the student government, the administration should not feel that it has abrogated all of its responsibilities in student affairs. Rather, the administration must be quick to support and assist the student government whenever major problems arise.

Athletics. Efforts at forming an organized athletics program in the junior college began with the preliminary work which led to the formation of the National Junior College Athletic Association in 1938. This organization now administers guidelines for junior college athletics. Unfortunately, some junior colleges have tended to copy senior college athletics; and incidents have arisen which have brought bad publicity to the junior college athletic program. Many elements of the junior college athletics program also resemble the programs of good secondary schools; however, the junior college does have some problems which are related to small enrollments and to age range.

Since many of the junior colleges of past years have been fairly small, the opportunities for developing successful teams were limited both for interscholastics and intramurals. Since junior college students are neither high school nor senior college students, it has been very difficult to find good interscholastic competition on the same level. As the number of junior colleges grows, and as their sizes increase, these problems will abate for the most part. A detailed look at the concepts involved in physical activities is presented in Chapter 7.

As in the secondary schools, junior college athletic programs also give rise to related activities such as cheerleading, pep clubs, lettermen's organizations, and homecoming. While most of these related functions are valuable at the junior college level, some are not. For example, Graham has pointed out that homecoming is not a valid function for junior colleges to include in their student activities programs. He feels that these festivities are timed to be of convenience to the institution, and not to the alumni.

The following statement gives significant indication of problems related to homecoming on the junior college level:

> At a recent homecoming dance on a junior college campus not a single alumnus showed up. Homecoming activities are justified solely because they are collegiate activities.[3]

Other Activities. Hillway has reported that junior colleges "have a larger proportion of their students engaged in extracurricular activities than do four year institutions."[4] This is at least partly due to the wide variety of student activities which are found among the junior colleges of this country. In a recent survey of junior college student activities the following student activities (among many others) were found in one or more institutions:

> Interscholastic soccer, wrestling, water polo, gymnastics, riflery, and fencing.
> Intramural volleyball, table tennis, badminton, boxing, archery, checkers, chess, softball, bowling, horseshoes, fencing, hand ball, flagball, cross country, flickerball, bridge, and swimming.
> Clubs: Naturalists, Engineers, Young Republicans, Young Democrats, Ski, Veterans, Forestry, Press, Business, Aviation, Journalism, Pre-nursing, Geology, Electronics, Teaching, International Relations, Sports, Service, Business, Radio-TV, Speech, Home Economics, Marketing, Fine Arts, Architecture, Dentistry, Accounting, Secretaries, Young Farmers, Chess, Music, Electrical Engineering, Medical Science, Rodeo, Sports Car, Surfing, Rifle and Pistol, Writers, English, Photography, Petroleum, Business Leaders, Biology, X-Ray, Archaeology, Draftsmen, Agriculture, Cosmeltology, International Planning, Political Actions, Judo, Ice Skating, Modern Dance, Life Science, Pan-American, Circle K, Forensics, Criminology, Spectators, Philosophy, Art, Building Trades, Sky-Diving, Italian, Coin, Psychology, Sales and Marketing, State Historical, Agricultural Equipment, Distributive Education, Pre-veterinary, 4-H, Ham, Toastmasters, Education, Russian, Bacteriology, Human Relations, United Nations, Boots and Saddle, Jazz, Food Marketers, Square Dancing, Physical Education Majors, Social Philosophy, Trail, Outing, Lawyers, Conservatives, Soil Conservation, Mechanical Technology, Retailing, Practical Nurses, Bridge, Projection, Audio-

---

[3]R. William Graham, "A Look at Student Activities in the Junior Colleges," *Junior College Journal,* 33:43-45, September, 1962.

[4]Tyrus Hillway, *The American Two-Year College* (New York: Harper and Brothers, 1958), p. 172.

Visual, Patriotic American Youth, Driver Education, Parliamentary Procedure, Gourmet, Winter Sports, Red Cross, Industrial Chemistry, Model Car and Railroad, Houseplans, Physics, Insurance, Dairy, Horn and Hoof, Constructioneers, Cattle, Metals, Thermal Technology, Indian, Great Issues, Luncheon, Married Students, Slide Rule, and Bachelors.

Others: Athletic Honor Society, Dramatics Honor Society, Student Teachers Association, Inter-Varsity Christian Fellowship, Inter-Club Council, Police Cadet Corps, Dental Hygienists Association, Verse Choir, Collegiate Civitans, Pep Band, Society for the Advancement of Management, Student Chapter of American Chemical Society, Folk Swingers, American Society of Tool and Manufacturing Engineers, African-American Culture Study Society, Society of Broadcasters, Institute of Electrical and Electronics Engineers, National Association for the Advancement of Colored People, National Association of Gardeners, American Welding Society, String Band, and People-to-People.[5]

Religious groups and secret societies are sometimes found on junior college campuses and reflect the influence of the senior college. The Baptist Student Union, Canterbury Club, Hillel Club, Newman Apostolate, Wesley Foundation, and other similar groups function in conjunction with local churches. Such groups are particularly effective on residential campuses where school surroundings must become "home." On nonresidential campuses, such groups do not have as great an effect on the student body, because it is not necessary to duplicate the major elements of the surrounding community on the campus.

Secret societies do exist in the form of fraternities and sororities on some junior college campuses. In some cases, state laws prohibit their existing on campuses; and, in others, local regulations and policy forbid or discourage such organizations. Where they do exist, generally on a residential campus, they may provide a valuable service by offering their members social and fraternal opportunities that do not exist elsewhere on the campus. Their internal organizations provide practical training in leadership and cooperation. Providing houses, other than perhaps meeting rooms, for these groups cannot be justified either administratively or financially on a junior college campus of moderate size. The matter of the expenses

[5]Robbins, *op. cit.*

involved for a two-year stay at a junior college makes such student investments of questionable nature. Certainly such groups should be recognized if they exist, so that they may be effectively integrated into the student activities program and controlled by the institutions.

THE ELEMENTARY SCHOOL

The elementary school, like the junior college, has undergone significant changes in the last few decades. The four gloomy walls of the dungeon-like classroom — traditional marks of the "little red schoolhouse" — are now gone. As the physical setting of the elementary classroom has changed and become more flexible and informal, so has the curriculum of the elementary schools. New techniques of teaching coupled with strides in educational technology have made significant improvements in the academic portion of the curriculum. In an effort to bring balance to school life and student development, elementary schools, particularly in recent years, have made strides in developing a formal program of student activities.

Few of the student activities found in the elementary school are unique; in fact, Allen, Alexander, and Means wrote some while ago that many "activities formerly found only in the secondary schools are becoming regular activities in the elementary schools."[6] A similar statement, unfortunately, may be made about the activities programs developing in the newest educational division: the middle schools. According to a statement by Cuff,

> Extra-class activities [in the middle schools] are usually limited to band, orchestra, chorus, student councils, and intramural sports. Instances of interscholastic athletics were not found[in 499 middle schools]. Activities are scheduled at lunchtime, after school, during a special period, or in competition with regular classes.[7]

Among the goals of modern education in the elementary schools listed by Petersen and Hayden are two specific goals of particular importance to the development and encouragement of an

---

[6]C. F. Allen, T. R. Alexander, and H. W. Means, *Extra-Curricular Activities in Elementary Schools* (St. Louis, Missouri: Webster Publishing Company, 1937), p. 7.
[7]William A. Cuff, "Middle Schools on the March," *NASSP Bulletin,* 51:84, February, 1967.

organized student activities program in the elementary schools. These two goals are the "importance of the physical development of each [child and the] development of social intelligence."[8] Generally, student activities in the elementary school may be said to include student government groups, publications, and special interest groups.

Types of Activities

Student Government. As in the junior college and the secondary school, student government activities provide student participation experiences that are valuable in later life as well as for the present. Operating through homerooms, elementary school student body organizations provide cooperation between students and administration on a limited basis. Especially in departmentalized elementary schools, the student government organization provides student unity that may become lost in the transition of moving to different teachers and different classrooms. Since this book deals mainly with student activities on the secondary level, this discussion of elementary school student body organizations will simply differentiate between the secondary and elementary organizations.

Some considerations that are unique to the elementary school must be made in setting up the system of providing council representatives. While election of representatives is possible in middle schools and in grades four, five, and six in traditional elementary schools, a means of teacher representation from the lower grade levels must be included. A primary-grade teacher should advise the student council on primary affairs. Careful selection by the administration of the teacher must be made, and the student council should understand the function of the teacher who represents the primary grades. Qualifications mentioned for a good sponsor (see Chapter 14) may serve as a basis for the selection of this faculty member.

Other problems unique to the elementary school student-body organization follow from the duties of the council, proper council procedure, and the council elections. In all cases it must be pointed out that a respected student group in the elementary schools will have a tremendous strengthening effect on student body organizations in secondary schools. Because of the age and maturity of the

---

[8]Dorothy G. Petersen and Velma D. Hayden, *Teaching and Learning in the Elementary School* (New York: Appleton-Century-Crofts, Inc., 1961), p. 36.

students involved, the council in the elementary school will not be able to carry out the major functions executed by councils on the secondary level. The council can provide, however, useful services for the school and students by arranging such activities as monitors in hallways, street crossing guards, and directors of school assemblies.

While the older students will play the major role in managing and executing these actions, provision must be made for either the participation by the lower-grade students or the recognition by the lower-grade students of the services provided by the older students. The concepts of *leadership* and *followership* may be taught and encouraged in such situations.

Elementary students may not be expected to use detailed parliamentary procedure in conducting business, but it would be wise for the sponsors to teach the basic concepts of such procedure. Printed forms outlining a simple agenda and reviewing the procedure for making a motion are most useful. Since elections must be carried out either for representatives or officers, or both, much adult direction will be necessary for both pupils and the campaigners to ascertain that the election is carried out properly.

Publications. Very few, if any, elementary schools produce a yearbook. Such an undertaking would be almost too ambitious for elementary pupils. In numerous instances of twelve-grade schools, the elementary division is alloted a number of pages in the high school yearbook. Designated elementary students are responsible for designing and executing the layout of the section. In such cases, the services of an elementary sponsor to coordinate the work of the youngsters is advisable.

A number of elementary schools have had somewhat more success with school newspapers than with yearbooks. Leonard Kaplan has termed this number as "relatively few,"[9] however. Among the readily obvious reasons for lack of success are lack of time by students and teachers, lack of content for a periodical of any frequency, lack of ability and equipment to produce a suitable periodical, and lack of financial support. Lack of financial support is a limiting factor for any type of publication similar to those of the secondary school, for elementary students cannot sell advertisements

[9]Leonard Kaplan, "Why Have An Elementary School Newspaper?" *The Instructor,* 74:53, May, 1965.

to local merchants as do their counterparts in secondary schools. The most successful elementary papers have been the result of class publications committees who had mimeographed the stories written by their class members. Additional copies were distributed to other rooms.

Leonard Kaplan has written of the beneficial uses of such a newspaper. The newspaper of which he speaks was a duplicated story sheet with student contributions from slow learners as well as from the better students. Kaplan found that the newspaper "instilled in many children the motivating feelings of accomplishment, security, and success."[10]

Special Interest Groups. Elementary schools offer a great, but often little-used, opportunity for the encouragement of special interest groups. Organizations such as the Earth Club, Science Club, Music Club, and others may be developed to pursue special interests of short duration or can become important and lasting portions of the student activities program. Student interest and capable, willing faculty leadership are essentials.

School playdays, with picnics, ball games, numerous races, and other events have long been a part of the elementary school activities program. Now that an increasing emphasis has been placed on physical fitness, elementary schools have developed intraschool and, to some extent, interschool athletic programs. Softball, touch football, basketball, swimming, and running, for both boys and girls, easily lend themselves to such programs if adequate facilities and proper scheduling are available. Students and parents must understand that such activities are only an extension of the school's physical education program, and that such a program is not designed to place excessive demands on body and time.

SUMMARY

Student activities are no longer found primarily in the senior high school. Many elementary schools have recently adapted student activities from the junior and senior high schools. These activities will, of necessity, have to be limited in several ways because of the

---

[10]*Ibid.*, p. 96.

nature of the student body. In grades 13-14, the junior college, there is great need for unique junior college activities, not those handed down from the senior colleges. This chapter has presented the problems and suggestions for the student activities programs in both the elementary school and the junior college.

REFERENCES

Allen, C. F., Alexander, T. R., and Means, H. W. *Extra-Curricular Activities in Elementary Schools.* St. Louis, Missouri: Webster Publishing Co., 1937.

Cuff, William A. "Middle Schools on the March," *NASSP Bulletin,* 51:82-86, February, 1967.

Geiger, Evangeline. "Group Guidance Through Student Activities in an Elementary School," *Educational Administration and Supervision,* 44:338-348, November, 1958.

Graham, R. William. "A Look at Student Activities in the Junior Colleges," *Junior College Journal,* 33:43-45, September, 1962.

Hillway, Tyrus. *The American Two-Year College.* New York: Harper and Brothers, 1958.

Kaplan, Leonard. "Why Have an Elementary School Newspaper?" *The Instructor,* 74:53, 96, May, 1965.

McKown, Harry C. *Activities in the Elementary School.* New York: McGraw-Hill Book Co., 1938.

Mehl, Marie A., Mill, Hubert H., and Douglass, Harl R. "Participating in Extraclass Activities." *Teaching in the Elementary School.* 2nd ed. New York: Ronald Press Co., 1958.

Misner, Paul J. "Pupil Activities in the Elementary School." *Elementary School Administration.* Columbus, Ohio: Charles E. Merrill Books, 1963.

"News and Trends," *NEA Journal,* 57:3, February, 1968.

Otto, Henry J., and Hamrin, S. A. *Co-Curricular Activities in Elementary Schools.* New York: D. Appleton-Century Co., 1937.

Petersen, Dorothy G., and Hayden, Velma D. *Teaching and Learning in the Elementary School.* New York: Appleton-Century-Crofts, Inc., 1961.

Reavis, William C., *et al.* "Extra-Class Learning Experiences." *Administering the Elementary School.* New York: Prentice-Hall, Inc., 1953.

Reed, Calvin H. "Sense of Responsibility: Are Classroom Activities Nourishing It?" *Elementary School Journal,* 58:394-397, April, 1958.

Robbins, Jerry H. "Student Activity Offerings in Public Junior Colleges," Faculty Research Grant No. 5654-M, The University of Mississippi, 1967.

Tickton, Sidney G. "What's Ahead for Public Junior Colleges," *Junior College Journal,* 34:46-48, November, 1963.

Part III

TYPES OF
STUDENT ACTIVITIES

The innovative high school will probably offer many types of student activities, many of which are also found in elementary or junior high schools or in junior colleges. While aimed at the senior high school, these chapters give useful information that may be applied to similar student activities at other academic levels.

Student participation in school government, athletics and physical activities, publications, subject matter and special interest groups, service and recognition groups, fine arts activities, and social activities are discussed in Chapters 6 - 12.

Chapter 6

STUDENT PARTICIPATION IN SCHOOL ADMINISTRATION

Most American secondary schools make some provision for the students to have an official voice in school affairs. Like many other aspects of the student activities program, the organizational pattern, the name, the responsibilities, and the activities of student government organizations vary considerably.

A MATTER OF SEMANTICS

The student council is the name most often given to the body of student representatives, although many other names, such as the general organization, the student organization, the student association, and the school council are sometimes used. Even though some authorities prefer the term school council, the fact that the influential National Association of Student Councils is so named indicates that the use of the term student council will continue in favor.

Student government, student participation in school government, and student self-government are among the various names that have been applied to the students' role in school affairs. The use of the term government seems out of place, as students do not govern, nor do we ordinarily think of schools as being governed. Further, some of these terms have applied in the past to several more-or-less separate student organizations – a council *and* a student court in most instances. Today's secondary schools usually consolidate all student involvement into one body – a council – and student council has become more and more a generic name as well as a specific name.

The concept of the school council – a broader concept than student council – has considerable merit, but it does not seem to have been accepted to any great extent. The school council is an organization consisting of representatives of each type of school citizen – students, teachers, administrators, noncertificated personnel, (sometimes parents, board members, and community leaders) — whose chief function is to improve the school community in any or all of its many and varied aspects. Perhaps the very breadth of this concept is its main shortcoming. Relatively few problems directly and legitimately concern all groups of persons connected with the school, and it may be difficult to maintain interest among all these factions.

The definition of student council has changed with changing views on student activities. One early reason for the student council was to keep the students informed of school policies and activities; later the teaching of basic skills in group procedures came into vogue. Still later, the student council was used for discussing school policies and programs, but the student council had little opportunity to take action. In recent years, it has been common for the student council to assist in forming policies and procedures.

How, then, is student council now defined? A student council might be defined as a group of students selected by their fellow students to manage student affairs and to represent the student body. A recent definition says that the student council is "a group of elected citizens in a school who meet together regularly to: Promote Citizenship... Promote Scholarship... Promote Leadership... Promote Human Relations... and Promote Cultural Values."[1] Another, perhaps better, definition is that a student council is a group of students elected by students to represent students in school affairs. Inasmuch as student councils and other similar organizations vary greatly in organization and function, perhaps it is pointless to try to define the term more specifically.

Misconceptions of the Student Council

While it is difficult to say exactly what the student council *is*, it is fairly easy to say what the modern student council is *not*.

1. It is not student self-government; it is student participation in school life.
2. It is not an administrative device to get things done; it is a part of the total educational program.
3. It is not intended to relieve the school staff of any of its responsibilities; it enriches the teaching and learning of democracy.

[1] Earl Reum, "And Finally — A Definition," *School Activities,* 37:17, May, 1966.

4. It is not limited to discipline and conduct; it sponsors a broad range of activities.
5. It is not merely a legislative body; it is a representative body that functions in all phases of school life.
6. It is not an elite or privileged group; it represents all students.
7. It is not just another club; it is the most important group in school.

PURPOSES OF THE STUDENT COUNCIL

Each student council constitution has (or should have) a list of the purposes — the aims and objectives — of the organization. Among the many purposes often stated for student councils are these:

1. To provide for citizenship training; to prepare for life in a democracy; to foster sentiments of law and order.
2. To allow students to participate in and/or manage their own affairs; to assist in the internal administration of the school.
3. To promote proper student-faculty-staff-community relationships; to increase the interest of each group in the school; to more closely integrate the school and the community.
4. To promote the general welfare of students, and to improve the school community.
5. To capitalize on certain "fundamental drives" of adolescents; to better acquaint students with adult patterns of living.
6. To make students increasingly more self-directive; to teach them how to assume responsibility and initiative; to encourage self-discipline.
7. To teach social cooperation and sharing; to improve attitudes.
8. To increase school morale; to provide for emotional satisfaction.
9. To discover and develop special qualities and abilities; to develop leadership and followership.
10. To assist with organizing, promoting, administering, articulating, and supervising other student activities.

The school is, by definition, an educational institution. Therefore, every aspect of the program of the school, especially the student council, must have an educational objective. This educational objective must be the primary reason for the establishment and maintenance of student councils. As Bear has said,

The main function of the student council is to provide learning experiences for students. Its principal contribution to learning is the development of good citizenship which is one of the cardinal objectives of the schools, both public and nonpublic. For this reason, the student council is no longer considered to be extra-curricular or an adjunct to the curriculum, but an integral part of it.[2]

Bear continues by saying that a second function is that of providing a climate conducive to the intellectual, physical, social, and moral development of every member of the student body. A third, but less important, function is that of assisting the administration in managing the student activities program.

ORGANIZATION

Source of Authority

Legally, education is a function of the state. States have created school districts, each with a governing board to which the state has granted considerable authority. The board employs a heirarchy of administrators and delegates the operational aspects of the school to them, such that the principal is the responsible head of each school attendance center. The principal has granted whatever authority the student council has; and he retains the right to expand on, withdraw, or modify this authority. The source of authority is frequently misunderstood, and many student council constitutions are mis-leading or in error. The source of authority for student "govern-ment," unlike that of political government, does not arise from the populace.

The Constitution and Bylaws

In some small schools, and in others with an informal system, a written constitution is not used. A few schools conduct affairs using a "town meeting" type of action, or using an appointed body of students as a sounding board and communications device. Most student councils, however, have a written constitution to formalize

[2]Williard Bear, "Functions, Objectives, and Basic Principles of the Student Council," *The Student Council in the Secondary School* (Washington, D.C.: The National Association of Student Councils, 1962), p. 7.

the organizational scheme. For most modern schools the only occasion to write a constitution comes when the present one becomes so out-of-date or inadequate that it is easier to start over than to amend the present one.

In reviewing the organization of a student council, either present or proposed, the following points may be helpful:

1. The constitution should be short and simple. Items likely to be changed often, such as meeting times and places, election procedure, and so on should not be incorporated into the body of the constitution, but should be placed in the bylaws.

2. The source of authority and the areas for which the student council has some or complete authority should be carefully spelled out.

3. The constitution should be tailored for a particular school. A school should not imitate a governmental constitution, transplant one from another school, or copy verbatim a "model" constitution.

4. Most constitutions provide for a unicameral body, preferably of not more than about 40 people.[3] Routine matters may be handled by an executive committee in a large student council.

5. Each student should be represented exactly once. The "one man, one vote" concept is as valid for student councils as it is for Congress. The basis of representation should be by homerooms, by classes, or by students selected at large. It is undemocratic to give disproportionate representation to upper classes or to require a certain number of members of each sex.

6. Sponsors should be faculty members appointed by the principal, but ordinarily should not include the principal himself.

7. There should be few qualifications for members and officers, other than being bona fide members of the school and passing most, or all, school work.

8. The student council should be organized in such a way that it is primarily a deliberative group rather than a service group or fund-raising group. Many proposals should be referred elsewhere for action, rather than taken up by the student council.

9. Meetings should be held at least once every two weeks, but a weekly meeting is better, and a daily session is the best. If time is

---

[3] A notable exception may be found in Charles M. Russell High School in Great Falls, Montana, where a three-branch, bicameral organization, patterned after the United States government, appears to be highly successful.

available daily, only one or two formal meetings per week are necessary; the remainder of the time for each week should be used for committee work and study sessions. Meetings should be held on school time and in a student council room.

10. At least the four usual officers are needed. A large student council usually provides for additional officers such as corresponding secretary and a parliamentarian. Major offices should be filled in school-wide elections; minor offices may be filled from within the membership of the student council.

11. Committees should ordinarily be chaired by a student council member, but should contain nonmembers of the council, if at all possible. Most committee work should be done by *ad hoc* committees, and standing committees should be kept to a minimum. It is often helpful to have a faculty member available to serve as a consultant to major committees. Some committees may be made up of both students and faculty — the students should be appointed by the student council president and the faculty members by the principal.

12. The local student council should be affiliated with regional, state, and national associations of student councils.

13. Bylaws should spell out the nomination procedures, election mechanics, installation provisions, the committee structure, details of meeting times and places, budgetary items, and any other provisions that might need frequent changes.

The items above are merely intended as guidelines; for the form of organization is of much less importance than its adaptability to the unique needs of a particular school. As Gerald Van Pool has said, "The best kind of student organization is that type which actually works best."

The Student Court

At one time the student court was considered a proper part of the arrangement of student government. This position has been reversed in recent years. As Earl Reum has stated,

> Student Councils should never have student courts; the council
> is not a judicial structure. It is the moral, legal, cultural responsi-
> bility of the school, the school administration, to judge youngsters

and to hand out punishments. This is not the function of the Student Council.[4]

The student council should be a positive, constructive organization, and its time and energy should not be wasted on being a "junior Gestapo" or in devising punishments for those who fall into its hands.

To be sure, a few schools have used some variant of the student court with considerable success.[5] The following statement should be considered in evaluating student courts: "If you don't have one, don't organize one, if you do have one, evaluate its work carefully."

SPHERES OF RESPONSIBILITY

Increasingly, administrators and student councils are agreeing on áreas in which the student council has degrees of authority or responsibility. This concept of "budget of power," "areas of sovereignty," or "spheres of authority" recognizes that in certain aspects of the administration of the school the student council has no authority; in certain aspects it shares authority with the school administration; and in certain areas it may assume complete responsibility.

In answering the question "How much power does the student council have?" Earl Reum has said,

> The question is relevant because it is asked again and again, but the answer lies in the realization that in American public educatiion (*sic*) the voice of the people controls the curriculum, the attitudes, the activities program, and the faculties. Everything significant about the schools is determined by the people through their representatives selected to serve on their school board. The school board, then, is the basic fundamental power-giving group. They have been invested with all the power of the people to do the best job they are capable of doing in relegating that power to groups

[4]Earl Reum, "How Much Power Does the Student Council Have?" *School Activities,* 37:12, May, 1966.

[5]A show of hands of approximately 200 secondary administrators attending a panel discussion on student activities at the 1968 National Association of Secondary School Principals convention revealed only four schools of those represented with a student court. Statements of effectiveness from these individuals ranged from "unsuccessful" to "very effective."

– that authority to groups – that responsibility – in terms of basic objectives of education.[6]

The student council derives its authority from the administration rather than from the students, and in this sense it is not democratic. It may, and should, operate in a democratic manner within the latitude granted by the administration; but it has no right to attempt to exert authority outside these bounds. The student council constitution should include a statement of the source of authority and general statements defining the areas of student council responsibility. The principal and the student council should have a complete understanding as to what is included in each of the spheres of authority. Hopefully, the student council in a given school will be granted additional areas of responsibility and authority as it becomes more sophisticated.

To illustrate the types of items often found in each of the three major spheres of influence, Table I may be helpful. It should be noted that the items under each heading are not mutually exclusive as they have been gathered from a number of sources.

ELECTIONS

Election procedure should be spelled out in detail in the bylaws of the student council. In addition to being a device for obtaining members and officers, the election should provide experience for the future voting population. The election process includes establishing eligibility requirements, nomination, campaigning, voting, and installation.

Eligibility Requirements

Eligibility requirements should be minimal for maximum consistency with the democratic concept, for "when standards for membership are high, pupils do not have an opportunity to weed the good from the poor at election time."[7] It is far more realistic to train students to select good leaders by comparing qualifications of those running than to permit only those with high qualifications to run.

[6]Reum, "How Much Power?" p. 11.
[7]Herbert W. Wey, *Handbook for Principals* (New York: Schaum Publishing Company, 1966), p. 68.

TABLE 1

Representative Items in Each of Three Spheres of Influence Found among Student Councils

No Responsibility	Shared Responsibility	Complete Responsibility
1. Hiring and firing of personnel	1. Assemblies	1. Homecoming
2. Teachers' pay	2. School spirit	2. Social events
3. Noncertified personnel	3. Athletics	3. Charity drives
4. School maintenance	4. Election of cheer-leaders	4. Special committees
5. Purchase of equipment	5. Interscholastic relations	5. Elections
6. School buses	6. Organization of new clubs	6. Leadership-training workshop
7. Cost of school lunches	7. Student-faculty relations	7. Publicity for activities
8. Course offerings	8. Welfare of students and faculty	8. Chartering of clubs
9. Teaching methods	9. School calendar	9. Congratulatory and condolence expressions
10. Length of school day	10. Promotion of citizenship and leadership	10. Executive committee agenda meetings
11. Length of vacation	11. Code of dress	11. Suggestion box
12. Hall passes	12. Code of conduct	12. Evaluation of year's work
13. Discipline and punishment	13. Foreign exchange student	13. Interschool visitation
14. Homework	14. Promotion of health and safety	14. Cleanup programs
15. Grades and honor roll	15. Sales projects	15. Constitution revision
16. NHS selection		16. Information and welcoming service
17. Counseling		17. Orientation activities
18. Student enrollment		
19. Academic credits		
20. School finance		
21. School policies		

Johnston and Faunce pointed up the importance of low eligibility requirements with this statement:

> As a plan for civic training through civic participation, the student council has not been notably successful. Through minimum scholarship plans, we have often limited participation in the council to those students who can be trusted, as evidenced by their marks in our classes. In some schools, candidates for the council are first screened by the faculty. In a few schools, the faculty actually does the nominating. Perhaps even more serious is the degree to which participation tends to be limited to the elected representatives rather than extended to every student in the school. Ideally, the council should be the voice of all the people. The youngest, poorest, least articulate, and the least influential student in the entire high school should firmly believe, with all of his fellows, that he may present an idea which will affect the whole school through its transmission to the floor of the student council. Actually, as a result of our typically extra-curricular elective base, little time is ever spent on school-wide discussion and group decisions on the constituent level. The identity of the council members is seldom remembered by the average student. He feels little concern about their decisions, or the reasons which prompted them — for they are not *his* decision, *his* reasons.[8]

Before nominations are made, faculty members should discuss desirable qualities for student council members and officers with the student body. Often this is done in social studies classes, but it could also be effectively handled in homerooms or other small groups. Characteristics such as the following usually emerge from such discussions:

It is highly desirable for student council members and officers:
1. To be greatly interested in the school.
2. To be respected by their associates.
3. To have sound ideas for school improvement.
4. To be able to communicate their ideas to others.
5. To be willing to compromise.
6. To be willing to assume responsibility.
7. To be able to carry through with responsibilities accepted.
8. To represent effectively their constituencies.
9. To be willing and able to attend all meetings.

[8]Edgar G. Johnston and Roland C. Faunce, *Student Activities in Secondary Schools* (New York: Ronald Press Co., 1952), pp. 37-38.

10. To be good followers as well as good leaders.
11. To like people and to work well with others.
12. To have a desire to serve.
13. To be willing to undertake self-improvement, and to take criticism.
14. To have initiative.
15. To be sincere and honest.
16. To have a basic knowledge of parliamentary procedure and leadership skills.
17. To think clearly and speak effectively.

Nominations

Before campaigns or voting can take place, some method of nomination must be provided. There are four major methods of nomination.

Self-nomination. Any eligible student who wishes to run may announce his intention to some designated person.

Petition. Any eligible student who wishes to run may gather the signatures of a certain number of students and file the petition with some designated person.

Nominating Committee. A comittee of students or students and faculty may nominate one or more persons for each position to be filled. Provision is usually made for nominations "from the floor" in connection with this method.

Convention. In an assembly called for the purpose, the student body, or delegates therefrom, may nominate candidates in the same manner as the national political convention. For student council members, the homeroom or class may nominate from the floor.

Campaign

Between the time of nomination and the election, provision should be made for a campaign. Even for positions as representatives from homerooms or from a class, the election should not take place on the day of nominations, but should be at least several days later.

The campaign should be dignified and well-planned; well-defined provisions for "electioneering" should not only be tolerated but encouraged. The bylaws of the student council constitution should contain regulations for the conduct of elections. Costs should be kept low, and for verification of costs many schools require candidates to file lists of campaign expenses. Posters and other signs may be used, although in most buildings it will be necessary to specify when, where, how, and by whom they may be attached to the surfaces of the building. Use of pep bands, rallies, and informal parades are among the many devices that are often used as part of the election campaign. Often it is difficult to anticipate the devices that creative campaigners will design.

Care should be taken by the student council sponsor, the election committee, and the administration to insure that all candidates are treated fairly during the campaign. "Mud-slinging," removal of posters, and similar malpractices *do* take place even in the best-supervised canpaigns. If this becomes a problem of any magnitude, steps should be taken to educate the student body on the importance of "clean" campaigns.

Provisions should be made for each candidate to speak at least once before the group that will elect him. For representatives, this will ordinarily be before a homeroom or class meeting; for officers, this will usually be before the entire student body.

Voting

All students should have the *right* to vote, but many schools are using some form of registration or qualifying procedure, which usually takes place during the campaign.

Students should be encouraged to vote; bad officials are often elected by good citizens who do not vote. On the other hand, students should not be required to vote, or to vote on every race, for if a student has no basis for making a choice, then he makes a chance selection which is of no value.

All voting should be by secret ballot. Election committees should establish polling places, they should make sure that the opening and closing times are carefully adhered to and that the election is conducted in a dignified manner. The counting of the ballots should be handled by disinterested students. Seniors or outgoing officers are often used for this purpose.

In addition to the traditional voting practices used by schools, several devices exist for obtaining election results quickly and accurately. The Memphis City Schools use the voting machines of the County Elections Commission, and the Cleveland, Mississippi, Public Schools use the data processing equipment of nearby Delta State College for vote counting.

The constitution, bylaws, or election committee regulations should carefully define the procedures to be followed in the event no candidate receives a majority of the votes cast, and write-in votes are used.

Should seniors vote for the next year's officers? Preferably not. Should the incoming class vote for the next year's officers? Yes. However, there are obvious problems connected with these recommendations.

Elections should be held in the spring of the year so that officers and members may be installed before school is out and the summer may be used for evaluating, planning, and orientation.

Installation

An impressive, dignified installation ceremony lends prestige and status to the student council and to its members. Many schools write their own ceremony, or have a traditional ceremony to use. The ceremony should be held at or near the end of the school year; it is frequently held in connection with an awards day or with other honors. Some schools have found it helpful to review the purposes and functions of the student council for the student body during the installation ceremony.

Several good ceremonies may be found in the National Association of Student Council's *The Student Council in the Secondary School.*[9]

PRE-SERVICE AND IN-SERVICE TRAINING

Effective student councils are devoting more and more time to pre-service and in-service training of members and officers. A variety of methods are utilized; and the training or orientation ranges from very simple, brief sessions to elaborate series of workshops, leadership training camps, leadership classes, and the like.

Leadership training and orientation patterns fall into two general categories: (1) multischool summer leadership training camps, conferences, student council workshops, etc.; and (2) various local programs.

[9]See installation recommendations in *The Student Council in the Secondary School* (Washington: National Association of Student Councils, 1962), Chapter VI.

When a number of schools combine to provide leadership training, great things can be accomplished. A leadership training workshop on the national level has been held every summer since 1951 near Estes Park, Colorado, and other national leadership training conferences, sponsored by the National Association of Student Councils, are held elsewhere each summer. Each state student council association may send at least five delegates to the four-day conference of the National Association of Student Councils held each summer. Many state and regional associations hold one- or two-day conventions or conferences.

Most state student council associations now have a summer workshop for leadership training. One of the first states to have such a workshop was Arkansas. The Arkansas Association of Student Councils workshop meets on a college campus in August for five days. Two delegates and a sponsor from each school that is a member of the AASC may attend. The schedule each day consists of an assembly with inspirational and informative sessions (pencil-pushing-periods); "council" meetings, both adult-led and student-led, in which the students, in small groups, tackle hypothetical but realistic problems; another informational assembly; and assorted recreational, social, and entertaining activities. The objectives of the AASC workshop are:

1. To provide instruction for new student council sponsors and student leaders.
2. To further the growth of the student council as a medium of citizenship training in our schools.
3. To promote a common philosophy of the aims and objectives of the student council.
4. To bring about more uniform practices in student council work within the state.
5. To encourage the growth of the Arkansas Association of Student Councils.

On the local level, there are three major approaches to the development of student leadership. One is to develop and improve status leadership. Under this concept, the officers of the student council, and often other organizations as well, receive separate, intensive instruction in leadership. Sometimes this takes place during the school day, but more often this instruction takes place in the summer, on weekends, or outside school hours. The usual organization consists of lectures on parliamentary procedure, public speaking,

the responsibilities and duties of officers, and local policies. Sometimes practice in parliamentary procedure and public speaking is
included. The method of training status leadership assumes that
"leadership" is exercised primarily by officially elected officers.

A second method is to develop and improve a leadership elite.
Under this concept, students with high intelligence, academic success, and polished social graces are selected, usually by the faculty or
administration, and trained for leadership roles. The organization of
this type of instruction is oriented toward parliamentary techniques,
human relations, and group psychology. In brief, it is slanted toward
the efficient manipulation of groups, and assumes that the elite
students of the school can be trained for leadership outside the group
in which the leadership is to be exercised.

The third, and best, method is to develop group leadership
techniques in a group situation. In this method, leadership is seen as
a series of functions to be performed, rather than as a series of
inherent qualities, or as group manipulation. The techniques lean
heavily on group problem solving, role playing, self and group
evaluation, and various other cooperative efforts.

At San Bernardino (California) High School, following the
spring election, the incoming and retiring student council officers
spend a weekend in evaluating the year's activities and in planning
for the coming year. Each retiring officer has major responsibilities
for orienting his successor. During the summer months, a regular
weekly meeting of the student council is held at the school, at night,
with the sponsor and principal present. These meetings are devoted
to planning, orientation, and leadership training.[10]

Each fall the Oak Park and River Forest High School at Oak
Park, Illinois, holds a Student Leadership Colloquium to honor
student leaders and to help improve their understanding and thereby
their fulfillment of their roles as student leaders. A student leader
from each activity and the activity sponsor are invited to attend. The
program begins with a keynote address by a prominent leader and is
followed by a question-and-answer period and dinner. The administration feels that the participation of both students and faculty in
the program is a direct way to increase the student leader's pride in
and concern for his office and/or position.

[10]See "Student Council on a 12 Month Basis" by G. Keith Dolann, *School Activities,*
37:7-8, May, 1966.

In some schools, as at Mapleton High School in Denver, Colorado, the student council is organized as a regular class, and credit is given for participation. With five meetings a week, one or two might be devoted to business sessions, one or two devoted to formal learning activities, one to committee meetings, and one to sponsor-chairman and sponsor-officer individual conferences.

In some schools a leadership training class is organized which often includes students other than student council officers and members. Practices vary in the organization of the leadership training class. The length varies from a few days to a full year. Sometimes they are held within school hours, sometimes not. Credit is sometimes given, more often it is not. The content and approach vary, as indicated on the following pages.[11]

Regardless of whatever method of organization seems best for a particular school, the learning experiences of the pre-service and in-service training of the student leaders should include the following:

1. The organizational structure of the group with which the student will be concerned.
2. The aims, objectives, and purposes of the organization.
3. Communication.
   A. The importance of good communications.
   B. Definition of communications.
   C. Dangers in communication.
   D. Modes of communication.
   E. Qualities of a good speaker.
   F. Qualities of a good listener.
   G. Ways to communicate with various publics.
4. Problem-solving techniques. A possible sequence of steps to be included in the problem solving process would be:
   A. Recognize that the problem exists.
   B. Define and state the problem.
   C. Get the facts.
   D. List several possible solutions and the advantages and disadvantages of each.
   E. Make a choice, and map out a plan of action.
   F. Carry out the plan of action.

[11]See also Fred R. Petrillo, "A Survey of Leadership Education Programs in Selected Colorado High Schools" (unpublished dissertation, The University of Denver, Denver, Colorado, 1964.)

G. Evaluate.
5. Parliamentary procedure techniques.
6. Techniques of group leadership, such as the following:
   A. A philosophy of good group leadership.
   B. Characteristics of an effective group.
   C. Types of groups.
   D. Forces operating within a group.
   E. Behavior patterns of members of groups.
7. Types of leaders.
8. Roles of elected officials.
9. Supervised experience.
10. Sources of help and additional reading.

MEETINGS

The student council should have a regular meeting time and place. Preferably, the meetings should take place during the school day and at least one business meeting per week will probably be needed. More and more schools are providing special quarters for student council meetings, as well as storage and office space for the student council's activities.

An agenda must be prepared before each meeting. Usually, the executive committee and the sponsor determine the agenda. Sources of items for the agenda will include such routine items as reading the minutes and the treasurer's report; semi-routine items will include such things as committee reports and projects that have been planned on a long-range basis; and items of new business arising from new ideas and changing conditions. If possible, the agenda should be prepared, reproduced, and distributed to the student council membership at least a day or so ahead of the meeting.

The presiding officer and the membership should be well-versed in, and encouraged to use, proper parliamentary procedure during the meetings, especially in large student councils. The presiding officer is responsible for the physical arrangements of the meeting room being in good order prior to the meeting. Chairs, tables, the lectern, the gavel, and copies of the minutes, financial report, committee reports, and other written materials are among the important items to be checked before the meeting starts.

The sponsor has a difficult role to play during the meetings. Generally, the sponsor should work "behind the scenes." If student council members have been well-educated to their responsibilities and limits of authority, and if meetings have been well-planned, then the sponsor's role during the meetings can, and should, be passive except when he is serving as a resource person.

Should student council members be required to attend meetings? Fortunately, the problem seldom arises. Generally, however, if the meeting is held during school hours, the meeting is considered the student's responsibility for that time, and the administration and the faculty should have a firm agreement on this point. If the meeting is held outside school hours, it is questionable whether or not a student could be required to attend, especially from a legal point of view. In any case, absences excusable by school policy must be honored by student council regulations, and a quorum as defined in the bylaws must be present to conduct business.

In many schools provision is made for persons other than members of the student council and the sponsor to attend, but not participate, in student council meetings. Often the Director of Student Activities or a member of the administrative staff will be present; sometimes a representative of the custodial staff, or other nonprofessional staff member will be present; and sometimes arrangements are made for nonmember students to visit student council meetings. For example, Conway (Arkansas) High School, for a number of years, permitted members of the student council, in rotation, to bring a student guest to the meetings. The attendance office was to be notified ahead of time, and the student guest was excused from class to attend the meeting.

STUDENT COUNCIL ACTIVITIES

What does the effective student council do? This, of course, varies widely from school to school. The NASC publication *The Student Council in the Secondary School* devotes almost two hundred pages to brief descriptions of outstanding student council projects. Issues of *Student Life Highlights, School Activities,* and the *Student Council Yearbook* contain ideas for projects. In general:

1. Student council projects should be in the areas where the student council has complete or partial authority.

2. Projects should be student-initiated and should come from student interests.

3. The student council should be concerned with real and significant problems.

4. Student council projects should always be positive in nature and educationally sound. They should conform with the objectives of the school and the student council.

5. Each project should involve as many students as possible, especially students who are not members of the student council.

6. There should be a reasonable probability of success on each project undertaken. However, if all projects succeed, the student council is probably not undertaking very challenging projects.

7. Most projects should be completed within the year they are begun. For very large or long-term projects a series of intermediate goals should be established, each of which can be attained in a reasonable amount of time.

8. Projects should be appropriate for the group, considering the age of the students, the size of the school, the resources available, and so on. As student bodies and student councils become more sophisticated, they may and should undertake more sophisticated projects.

9. Adult assistance should be available for all projects. The sponsor will assume this role for most projects, but at times it may be advisable to ask another faculty member, a parent, or a patron to assist with a project.

10. The student council should *not* become another service organization; it should strive to maintain a role as a deliberative body, and its projects generally should be those of concern to the entire school.

PUBLIC RELATIONS

Public relations, in its broader sense, means communication *with*, not *to*, various publics. Among the publics with which the student council has concern are the following:

The Administrative Staff. Student council officers should confer frequently with the principal and his assistants. These members of the school administrative staff should be regularly invited to attend student council meetings.

The Faculty. The faculty should be kept well informed of the student council's activities. In turn, the faculty should make suggestions to the council for their consideration. The sponsor has an important role in student council-faculty relationships.

Parents. Most schools have organized channels for communication between parents and the school. In addition to devising its own methods of communication with parents, the student council should utilize the channels established for general school communication.

The Student Body. Communication with the constituency is of great importance. While many schools have adequate provisions for communicating *from* the student council *to* the student body, relatively little communication from the student body to the student council occurs. Strong efforts should be made to correct this problem.

Other Student Organizations. Often little official communication takes place between the student council and other student organizations. Chartering organizations, reviewing and evaluating their activities, working on common financial problems, and the like are steps in the right direction, but these are not enough.

Other Schools. Interschool visitation and regional, state, and national conventions and workshops are *musts* for good student councils. The pooling of ideas and capitalizing on the mistakes of others are of great value.

Local Patrons. As is often done with parents, most schools have organized channels for communication with local patrons. These channels should be utilized and additional channels should be developed.

Community Organizations and News Media. Good rapport with churches, charitable organizations, civic groups, newspapers, radio and TV stations, and other local agencies will pay many dividends. Student councils should cultivate these relationships carefully.

Governmental Groups. Police, fire departments, city and county officials, the school board, hospitals, and other public agencies are usually happy to work with student councils in a variety of ways. Communication that is carried out at regular intervals gets better results than communication "when you want something."

EVALUATION

It has been said that evaluation is "looking back so you can move forward." All aspects of the student council should be continuously evaluated with periodic intensive evaluation. Questions such as "Why will we evaluate?", "What criteria will we use for evaluation?", "Who will do the evaluating?", "What procedures will we use for evaluation?", and "What use will be made of the results?", must be answered prior to undertaking an evaluation.

The purposes of evaluation include (1) making improvement; (2) ascertaining progress and growth; (3) giving direction to planning; and (4) serving as a record. It cannot be stressed too strongly that all evaluation should be in terms of objectives.

Every student council should have an extensive planning session prior to the opening of school each year. This planning session should include an evaluation of the previous year's work of the student council in order to move forward in a productive way. The planning session should also include the establishment of goals for the year, the means for attaining these goals, and the ways in which each goal will be evaluated.

There are numerous techniques for evaluating. Section II of Part E of the 1960 *Evaluative Criteria*[12] may be of use in evaluating the student council program. Informal questionnaires are often used. Open discussion is frequently of value. Some activities, such as dances and other social events, may be evaluated in a quantitative manner by counting the number who participate.

The preparation of an annual report is a useful device for evaluation purposes. A typical annual report comprises the following:

1. personal data concerning members including names, addresses, phone numbers, why they are on the council, and the class schedule
2. schedule of meetings and attendance
3. treasurer's report (budget and final report)
4. the basic annual report, which is the summary of the council's activities and recommendations for the coming year
5. minutes of the meeting *[sic]*
6. standing committee reports including membership, projects completed, and recommendations for new committees
7. the constitution

[12]National Study of Secondary School Evaluation, *Evaluative Criteria, 1960 ed.* (Washington, D.C.: NSSSE, 1960), pp. 241-256.

8. miscellaneous items such as the code of ethics and school pledge[13]

The "leg work" of evaluation of student council activities should be done by student council members. Individuals, temporary committees, and standing committees may be used depending upon the size and complexity of what is being evaluated. Often the student body should be involved in evaluating. Student-faculty committees are valuable. At times it may be valuable to have evaluation by a group of students from another school, by an authority in student council affairs, by teachers or administrators from another school, or by parents and patrons. The administrative staff of the school should frequently be involved.

Self-evaluation is the best evaluation. Anyone who has a legitimate interest or concern in student council affairs should be involved in the evaluation process. Evaluation is complete when some action is taken on the recommendations of the evaluation.

SUMMARY

This chapter has considered the most important of all student activities — the student council. Emphasis was placed on the fact that the student council is not student *government,* but student *participation* in school administration. The scope of authority and areas of responsibility for the student council were presented. Innovative practices for the student council were suggested.

REFERENCES

Allen, Charles F., *et al. Extra-Curricular Activities in the Elementary Schools.* St. Louis, Mo.: Webster Publishing Co., 1937, pp. 152-188.

Austin, David B., French, Will, and Hull, J. Dan. "School Activities and Student Organization." *American High School Administration: Policy and Practice.* 3rd ed. New York: Holt, Rinehart and Winston, 1962.

Bear, Williard. "Functions, Objectives, and Basic Principles of the Student Council." *The Student Council in the Secondary School.* Washington, D.C.: National Association of Student Councils, 1962, pp. 7-15.

[13]"How the Annual Report Helps to Evaluate the Student Council," Report of Discussion Group 69, National Association of Student Councils, *The 1967 NASC Yearbook* (Washington: NASC, 1967), p. 121.

Bloland, P.A. "Role of the Student Organization Adviser," *Personnel and Guidance Journal,* 46:44-49, September, 1967.

Dolan, G. Keith. "Student Council on a 12 Month Basis," *School Activities,* 37:7-8, May, 1966.

Fretwell, Elbert K. *Extra-Curricular Activities in Secondary Schools.* Boston: Houghton Mifflin Co., 1931, pp. 89-117, 159-189.

Gruber, Frederick C., and Beatty, Thomas Bayard. *Secondary School Activities.* New York: McGraw-Hill Book Co., Inc., 1954, pp. 86-107.

Johnston, Edgar G., and Faunce, Roland C. *Student Activities in Secondary Schools.* New York: The Ronald Press Co., 1952, pp. 28-110.

Kilzer, Louis R., *et al. Allied Activities in the Secondary School.* New York: Harper and Brothers, 1956, pp. 139-173.

McKown, Harry C. *Extra-Curricular Activities.* Rev. ed. New York: Macmillan Co., 1949, pp. 89-123.

Miller, Franklin A., *et al. Planning Student Activities.* Englewood Cliffs, N. J.: Prentice-Hall, Inc., 1956, pp. 215-269.

National Study of Secondary School Evaluation. *Evaluative Criteria, 1960 Edition.* Washington, D.C.: NSSSE, 1960, pp. 241-256.

The 1967 NASC Yearbook. Washington: National Association of Student Councils, 1967.

Petrillo, Fred R. "A Survey of Leadership Education Programs in Selected Colorado High Schools," Unpublished dissertation, The University of Denver, Denver, Colorado, 1964.

Reum, Earl. "And Finally — A Definition," *School Activities,* 37:17, May, 1966.

Reum, Earl. "How Much Power Does the Student Council Have?" *School Activities,* 37:11-12, May, 1966.

Strang, Ruth. *Group Work in Education.* New York: Harper and Brothers, 1958, pp. 98-119, 230-256.

The Student Council in the Secondary School. Washington: National Association of Student Councils, 1962.

Wey, Herbert W. *Handbook for Principals.* New York: Schaum Publishing Co., 1966, pp. 66-71.

Chapter 7

PHYSICAL ACTIVITIES

Perhaps no element of the student activities program of American high schools is as visible to all elements of the public — student, teacher, parent, taxpayer, and the like — as the student activities related to those of a physical nature. Critics of student activities in general often focus on interscholastic athletics and the accompanying marching bands and twirlers, homecoming courts and football heroes, half-time musical numbers and "chorus-girl" routines, and the inherent expenses and dangers. One writer has gone so far as to state that "football bears the same relation to education that bullfighting does to agriculture."[1]

Regardless of one's attitude toward interscholastic athletics, a wide range of student activities have evolved as a result of "supporting" various team sports. Around the nucleus of interscholastic athletics have come pep clubs, pep bands, cheerleaders, various performing and entertaining units, and various clubs for lettermen and even parents. Typical of American ingenuity, the types of teams and the number of supporting activities that are possible are limited, in general, only by student desire, school policy, administrative decree, and — unfortunately — budgetary inadequacies.

THE PHYSICAL EDUCATION PROGRAM

Little training in physical education took place in American schools until the post-Civil War period. A number of enthusiastic persons acquainted with the German *Turnverein* movement eventually managed to have physical training brought into the schools, although the movement advanced slowly. As late as 1918 Inglis called

---

[1]Quoted in Harold B. Gores, "New Trends in Athletics," *Administration of High School Athletics* (Washington, D.C.: AAHPER, 1963), p. 15.

provisions for physical education in public schools "woefully inadequate."[2]

A variety of societal, health, and educational factors has led to the addition of physical education in school curricula within recent years. Emphasis on physical fitness by U.S. Presidents beginning with Eisenhower has now led to the rapid expansion of physical education throughout the secondary grades and into the elementary grades.

Too often the program of physical activities (centered around interscholastic football and basketball) has developed in a rather uncoordinated manner, and is directed mainly toward the winning of a conference or state championship. In such a program, the graduation of a few key players, the changing of schools by a certain coach, or the reassignment of a cooperative administrator may bring havoc to the entire school.

A well-organized — in our opinion, the only justifiable — program of physical activities must have developed from a well-planned physical education program for all students. From this beginning, student activities may be provided to include an intramural program and a recreation program. Only when there is a sound, well-organized extensive program in physical education, intramurals, and recreation can a justifiable program of interscholastic physical activities be added to the program of the school. Certainly, the physical education classes should *not* have as their goal the preparation of personnel for the varsity teams. A program emphasizing physical fitness is the ideal when the physical fitness is creatively planned and executed to appeal to a variety of student interests.[3]

Additionally, skills other than physical fitness must be developed through the physical education classes to insure appropriate background for the various physical student activities. Explanations of games and rules not only serve students' immediate participation needs but also lead to enlightened spectators. Once a student has participated in some sports in physical education class, no matter how modestly, his appreciation and recognition of requisite skills, plays, etc., are enhanced. And, at least, he becomes a spectator that is more aware of the various processes making up any sports contest.

[2]Alexander Inglis, *Principles of Secondary Education* (Boston: Houghton-Mifflin Company, 1918), pp. 641-642.

[3]Much information of a highly useful nature is available from the President's Council on Physical Fitness, Washington, D.C. 20203.

Above all, it is imperative that the development of both the intramural and interscholastic physical activities programs must begin with a comprehensive physical education program for every student, every day, every year. Until this goal has been reached, it is difficult to justify developing the physical activities program to any further degree. Later steps should include programs in intramurals, recreation, and then interscholastic athletics. A "step" in this sequence must be fully developed, implemented, and evaluated before the sequence may be advanced. If a school has an imbalance in its curriculum between the academic portion (the physical education program) and the student activities portion (the intramurals, recreation program, and interscholastic sports), then the latter should be held at present levels or perhaps even reduced until the former can be strengthened.

INTRAMURAL SPORTS

If a school wishes to step beyond the physical activities contained within required physical education classes, the development of intramural sports should be considered. Intramurals are an excellent addition to the program of student activities. By definition, intramurals are carried out within a school and involve only members of that particular school's student body. Historically, as interscholastics became increasingly competitive and demanded great sacrifices from the participants, intramurals were given increased emphasis. Even today, many schools have elaborate intramural programs but attach relatively little significance to interscholastic physical competitions. Unfortunately, in certain schools this valuable student activity has been overlooked.

The innovative high school should provide within its physical activities program opportunities for high-caliber competition, as well as friendly voluntary competition. In a comprehensive program, provision should be made for both interschool rivalries and intraschool rivalries. Unfortunately, too often intramurals have been forsaken for the more prestigeous interscholastic program when there have been a lack of funds, participants, interest, and facilities for the support of both programs.

Intramurals must be viewed as the logical outgrowth of the physical education program. Within the intramural program, every student who wants to should have an opportunity to participate. The program should be geared for students with modest skills and should not consist of only the "best" physical education students or operate as the vehicle of moving students from the physical education class to interscholastic competitions. Naturally, intramurals will receive their share of "good" physical education students and because of the outstanding experiences obtained in intramurals, an exceptionally capable player would join the high school varsity team.

Some goals of the intramural program closely resemble the basic concepts underlying the interscholastic athletics program. According to The Athletic Institute:

> A major role of intramurals is the development of wholesome attitudes regarding the value which physical activity has in modern living. The hurry-fast pace of living requires a body "which knows itself" and which can successfully meet the problems encountered in everyday living.[4]

To adequately carry out this goal, intramurals must provide both team and individual sports. All too often intramurals are composed merely of team sports. Yet there certainly is a place for individual intramural competitions such as golf, tennis, swimming, gymnastics, and running.

Perhaps it may be said that the main difference in interscholastic sports and intramural sports is that intramurals exist mainly for fun and recreation, while interscholastics develop rigid team discipline and tend to become a rather expensive "cause" carrying the school's honor. Nevertheless, intramurals require organized administration, competent officials, facilities, and equipment similar to that required for interscholastics.[5]

When both programs exist side-by-side, the administrator should see that each program is allowed to function without interfering with the other. Highly unsuccessful intramural programs have resulted from a lack of definition of the purpose of these two programs.

[4]David O. Matthews (ed.), *Intramurals for the Senior High School* (Washington, D.C.: The Athletic Institute, 1964), p. 3.
[5]A detailed listing of suggested intramural activities mentioned in Matthews, *op. cit.,* pp. 9-10, lists 78 activities under four headings. This should give the educator a great many possibilities that can be included in an intramural sports program.

RECREATION PROGRAM

The recreation program is often overlooked in planning a complete physical activities program. Such an oversight is unfortunate, because a correctly developed recreation program provides an outlet for coeducational activities geared to developing leisure-time skills.

The recreation program that could easily become an adjunct of a community recreation program as well as fulfill a major role in the school should provide facilities and equipment for use before school, after school, during lunch periods, and during "free" periods for both students and faculty. The following points are characteristics of a good recreation program:

1. *Minimal internal organization.* No set teams exist, but for example, a group of girls wishing to play volleyball could form a team to function in that particular instance.

2. *Coeducational participation.* Activities should not be geared to only one sex. Tennis, hiking, swimming, and riding (as examples) would be available to any one who wished to participate.

3. *Pleasure orientation.* Recreation activities exist for the enjoyment of the participants; no trophy, no title, no recognition should exist. Individuals may participate to their own desired degree.

4. *Future usefulness.* Activities offered in a recreation program should be those that participants may enjoy in later life in their leisure time. Thus, camping, golf, tennis, and other activities might be offered, as well as chess, karate, and fly-casting.

5. *Creative planning.* The recreation program must always be dynamic: a static program often loses the interests of the participants. Activity "fads," such as the recent national interest in soccer (or the earlier interest in 50-mile hikes), should be considered for inclusion in the recreation program — even for an ephemeral existence.

6. *Good administration.* While a minimal degree of organization is essential to the success of the program, good administration must be provided. Personnel with knowledge in the area of physical education and recreation must be sought to work with this program.

A variety of activities is essential to a good recreation program. Training in marksmanship, as well as archery, is readily adapted to inclusion in the recreation program. The Cuba (New Mexico) Independent Schools have indicated a fine response on school trips to different sections of that state. The public schools of Bristol, Pennsylvania, have reported wide acceptance of school camping.[6]

INTERSCHOLASTIC SPORTS

Interscholastic sports should be the logical conclusion of a sequence of physical activities that stem from the physical education class — enriched with a program of intramurals and recreation for all students who choose to participate — and end with the specialized and highly organized undertaking of interscholastic sports for the physically talented. As a result of the background in physical education, interscholastic sports include some of the objectives of all physical education. Specht has listed the objectives as development of "strength, endurance, stamina, coordination, and agility in each child."[7] Others, like Williams, would stress training and development of the "wholeness of the individual," which he terms "education *through* the physical."[8]

Although there is a tendency to create objectives as a rationale for an existing or desired program, from various sources there has come a desire to enrich the basic skills and achievements taught in high school physical education.[9] Enrichment of the basic physical education program has sometimes resulted in interscholastic athletic programs, although in a great many instances the development has occurred the other way around. As Daniels pointed out, this development first occurred on the college level through the evolution of organized student teams from chance "pick up" teams. By the end of the nineteenth century most of the present collegiate interscholastic sports had been established;[10] and again, as in so

[6]For further information on camping see John W. Gilliland, *School Camping* (Washington, D.C.: Association for Supervision and Curriculum Development, 1954).

[7]Bess A. Specht, in William T. Gruhn and Harl R. Douglass, *The Modern Junior High School* (New York: The Ronald Press Company, 1947), p. 179.

[8]Jesse Feiring Williams, *The Principles of Physical Education,* 6th ed. (Philadelphia: W. B. Saunders Company, 1954), p. 2.

[9]It is to be noted that little effort so far has been made to carry out a wide-scale elementary interschool program. Chapter 4 of this text includes a discussion of the objections voiced against junior high school interscholastic athletics. Therefore, this discussion will necessarily be limited to senior high school athletics.

[10]Arthur S. Daniels, "The Inter-Relationship of Physical Education and Athletics," *Administration of High School Athletics,* (Washington, D.C.: AAHPER, 1963), p. 41.

many instances in student activities, the college served as the model for the high school.

As the History Club is justified as an enrichment of classroom activities for tenth-grade world history, so are interscholastic athletics now recognized as a justifiable enrichment of physical education class. While the physical education teacher seeks to develop the physical qualities of strength and endurance and the nonphysical, but highly important, qualities of teamwork and spirit in all boys and girls, the athletic coach will develop this strength and endurance into stamina and interest of selected students to achieve a specific objective — a winning team. The results of the physical education teachers' work are the informal games of various sports introduced in class, while the coach of interschool athletics molds a physical and mental entity — a team — into a vehicle to compete within the formal confines of competitive rules and regulations for a series of games of one sport over a set period of time.

In justifying a program of interscholastic athletics, the "values" of such a program are often cited. Indeed, interscholastics do often offer a valuable experience for the participants — be they girls on a basketball team or boys on a football team.

Interscholastic athletics supply a vehicle for the development of special skills by some interested and talented students. In this function a parallel may be drawn to any number of classroom enrichment activities. Unlike most other activities of an enrichment nature, interscholastic athletics provide a source of school spirit and a point from which many additional student activities may radiate.

Interscholastic sports provide the means of enhancing a person's physical fitness, his capacity to work cooperatively with others, his leadership ability, the development of his character, his ability to evaluate his efforts in the light of their contribution to team accomplishment, as well as his individual satisfaction. In the joy of victory or the tears of defeat these qualities are often overlooked, but to the players these qualities remain with them for life.

Gores pointed out the value of interscholastic athletics in the following statement:

> ... in athletics ... youngsters [are put] under stress ...
> physical stress, under social and intellectual stress. When a kid is part
> of a team, he knows that if he comes up with the wrong answer, if
> he makes the wrong response, he will either get knocked on his back
> or he will look ridiculous in the eyes of his colleagues and the

spectators — there's the social stress. The intellectual stress would indicate that he got the subject matter, which in many of the games today is as complex as geometry. Youngsters have the opportunity, therefore, to learn to operate under total stress.[11]

While an interscholastic athletics program is easily justified as an enrichment of the curriculum, the program is just as often easily criticized. Most of the criticism comes from people — not necessarily connected with the school by any means except in their role as taxpayers — who think that the time and other resources alloted to athletics should be spent in Latin, geometry, or music classes. They do not understand, nor do they take the time to investigate, the rewarding experiences which the players and coaches receive in working together toward their goal of a team. Nor do they grasp the important influence that athletic teams have in developing a school spirit that carries over from the playing field to many other school undertakings.

There are, perhaps, some few instances where criticism is just. Under no conditions should high schools compete for players; a player should attend school — and play — in the district or attendance area in which he resides.[12] Recruiting on the high school level is an atrocious practice, but not unknown in some areas. The developing of a high school team as the "training camp" for a nearby college or university is equally deserving of contempt, for it robs players and coaches alike of much of the enjoyment of participation and substitutes unnecessary exploitation in its place. Using various athletic teams to produce large gate receipts for other school activities often leads to excessive demands for winning teams.

Indeed, the administrative considerations of operating an interscholastic athletics program are great, and often onerous. These considerations involve the selection and appointment of the coaching staff,[13] the organization of the interschool sports program,[14] and the allocation of finances[15] and other resources.[16]

[11]Gores, *loc. cit.*

[12]Recent court rulings involving "freedom of choice" have created a considerable amount of confusion and uncertainty about residence requirements for athletic eligibility, although, in general, it seems that any student who is entitled to attend a particular school is entitled to participate in that school's interscholastic athletic teams.

[13]See Chapter 14.

[14]See Chapter 13.

[15]See Chapter 16.

[16]See Chapter 15.

There are many problems pertaining to the scheduling of sports events. Week-night games are not wise for academic and other reasons — recently, the riot-like outbursts during and after the game by students in some localities have been of particular concern. Recent trends favor the elimination of night games, which is now being done by the Memphis schools, and the use of afternoon contests, including Saturday afternoons. Games played immediately after school allow spectator participation by a large part of the student body and eliminate conflicts with night study hours. A greater participation by the student body usually creates more interest in interscholastic competition, and other teams may be created — particularly those of the less prestigeous sports such as swimming, polo, and hockey.

The problem of assuring the safety of all participants is an administrative consideration of primary importance. A program of school-paid insurance is functioning in most schools with interscholastic sports programs. More than insurance is needed, however. A thorough physical examination of participants must be conducted immediately prior to the sports season. Conditioning and training periods must be carried out, and close attention should be given to physical reactions of participants. Coaches should be thoroughly trained in first-aid, and a doctor should be present at contests in contact sports.

"What will the line stretch out to the crack of doom?"

This protestation from *Macbeth* appears a proper remonstrance for the athletics program. It would appear that the "line" of possibilities for physical activities reaches to the limit of a school's imagination. More and more schools are evaluating their programs of physical activities to be certain that a program accommodates a wide range of interests. The increasingly widespread construction of tennis courts, swimming pools, handball courts, and other facilities that can be used the year-round have allowed the introduction of valuable physical activities into the student activities program. Geographical considerations have allowed some schools to offer snow skiing, surfing, mountain climbing, and other regional physical activities.

Almost any physical activity can be included in the student activities program, if it meets the objectives of the school. The Atlanta school system has undertaken a unique and commendable physical training program. "Operation Upstream" provides rescue and survival training during a summertime 26-day program of intense physical fitness training and self-confidence building.[17]

SUPPORTING ACTIVITIES

To support the athletics program and to further develop school spirit, a multitude of supporting activities has developed. Among these supporting activities are some which do not fit within the definition of "student activities" as used in this book.

Among these are the various musical groups — band, pep band, marching band — for which academic credit is usually given. Other special marching units, including Junior Division ROTC drill teams, provide additional support for athletic contests.

From such groups, however, student activities such as precision dance groups, twirlers, and various female marching ensembles often originate. School policy and specific situations for these units cause variations in form and purpose.

Training Spectators

The most important supporting activity should be that of educating sports boosters in their responsibilities as spectators. Booing, trash-throwing, and fisticuffs are — lamentably — not unseen in the galleries at secondary school sports contests. The training of spectators is a joint responsibility of the PTA, the athletic booster club, the student council, the lettermen's club, the faculty, and other bodies.

The overzealous spirit of persons wanting a winning team at all costs has always plagued those responsible for administering an interscholastic athletics program. An admirable attempt to teach appropriate audience behavior is reflected in the Sportsmanship Code of the Iroquois League Student Councils. The Code, formulated by representatives of the League, is designed to be passed out to fans at athletic contests. It reads as follows:

> Good sportsmanship should play a basic role in the spirit of the school. It should not be altered whether the game is won or lost and should include each of the following:

[17]For further information contact the Director of "Operation Upstream," c/o P. E. Department, Instructional Center, 2930 Forrest Hills Drive, S.W., Atlanta, Georgia.

1. Referees, being human, are bound to commit a few errors in judgment. However, they are well trained for their jobs and decisions are final, and they should be respected at all times.
2. Booing is not an accepted method of showing disapproval and is not conducive to good sportsmanship.
3. Keep the game on the playing area. Violent reactions by spectators will not be tolerated. They may result in the removal of spectators from the games.
4. Derogatory remarks should not be directed to (or by) the opposing team or spectator.
5. Follow the cheerleaders. They are the ones who should stimulate and lead spirit.
6. Respect should be shown toward each school's traditional half-time display and Alma Mater.
7. Remain in your seats during the action of the games (especially basketball) until the final whistle.
8. Applaud an injured player when he leaves the field.
9. Post-game conduct should exemplify the high esteem in which you want your school and community to be held.

We must realize that the school gets the blame or praise for its conduct. Remember an athletic contest is only a game, not a matter of life and death, for a player, a coach or a school. Losses should be expected in sports, but not in sportsmanship.

The student body of the school has pledged itself to adhere to the above code. Will you as adults do likewise?[18]

Cheerleaders

Probably the most common of the auxiliary activities which exist to support athletics are the cheerleaders. Since the position of cheerleader places these selected students in a representative capacity for the school, cheerleaders should possess outstanding personal qualities worthy of their position in the public eye, as well as physical stamina. The procedure for selecting cheerleaders should be generally available in written form to serve as a reference for conducting consistently impartial selections. The "try-out" system of selection is preferred. Under this system any student is eligible to try out for the cheerleader corps. Preferably, faculty-student committees should observe the aspirants as they execute cheers and routines. The

[18]Taken from "The Student Handbook" of Norwich Senior High School, Norwich, N.Y., p. 19.

final decision is then made on the basis of the number of positions to be filled, the enthusiasm, cooperation, and the creativity of the candidates who have also passed the academic and additional standards which may apply. In other less desirable instances cheerleaders are elected by the student body, often after a public demonstration of their skills. In some schools, cheerleaders are even selected by the members of the pep club or the student council.

As the name implies, cheerleaders exist to encourage and lead school spirit; other duties, such as the selling of season tickets, ribbons, etc. should be closely examined for relevance to the cheerleaders' purpose. Like any other school group, there should be at least one faculty sponsor for the group, written organizational guidelines pertaining to officers, election/selection, eligibility, male-female participation, finance, and other important considerations. Ideally, this organization should be integrated into the school's student activities program with a separate budget as in other student activities. A number of training opportunities are now available for cheerleaders, such as the one held each summer at the University of Mississippi, where not only new cheers but topics such as rules of games and crowd psychology are learned.

Pep Clubs

A pep club exists in many schools to assist the cheerleaders. This club may vary numerically from a handful of athletic "boosters" to a gigantic organized card section or cheering gallery for sports events. Membership, specific purposes, and other responsibilities vary from school to school. Again, a formal organization, adequate sponsorship, written regulations, and integration into the total student activities program are essential requirements.

Lettermen's Clubs

As a reward for athletic excellence most schools — from the junior high school level through college — award athletic letters. Holders of these letters are often organized into clubs.

These clubs, no matter what the school or situation, should have objectives similar to those listed by Sells:

1. Maintain highest standards of sportsmanship.
2. Direct the leadership ability of the athlete.

3. Stimulate individual and group initiative.
4. Engender a feeling of cameraderie among the members.
5. Encourage club members to seek excellence in the classroom.
6. Inform members about careers in physical education and coaching.
7. Take an interest in and work with student government.
8. Promote good deportment and sportsmanship at games.
9. Encourage participation in all sports.
10. Support the activities of reserve teams.
11. Encourage an interest in intramurals.
12. Develop patterns of good citizenship.
13. Help athletes better prepare themselves to participate in community service after graduation.
14. Help faculty and administration better understand the competitive sports program.
15. Enlist the support and stimulate the interest of townspeople or of the local school neighborhood.
16. Foster a spirit of cooperation among parents.
17. Establish good relations with athletes in other schools.
18. Improve conditions in athletics in schools and colleges.
19. Function to achieve the aims of education.[19]

To carry out the objectives the lettermen's organization is best organized along the guidelines set by the student government organization for chartering other student groups. Since the lettermen's club seeks to support athletics and school spirit in the *entire* school, a noncoaching staff member as the sponsor may help to assimilate athletics into the total school program. The practice of lettermen selling tickets, popcorn, and other merchandise is questionable unless such sales are conducted under businesslike circumstances which do not detract from their positions of leadership.

Other Activities

A number of other activities exist which are closely related to the various supporting activities. These are usually projects of some group such as the student council or the pep club. Pep meetings, homecoming, bonfires, victory dances, and other similar activities exist in most secondary schools. Since student organizations — the

[19]James L. Sells, *Varsity Lettermen's Clubs* (Washington, D.C.: AAHPER, 1964), pp. 6-7.

cheerleaders and pep band, for example — do participate in these undertakings, such activities should be planned and coordinated by the director of student activities.

SUMMARY

This chapter has stressed the concept that interscholastic sports are only one part of the physical activities program. All physical activities programs should be natural outgrowths of the physical education class. Programs of voluntary intramural sports and recreational activities should be established before the implementation of interscholastic athletics.

Resulting from the search for new methods, new ideas are continually arising to enlarge the physical activities offered by the innovative high school. The physical activities program is further enlarged when the various supporting activities are considered.

REFERENCES

Allen, Charles F., *et al. Extra-Curricular Activities in the Elementary Schools.* St. Louis, Mo.: Webster Publishing Co., 1937, pp. 375-484.

Coleman, James S. "Learning Through Games," *NEA Journal,* 56:69-70, January, 1967.

Daniels, Arthur S. "The Inter-Relationship of Physical Education and Athletics." *Administration of High School Athletics.* Washington, D.C.: AAHPER, 1963.

Fretwell, Elbert K. *Extra-Curricular Activities in Secondary Schools.* Boston: Houghton Mifflin Co., 1931, pp. 405-443.

Gilliland, John W. *School Camping.* Washington, D.C.: Association for Supervision and Curriculum Development, 1954.

Gores, Harold B. "New Trends in Athletics." *Administration of High School Athletics.* Washington, D.C.: AAHPER, 1963.

Gruber, Frederick C. and Beatty, Thomas Bayard. *Secondary School Activities.* New York: McGraw-Hill Book Co., 1954, pp. 151-168.

Inglis, Alexander. *Principles of Secondary Education.* Boston: Houghton Mifflin Co., 1918, pp. 641-642.

Johnston, Edgar G., and Faunce, Roland C. *Student Activities in Secondary Schools.* New York: The Ronald Press Co., 1952, pp. 200-222, 268-289.

Kilzer, Louis R., *et al. Allied Activities in the Secondary School.* New York: Harper and Brothers, 1956, pp. 174-195, 272-297.

McKown, Harry C. *Extra-Curricular Activities.* Rev. ed. New York: Macmillan Co., 1949, pp. 283-332.

Matthews, David O. (ed.), *Intramurals for the Senior High School.* Washington, D.C.: The Athletic Institute, 1964.

Miller, Franklin A., *et al. Planning Student Activities.* Englewood Cliffs, N.J.: Prentice-Hall, Inc., 1956, pp. 334-377.

National Association of Student Councils. "The Student Council Can Improve Sportsmanship." *The 1967 NASC Yearbook.* Washington, D.C.: National Association of Secondary School Principals, 1967, pp. 60-61.

Sells, James L. *Varsity Lettermen's Clubs.* Washington, D.C.: AAHPER, 1964.

Specht, Bess A. Quoted in Gruhn, William T., and Douglass, Harl R. *The Modern Junior High School.* New York: The Ronald Press Co., 1947, p. 179.

Strang, Ruth. *Group Work in Education.* New York: Harper and Brothers, 1958, pp. 160-181.

Williams, Jesse Feiring. *The Principles of Physical Education.* 6th ed. Philadelphia: W. B. Saunders Co., 1954.

Chapter 8

PUBLICATIONS

Student publications, particularly the school newspaper, have a rich and highly respected tradition which is said to have begun in the 1700's[1] with manuscript newspapers. Today, a wide range of student publications continues the tradition. Secondary and elementary schools throughout the nation produce, with increasing frequency, newspapers, yearbooks, handbooks, directories, magazines, and many other publications. Regardless of the specific nature of the publications, all publications exist to carry out certain functions.

FUNCTIONS OF SCHOOL PUBLICATIONS

The functions of school publications are as follows:
1. Recording school events.
2. Interpreting the school to the community.
3. Furnishing a means of creative expression for the students.
4. Making available opportunities for vocational exploration and preparation.
5. Providing *esprit de corps* for the school and its student body.
6. Furthering the learning experiences of the students.

Recording School Events

A major function of school newspapers and yearbooks is to furnish students and the school with a historical record of the events and activities of a particular academic year. Bound volumes of the newspaper and reference copies of the yearbook provide not only materials for a school archives but also information useful for formal research, alumni use, and school records. For this reason, both the

---

[1]Edgar G. Johnston and Roland C. Faunce, *Student Activities in Secondary Schools* (New York: The Ronald Press Company, 1952), p. 171.

newspaper and the yearbook must be accurate and complete in covering the main activities of the school.

Interpreting the School to the Community

While the school newspaper, handbook, and literary magazine, along with the other publications of the school, are considered to be of value and interest to the students of the school, too frequently not enough attention is given to the impression that the publications will have on the community. The community can gain knowledge of the general activities of the school through the articles in the school newspaper; of the organization and administration of the school through the student handbook; and of the scholarship of some part of the student body through the varied selections in the literary magazine.

For example the Oxford (Mississippi) Municipal Separate School District uses their student newspaper as a public relations device. The bi-monthly high school paper, *The Colonel Courier,* is distributed to the entire community on the date of publication as a supplement to the community's *Oxford Eagle.* This has resulted in an invaluable benefit for the school.

Furnishing a Means of Creative Expression for the Students

The newspaper, yearbook, and literary magazine provide the students with opportunities for self-expression. Even the covers of the student handbook, student directory, and other such publications — not usually considered outlets for creativity — may serve to allow art students and photographers to display their creative talents.

Opportunities for Vocational Exploration and Preparation

Working on a school publication can provide vocational exploration and preparation in a variety of areas. While not every student contributing to or working for a school publication will enter a field related to publications, the information and appreciations gained will be useful in later life.

Writing is a major area of concern in this respect, but there are many types of writing — reporting, historical, essay, editorial, fiction, poetry, etc. — that can be used in one or more school publications. An exploratory interest in historical research, contemporary issues, editing, broadcasting, business, and advertising can find an outlet in writing for a school publication.

Student photography is found in yearbooks, many school newspapers, and even to some extent, in other school publications. Students interested in careers as portrait photographers, reporters, TV cameramen, commercial artists, and models can get valuable information and experience through serving as a photographer for a school publication.

Students interested in design, advertising, commercial art, and related fields can prepare art work, covers, division pages, copy arrangement, and so on.

Advertising, printing, proofreading, and business operations are a few of the other areas of interest that may serve a prevocational function.

Providing esprit de corps *for the School and its Student Body*

This function is chiefly the responsibility of the school news-paper because of the frequency of its publication. Through editorials and news articles, support for projects can be obtained and maintained. Particularly in large schools, the school newspaper provides a valuable service in promoting unity of the student body through the information about students and student activities that it releases. A column by the school administration provides information to the students about policy changes, new policy, etc.

Furthering the Learning Experience of the Students

Work on publications provides opportunities to improve many general skills and to learn new ones. Practice with grammar, spelling, and the mechanics of form increases knowledge in addition to the journalism experience acquired. Typing, mimeographing, and printing skills will be improved by having meaningful projects to work on. Information learned from interviews, from gathering background information, and from sales and advertising are only a few of the many other learning experiences that may be of use to the student.

PUBLICATIONS COMMITTEE

To oversee all student publications a Publications Committee should be set up by the school administration to be responsible to the Director of Student Activities. A suggested committee (see Figure I) is composed of representatives from the publications, from the faculty, and from the student body. The sponsor and editor-in-chief of each publication serve on the committee along with the publication's business manager, if there is one. Preferably, the student council president should nominate two students as members on condition of student council approval. With the approval of the principal, the Director of Student Activities will name two faculty members who are not publications sponsors, one of whom shall be the committee chairman.

The major duties of the committee will be the following:

1. Appointment of editors-in-chief and business managers of the publications near the end of each academic year to serve during the next year.

2. Promulgation of a statement of general publications policy to be amplified by each publication.[2]

3. Financial management of all publications funds in the form of standardized bookkeeping procedures and periodic audits.

4. Recommendation to the Director of Student Activities of names of persons to fill sponsorship vacancies in the area of student publications. The recommendation would then be given to the principal for consideration in making appointments.

5. Encouragement of coordination and cooperation with all publications staffs. Such coordination will allow for wise use of resources and supplies. This could, and in large schools should, include utilization of centralized photographic services (cameras, files, personnel) and other common services that are used by two or more publications.

Financing of student publications will be one of the main responsibilities of the Publications Committee. Fortunately, today the students usually do not have to bear the entire cost of publications. Various plans for financial management of school publications are now in operation: (1) financing entirely by the

---

[2]This point is particularly stressed in the *1967 NASC Yearbook*, p. 56, where the following is urged:

> Develop a policy statement concerning student publications. School publications often run into difficulty with advisers and administrators because they lack clear-cut guidelines about what is printable and what is not. It is therefore essential that all schools adopt a school publications policy statement that covers all areas where questions might arise.

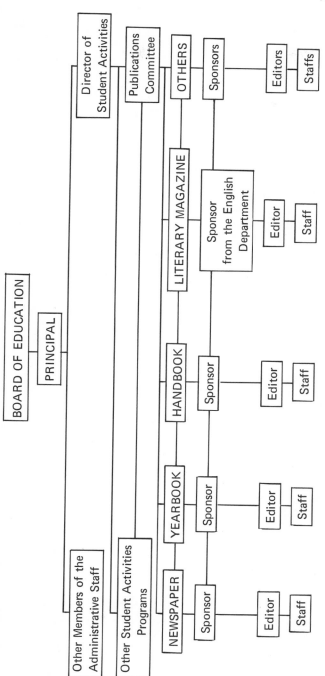

FIGURE 1

A suggested organization of the publications operations of a student activities program working through a director of student activities and a publications committee.

school, (2) partly by the school and partly by the students, and (3) partly by the school with students and commercial interests paying part of the costs. Detailed information about financing publications is contained in Chapter 16.

THE SCHOOL NEWSPAPER

Responsibility

Whatever its form — mimeographed or printed — the school newspaper provides the most varied experiences for student staff members. Duty assignments, organization, writing, editing, photographing, layout, and distribution must be carried out each time an issue is prepared. The newspaper, regardless of its form, must represent careful planning; for not only is it a reflection of the adequacy of the journalism and/or English instruction, but also it is a measure of the school itself. This is best seen in Spears and Lawshe's listing of the functions of the school paper as an aid to the school:

(1) To educate the community as to the work of the school
(2) To publish school news
(3) To create and express school opinion
(4) To capitalize the achievements of the school
(5) To act as a means of unifying the school
(6) To express the idealism and reflect the spirit of the school
(7) To encourage and stimulate worth-while activities
(8) To aid in developing right standards of conduct
(9) To promote understanding of other schools
(10) To provide an outlet for student suggestions for the betterment of the school
(11) To develop better interschool relationships
(12) To increase school spirit
(13) To promote co-operation between parents and school[3]

With such important responsibilities, the school newspaper must be adequately directed. The overall responsibility for the paper belongs to the Publications Committee. The sponsor and primary staff members are responsible for the performance of all tasks by themselves and the other staff members. The paper *must* remain a

[3]Harold Spears and C. H. Lawshe, Jr., *High School Journalism* (New York: The Macmillan Company, 1949), p. 8.

student enterprise although adult regulation is ultimately required. Responsible students and responsible student leadership lead to smooth working relations with the Publications Committee only if the Publications Committee shows similar interest and responsibility. Coverage should not concentrate on certain limited aspects of school life, such as sports and social events. Likewise, faculty supervision does not mean faculty writing or rewriting of the paper before press time. Furthermore, the newspaper must not become a bulletin of the school office. Responsibility is an essential element of all journalism; this includes student journalism.

Organization

Except in the very smallest schools, the newspaper should be, although sometimes it is not, a product of (or an outgrowth from) the journalism classes. As previously stated, publication involves certain responsibilities. The *teaching* of these responsibilities is the job of the journalism class; the *practice* of these responsibilities is the task of the students working on the school newspaper. Journalism classes are not vocational training courses; however, some prevocational training is available. Classes in journalism are offered as electives, and students interested in working on the newspaper — for whatever reason — may elect journalism. Such an organization provides proper standards of journalism before participation is allowed, while also providing for better administrative control. Paper assignments are less likely to be forgotten or done poorly if they are classwork. In most instances, at least some class time becomes paper staff time. In addition, if operated through a journalism class, student paper staff members will receive academic credit for satisfactory work on the publication.[4]

[4]It must be emphasized, however, that many students that can make a substantial contribution to a school newspaper will not be able to schedule journalism or are not interested in pursuing a study of all phases of journalism. Provision should be made for the staff to include nonjournalism students.

The *1967 NASC Yearbook,* p. 56, urges that schools do the following:

Develop ways to insure widespread student participation in and support of student publications. One of the best ways of encouraging student support of publications is to be sure that those publications do in fact represent the voice of all the students, not just a small elite group. Some suggestions follow:

a.   Each advisory room or homeroom should have a reporter for the school paper.

b.   Each English teacher should be encouraged to have classes write articles or stories for student publications.

c.   Social studies classes should be encouraged to write editorials and features on current world and local problems.

Although closely related to classwork, a staff including editor-in-chief, business manager, section editors, and other students may be set up as needed and given responsibilities for the makeup of the paper. In the portion of the work related to classwork, all students will be better able to evaluate one another's work and to see that staff positions are earned, and not given. Tests can be administered to see that all staff members have a command of fundamental skills, particularly grammar and journalistic form.

While ordinarily the journalism teacher would be the sponsor, the Publications Committee should feel free to recommend any qualified faculty member to the principal. A person, although a faculty member, who does not know a crossline from a dropline is of practically no value. The sponsor should have had, according to Williams, "college courses in journalism and creative writing and be capable of managing a lively activity situation."[5] It is difficult to evaluate whether professional training or mental attitude is more important. One case was noted where the faculty sponsor, although professionally prepared, was of little value to the staff because she frequently suffered spells of weeping when normal minor problems occurred. Fretwell has pointed out that expert faculty leadership is also a necessity because of an annual average turnover of 75% of paper-staff staff members.[6] Specific responsibilities of the activity sponsor are discussed in a later chapter.

To aid both the faculty members in charge of newspapers and other periodicals and to help student workers, much advice can be obtained from the National Scholastic Press Association, Catholic School Press Association, and Quill and Scroll.[7] Nearby institutions of higher learning frequently offer information through departments of journalism. In the staff rooms it is well to have a small reference library that contains various publications guidelines and basic journalism texts.

Evaluation

Evaluation of all work is a necessity, although, because of the widerange responsibilities of the school newspaper, evaluation is

[5]Stanley W. Williams, *Educational Administration in Secondary Schools* (New York: Holt, Rinehart, and Winston, 1964), p. 347.

[6]Elbert K. Fretwell, *Extra-Curricular Activities In Secondary Schools* (Boston: Houghton Mifflin Company, 1931), p. 302.

[7]See Appendix B.

difficult. However, the two statements which follow may serve as general evaluative criteria for staff members, sponsors, and administrators.

Fretwell writes,

> The school is an educational institution, and if the production of the paper is not a real educative experience for the group producing it, and to a lesser extent for the whole school, the paper has no place in the school.[8]

Reichley, in questioning the worth of student publications, has written the following:

> Where *good* [emphasis added] publications exist in a secondary school, they are, to a varying degree, an extension of the curriculum — laboratories where what one student learns from one teacher in one classroom can be tried out on a mass audience.[9]

For a goal of correct writing, the number of grammatical errors per article may be counted. For goals having to do with layout, photography, headlines, and so on, various check lists and rating scales are available in journalism textbooks, journal articles, and through organizations providing critical services. Readability tests are available to check levels of writing. The number of typographical errors per page (or issue) can be used to check the effectiveness of typists and proofreaders. The number of inches of advertising sold is a rough measure of sales proficiency. Ending the year "in the black" is a measure of prudent business management. Evaluative methods and instruments will need to be developed to measure the various goals that have been set up.

Only those directly concerned with the paper — sponsor and students — can truthfully evaluate their "experiences." However, the entire school and the community have the right to expect the best.

THE SCHOOL YEARBOOK

Of all the secondary school publications, the yearbook is perhaps the one most traceable to the college influence on secondary schools. The first yearbook-like publication is traced to Yale in the

[8]Fretwell, *loc. cit.*
[9]Robert A. Reichley, "Student Publications: Are They Worth It?" *NASSP Bulletin,* 48:17, October, 1964.

year 1806. It was not until 1873 when the Hopkins Grammar School of New Haven, Connecticut, published a yearbook that annuals entered the noncollege field. In the last three decades yearbooks, in various forms, have become quite common as secondary school publications.

Even more than the newspapers, the yearbook must be very carefully prepared; for not only must it be true to journalistic qualities, but it also must honestly represent the historical record of the school for that particular year. The archival and public relations functions of the yearbook are among its primary functions, as Reichley emphasizes in the following statement:

> How often do yearbooks engage in the same idle pattern of a "last will and testament" to members of the graduating class instead of publishing an opening and closing essay that will stand as evidence that someone on the staff has learned something in the past three or four years?[10]

Although the yearbook is assigned, by its nature, the important task of serving as a historical record for the school, and although the number and size of yearbooks continues to grow, yearbooks are often subject to very legitimate objections. These objections are as follows: (1) extravagant cost, (2) minimum indication of planning and originality, and (3) limited scope.

Extravagant Cost. The addition of color pages, elaborate photographic portraits of personalities, and highly decorative covers have caused the price of publication of yearbooks to increase greatly in the last few years. Quite naturally, yearbook publishing companies are encouraging these additions. As mentioned earlier in this chapter, it has become necessary for schools to assume an increasingly greater part of the financing of yearbooks, for yearbooks should be recognized as legitimate expenditures from school funds. Such enlightened attitudes will keep yearbooks within the financial reach of most students.

Minimum Indication of Planning and Originality. Too often secondary school yearbooks are poor copies of college publications or near-perfect reproductions of a previous year's high school issue. Lack of pictures of all students, activities, and organizations must be attributed to faulty organization and planning on the part of the

[10]Reichley, *op. cit.*, p. 24.

yearbook staff. Such hiatuses make the yearbook of little meaning for the unfortunate students who were "omitted by an oversight." While the seniors are the main persons to benefit from a yearbook, there is no reason that the activities of the underclassmen should be greatly slighted, as is sometimes common in yearbooks. The yearbook, as the name indicates, contains a review of the school activities for a year; no organized activity should be overlooked.

Limited Scope. Because of the demands placed on the staff by the publisher, it is all too frequent that many activities and events are omitted from the annual because a certain section was sent to the printer before some activities happened. A laudatory practice, begun some years ago by schools like East High School and South Side High School of Memphis, is to arrange for summer delivery of the yearbook. Deadlines are set later in the year, and pictures of all activities, including spring sports, spring social events, and commencement, can be included. Not only does the annual become a complete historical record, but often publishers offer reduced rates for slack-season publications. These factors outweigh the inconvenience caused by either an extra trip to the school to receive the yearbook or the cost of postage if the yearbooks are mailed to students.

Organization

While it might be best if a journalism class produced a yearbook, especially a second-year journalism class, the yearbook has a long tradition of being produced by extraclass staff members. There are several evident reasons that journalism classes have not been charged with the responsibility of producing the yearbook. Traditionally, the yearbook is a historical record; and all members of the student body participate in making that record, so they should have an opportunity to work on the yearbook staff. An administrative consideration also plays a part in not asking the journalism class to publish the yearbook. Journalism classes were offered by only 60.1% of public high schools in 1960-1961, and 64.3% of the journalism classes were in public schools with an enrollment of less than 1,000 students.[11] Thus, it would be an excessive demand to ask

[11]Grace S. Wright, *Subject Offerings and Enrollments In Public Secondary Schools,* United States Office of Education, United States Department of Health, Education, and Welfare (Washington: Government Printing Office, 1965), pp. 27, 29.

that the many small classes of journalism work on journalism *per se* and the newspaper, as well as the yearbook.

To publish the yearbook, a student staff and student assistants are needed. An editor-in-chief, a business manager, photography editor, and editors-in-charge of the various sections (classes, faculty, athletics, features, etc.) are the minimum necessary for publication. Other student staff members may be added as necessary. It is wise to train neophyte staff members, so that they can carry out the major tasks during the next year. As Kilzer, Stephenson, and Nordberg point out:

> With yearbook budgets averaging approximately $1800, [probably much higher now] a novice staff is an extravagance. One effective plan is to allow beginners to serve as assistants the year before taking office.[12]

To supervise this staff the Publications Committee should recommend to the school administration a qualified faculty member. As was mentioned for the sponsor of the newspaper, the yearbook sponsor must have had training in preparation of yearbooks and be able to supervise all of the operations of the yearbook staff. Qualities of effective activity sponsors are discussed in Chapter 14.

The yearbook staff and sponsor will find much assistance available from the previously mentioned press associations and from all the yearbook publishing firms. The professional assistance of the publishers is available for almost every facet of yearbook publication if the school can afford the service. Reference materials of a professional nature, as well as yearbooks from previous years and other schools, should be kept in the staff room for reference and inspiration, not duplication.

Evaluation

Johnston and Faunce have pointed out that the primary function of the yearbook is to serve as:

> a record which captures and preserves events and associations of school life for the years ahead when friends have scattered and familiar scenes have changed.[13]

[12]Louis R. Kilzer, Harold H. Stephenson, and H. Orvill Nordberg, *Allied Activities in the Secondary School* (New York: Harper and Brothers, Publishers, 1956), p. 240.
[13]Johnston and Faunce, *op. cit.*, p. 186.

The yearbook staff members, the sponsor, and members of the Publications Committee should carefully and honestly evaluate their recent yearbooks as well as the one being planned to determine if the publications have been true historical records for the students to cherish.

OTHER PUBLICATIONS

While the newspaper and the yearbook are the standard publications in secondary schools, several other publications are becoming fairly common. These publications are generally characterized by the following:

1. They are published once a year.
2. They are nonrevenue producing.
3. They are the outgrowth of some other activity.

The publications to be considered under this heading are the Student Handbook, the Student Directory, the Literary Magazine, and other publications.

Student Handbook

The publication of the handbook, one of the newest additions to the list of school publications, is necessitated by the growing size and increasing complexity of American high schools. Gruber and Beatty[14] have listed the functions of a student handbook as follows:

1. It informs the community of the organization and the workings of the school.
2. The handbook informs parents of new students about the kind of school their children will attend.
3. The handbook informs the new student of the rules and regulations of his new school.

Since the handbook is an easy way for an administrator to keep students informed about a plethora of facts — from commencement requirements to cheers — it is financed entirely by the school and furnished to all freshmen and new students, except at times of revision when all students are issued new handbooks. The

[14]Frederick C. Gruber and Thomas Bayard Beatty, *Secondary School Activities* (New York: McGraw-Hill Book Company, Inc., 1954), p. 210.

Publications Committee will select students and faculty to work together to provide the necessary information in an attractive format. Williams recalls when one principal had the schedule of the school's conference-championship basketball team printed on the inside cover of that school's yearly handbook to encourage students and parents to read the handbook.

Qualities of a Good Handbook

Attractiveness. Student art design, pictures, and other material may be utilized to make the handbook attractive. Page layout should be appealing, neither cluttered nor gaudy.

Comprehensiveness. Careful planning is essential to see that the handbook contains all the information needed by the new high school student. As an orientation instrument, the handbook must provide all needed information *accurately*. Information about the school, general regulations, and information about services, student activities, schedules, and counseling are essential. Numerous other items may be included.[15]

Since the cost of printing a handbook is considerable and the vast majority of the information to be included changes infrequently, it may be advisable to exclude information of a current and changing nature from the handbook. Inclusion of student government officers, current team schedules, and meeting times and places which change yearly might best be printed in the student directory or in a supplement. Such preplanning would allow large quantities of the handbooks to be purchased at a lower cost. Naturally, ordering too many copies should be avoided so that an oversupply does not accumulate and become damaged in storage. But, enough copies should be ordered to allow for the quantities needed for transfers and for replacement of lost or mutilated handbooks. A loose-leaf or spiral-bound handbook may be appropriate in some situations.

In many schools where handbooks are not elaborate, perhaps even mimeographed, the custom is to issue handbooks yearly. In more affluent schools, it is possible to publish a fairly elaborate handbook on a yearly basis, and yearly publication has much to offer. Names of student council and club officers and sponsors,

---

[15]For a detailed discussion of the contents of handbooks see Harry C. McKown, *Extra-Curricular Activities* (rev.ed.; New York: The Macmillan Company, 1949), pp. 484-489.

meeting times and places for activities, and schedules of intermurals and intramurals may be provided. It is the responsibility of the school administration and Publications Committee to determine if total comprehensiveness is worth the costs of yearly revision and publication.

Usability. This quality is related to several needed features of the handbook. Since the handbook provides a great deal of information, an index must be provided to aid the reader. The handbook should be designed so that the students will have the book available whenever they are in the school building. *Size* is the important element here. Many schoolmen prefer the small (approximately 4 in. x 6 in.) size so that the students may, hopefully, keep the booklet in their pocket or purse. We feel that a booklet of size 8½ in. x 11 in. is better; for, if the booklet is punched to fit a loose-leaf binder, it will be a ready reference for the students and will not be easy to lose or misplace.

Durability. Since the handbook is given to entering high school freshmen or sophomores to be used for three or four years, the materials used in printing should be durable enough to withstand three or four years use.

One such handbook is produced by the Yazoo City (Mississippi) High School. The booklet is approximately 8 in. x 10½ in. in size, punched with 5 holes for loose-leaf binders, and has a detailed table of contents. Good quality paper and printing technique were employed, and the contents of the book are attractively arranged.

The best evaluation of a handbook is the frequency with which it is used by students and the effective citizenship which the students display at school. To insure maximum use of the handbooks, many schools administer tests on the contents. Although time-consuming, the tests encourage the use of the handbook and thereby allow for a more effective community membership in the school.

Student Directory

The directory is an outgrowth of the administrative function of providing information about teachers and pupils. Since few students have telephone numbers and addresses listed in the city telephone directory, the student directory is particularly valuable in large urban high schools. Since they must be issued yearly, student directories need only a fairly durable cover, with an attractive student-made design, to protect the mimeographed listings of names, addresses, telephone numbers, and homerooms. Care must be taken to obtain the correct information for the directory. Since this publication is informative and administrative in nature, no charge should be made for it.

Literary Magazine

The literary magazine is usually an outgrowth of a project undertaken by the English department of a school. While the English department will arrange for and select the contents of the magazine, a staff under the Publications Committee should handle layout, printing, and distributing the work.

The literary magazine must be open to all students of the school, not only to seniors, as Reichley points out.[16] The content of the publication must also be varied and include all types of literary work. Since the publication is a representation of the entire student body, it should be financed entirely from school funds so that each student may receive a free copy. Additional copies may be printed for public sale at local bookstores, but not for door-to-door sales. Such a publication serves as a valuable public relations device. Therefore, the publication should be the best possible, in terms of literary merit and its public relations function.

Other Publications

Special situations existing in some school systems may provide opportunities for special publications. The criteria mentioned previously in this chapter should serve as the measuring devices for the suitability and effectiveness of these special interest works.

For example, the Little Rock (Arkansas) Secondary Schools publish a *Manual for Written Work* to terminate confusion resulting from numerous "standard" composition forms. It is set up to offer a quick reference for the principles of manuscript form, correct spelling, and correct writing.

[16] Reichley, *loc. cit.*

SUMMARY

The field of student publications has become an accepted part of both the curricular and the student activities programs of many schools — elementary as well as secondary. Millions of dollars are expended yearly on the varied types of school publications, including newspapers, yearbooks, literary magazines, and directories. The value derived from these publications is measured, not only by the printed page, but by the attitude of cooperation, the recognition of the importance of teamwork, and the training and prevocational experiences which have been acquired. Reichley has pointed out the following:

> Like athletic teams, student talent moves in cycles and publications will have their good and bad years. But like schools that consistently produce top-flight teams, there are certain publications that have good years and better years. There are no bad ones. These usually are schools where an energetic adviser seeks good talent and offers as bait the rewards of producing a good product. Happily, there are youngsters in every school who will respond to this type of challenge, and it doesn't take very many of them to produce an effective publication.[17]

REFERENCES

Fretwell, Elbert K. *Extra-Curricular Activities in Secondary Schools.* Boston: Houghton Mifflin Co., 1931, pp. 296-350.

Gruber, Frederick C., and Beatty, Thomas Bayard. *Secondary School Activities.* New York: McGraw-Hill Book Co., Inc., 1954, pp. 183-216.

Johnston, Edgar G., and Faunce, Ronald C. *Student Activities in Secondary Schools.* New York: The Ronald Press Co., 1952, pp. 171-199.

Kilzer, Louis R., *et al. Allied Activities in the Secondary School.* New York: Harper and Brothers, 1956, pp. 217-251.

McKown, Harry C. *Extra-Curricular Activities.* Rev. ed. New York: Macmillan Co., 1949, pp. 350-501.

Miller, Franklin A., *et al. Planning Student Activities.* Englewood Cliffs, N.J.: Prentice-Hall, Inc., 1956, pp. 420-494.

National Association of Student Councils. *The 1967 NASC Yearbook.* Washington, D.C.: NASSP, 1967.

[17]Reichley, *op. cit.,* pp. 20-21.

Reichley, Robert A. "Student Publications: Are They Worth It?" *NASSP Bulletin,* 48:17-24, October, 1964.

Spears, Harold, and Lawshe, C.H., Jr. *High School Journalism.* New York: Macmillan Co., 1949.

Strang, Ruth. *Group Work in Education.* New York: Harper and Brothers, 1958, pp. 182-197.

Williams, Stanley W. *Educational Administration in Secondary Schools.* New York: Holt, Rinehart and Winston, 1964, p. 347.

Wright, Grace S. *Subject Offerings and Enrollments in Public Secondary Schools.* Washington: Government Printing Office, 1965, pp. 27, 29.

Chapter 9

SUBJECT MATTER AND SPECIAL INTEREST GROUPS

Many authorities feel that the subject matter and special interest organizations are the heart of any student activities program. In these organizations the curriculum of a school is extended, enriched, and enlarged, and the general objectives of education are met — perhaps more so than in any other phase of the school's operation.

Although the subject matter and special interest groups are usually organized as clubs, this is not essential for effective operation. Nevertheless, since most such groups are so organized, the club program will be discussed in some detail.

THE CLUB PROGRAM IN GENERAL

Much has been written about school clubs in the past few decades; a great deal of this body of literature seems out of date to the contemporary reader. Nowadays one seldom finds Good Manners Clubs, Valet Clubs, Victory Garden Clubs, the Order of the Daisy, and other such groups that are mentioned frequently in the available literature.

Now one is much more likely to find students building rockets rather than pinhole cameras, discussing Salinger rather than Tennyson, and producing "The Sound of Music" rather than "H.M.S. Pinafore." Clubs need to change with the times and with student interests.[1] Sometimes it is difficult to separate club activities from class activities, especially in connection with subject matter clubs. This is perfectly legitimate even if this means eliminating the club, for the only logical rationale for a club is to accomplish an educational objective that can be accomplished in no other way.

---

[1] See Donald I. Wood, "Archaic Student Clubs; Those Entrenched by Tradition May Be at Odds With Enlightened Student Activities," *Clearing House,* 31:91-93, October, 1964.

An Interclub Council may be useful in coordinating the functions of the various clubs within a building. (See Chapter 14.)

Contests and Related Activities

In addition to many of the club programs, contests are held among high school students. These contests have certain obvious benefits; they serve to identify and recognize students with talent. On the other hand, they have been abused, and in some cases still are.

In an attempt to prevent the exploitation of students through contests, the National Association of Secondary School Principals each year issues a list of approved contests.[2] If schools only permit students to participate in those contests on the NASSP list, many problems can be avoided. From time to time new contests become available which appear to be worthwhile to local schools. In such a situation, the principal should call the contest to the attention of the NASSP, so that the NASSP Committee on Contests and Activities may consider its inclusion on the approved list.[3]

SUBJECT MATTER ORGANIZATIONS

Subject matter clubs will generally endure; special interest clubs, except for a few old standbys, tend to be a more transitory group. Gruber and Beatty referred to these as "knowing" clubs and "doing" clubs; however, this seems to be an inadequate description.

Potentially, there are at least as many subject matter organizations as subjects offered and in many cases there are more. From a general science course both a Meteorology Club and a Rocket Club might develop, and from an American History class separate groups interested in the Civil War and World War I might develop.

A few subject matter clubs are found in a great many high schools: The Future Homemakers of America,[4] a Spanish club, and a social studies club are some of the most frequently found. Some of

---

[2] See Appendix C for a list of the approved contests.

[3] Each state principals association has a member on the Advisory Board of the NASSP Committee on Contests and Activities. This person can be very helpful to local schools in matters of contests and activities.

[4] See "Future Homemakers of America," *American Education*, 3:13, May, 1967.

these are well-organized into regional, state, and national organizations: The Future Farmers of America, the Future Business Leaders of America, the National Scholastic Press Association, etc. Many others exist in only one school and have no affiliations.

Science and Mathematics Clubs

Science and mathematics clubs and related activities such as science fairs have had a large growth in recent years, especially since the enactment of the National Defense Education Act of 1958. Robbins, in a study of student activity trends in Arkansas, found large increases in frequency of the mathematics clubs and interscholastic science fairs or contests in that state between 1956 and 1967.[5]

In general, science and mathematics clubs and related activities permit (1) the identification of talented students; (2) the opportunity for talented students to pursue individual interests; (3) the opportunity to develop technical skills; (4) the development of the understandings and appreciations of scientific and technical developments not possible in the classroom; and (5) the opportunity to develop avocational and leisure time interests and activities.

There are two major types of science clubs — the general, concerned with all areas of science, which is more frequently found in the smaller schools; and the special, such as the Junior Engineering Technical Society, the Spelunkers Club, and the Zoology Club.

It is possible to develop a coordinated approach to the many opportunities currently available in science youth activities. An outstanding example of this is found in the small Mena, Arkansas, High School.

> The coordinated science extracurricular program now in its eighth year of successful operation in Mena High School involves affiliation with three principal source organizations, as shown in the accompanying flow sheet. [See Figure I.]
>
> Immediate affiliation is with Future Scientists of America, Science Clubs of America, Arkansas Science Fair Association, and Arkansas Junior Academy of Science.
>
> By use of the coordinated plan of activities described, the science potential of a number of students has been developed to a

[5]Jerry H. Robbins, "Trends in Student Activities," *Journal of Arkansas Education,* 38:22-23, December, 1965.

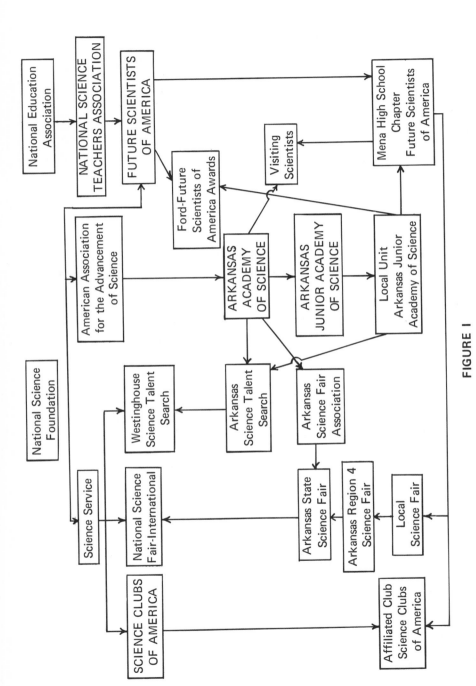

FIGURE I

Flow Sheet of Coordinated Science Extracurricular Activities.

degree beyond expectations. The success of the program has been highly gratifying.[6]

The Future Scientists of America school science club program sponsored by the National Science Teachers Association is prominent among the national science organizations. The FSA attempts to provide an atmosphere in which students with similar scientific interests and abilities may come together to pursue their own individual scientific inclinations and at the same time contribute to and benefit from the scientific interests of their fellow club members. Research activities, field trips, demonstrations, and exhibits are commonly found. The NSTA also sponsors the Ford Future Scientists of America Awards Program, the International Youth Science Fortnight and European Summer Tour, and the NASA-NSTA Youth Science Congresses.

Many schools participate in science fairs. Although in most schools science fairs have a short history, they originated in 1928 with the Children's Fair held in New York City by the American Institute of the City of New York. Today we find them almost everywhere — from those held in small elementary schools to the National Science Fair which draws entrants from each of our 50 states and several foreign countries.

The basic purpose of science fairs is to encourage students who are interested in science. In addition a science fair (1) gives students a chance to present their ideas publicly to people who are interested in seeing and hearing them; (2) teaches students new things by having them discuss their findings with those who have similar interests; and (3) gives students an opportunity to bring recognition to themselves, their school, and their community.

Science youth activities have a unique opportunity to be financed under the provisions of P.L. 85-875 of 1958. Certain nonprofit institutions, such as colleges, universities, state departments of education, and state academies of science may contract with the U.S. Office of Education for funds to support science activities which will, according to the provisions of the law, "encourage, foster, and assist in the establishment in localities throughout the Nation of clubs which are composed of boys and girls who have

[6]Aileen L. McWilliam, "Science Extracurricular Activities," *Pooling and Sharing*, (November, 1964), 47-52.

an especial interest in science."[7] Among the few states which have taken advantage of these funds are Arkansas, Kentucky, Minnesota, Ohio, Pennsylvania, and Virginia.

Mathematics clubs are in many respects similar to science clubs in their operation and activities. The outstanding national organization of mathematics clubs is Mu Alpha Theta, now under the co-sponsorship of the National Council of Teachers of Mathematics and the Mathematical Association of America.[8]

One interesting project involving mathematics students is that of the Tri-State Mathematics League, one of several operating in the New England states, which sponsors six meets per year. A meet is similar to a track or swimming tournament — one event after another. Each meet has five events, and each school enters six team members in each of the first four events. The fifth event in each meet is a team problem, which is done by three students working on the problem together. Each school has ten members on its team, but each team member may enter no more than three events. Furthermore, each team may enter no more than six of its members in each category and no more than four from a class. The winning team is the one with the largest total score, based on three questions per category — easy, average, and difficult, with scores of 2, 3, and 5 points, respectively. The topics, or categories (such as Arithmetic, Lines and Angles, Inequalities, and Quadratics) are well known in advance, so that students may practice and plan strategy for the meet.[9]

Vocational Organizations

Among the prominent national organizations for students in the vocational fields are (1) Future Farmers of America and (2) Future Homemakers of America, both sponsored by the U.S. Office of Education; (3) Distributive Education Clubs of America, Inc. and (4) Future Business Leaders of America. Especially in the smaller schools, the vocational organizations are often among the most

---

[7]For further information contact the Program Development Section, Bureau of Elementary and Secondary Education, U.S. Office of Education, Washington, D.C. 20202.

[8]See "NCTM to Cosponsor Mu Alpha Theta," *The Mathematics Teacher*, 60:528, May, 1967.

[9]Teunis J. Paarlberg, "The Mathematics League," *The Mathematics Teacher*, 60:38-40, January, 1967.

outstanding, at least partly because of the leadership and assistance which is available at the state and national levels. Yet, it is not uncommon to find home economics clubs or agriculture clubs in schools which do not have vocational programs. In addition, a business club, an occupations club, a secretarial club, an industrial arts club, a shop club, or the like is found in many schools.

Language Arts

Among the most popular types of student activities are those related to the language arts. There is some indication that these, especially those of the literary society-poetry club type are slipping in their popularity. These are discussed in greater detail in Chapter 11, "Fine Arts Activities."

Language clubs, especially modern foreign language clubs, are more popular than ever, largely due to the fact that more schools are teaching modern foreign languages, are teaching more languages per school, and are offering more years of those languages. Language clubs typically permit students to delve more deeply into the culture and literature of the countries speaking the language than is usually possible in the classroom situation.

An example of the variety of activities that a language club may indulge in may be seen in the list of contests and activities offered at the Arkansas State Latin Club conventions in recent years: Latin forms, Phrasing, Background, Translation, Composition, Comprehension, Grammar, Vocabulary, and Derivitives; costume competition in Goddess, Mythological character, Group of myth characters, Roman matron and child, Domestic slave, and Foreign slave; 50-yard dash; 100-yard dash; 220-yard run; 440-yard relay; Shotput; Discus throw; and Chariot races.

Social Studies

As schools have diversified their offerings in the social sciences, the variety of social studies clubs has also increased. Where formerly only a History Club or a Geography Club would be found, it is not uncommon to find clubs interested in the stock market, sociology, psychology, anthropology, civic affairs, current events, international relations, and the like. Mock political conventions are increasingly found during election years. As all the social sciences come into the secondary school, we will find students interested in an increasing variety of inter- and intrapersonal affairs.

Trends

In 1937 Harry C. McKown wrote:

> We are willing to go on record as making the prophecy that within a few years — perhaps a decade or two — in the modern school, with the exception of recreational, service, and honoring clubs, there will be no such activity as an organized school club; that these "club" activities will exist and be more highly developed than ever, but that they will have been accepted and incorporated in the regular work of the classroom.[10]

We have seen that his prophecy has not come true — at least not in the way that McKown visualized it. In recent months articles have appeared in the professional literature on the following clubs which are more-or-less subject matter related: Spelunkers Club, Indian Culture Club, International Relations Club, Mineralogy and Lapidary Club, Health Club, Distributive Education Club, Art Club, Business Club, English Club, Future Business Leaders of America, Future Farmers of America, Future Homemakers of America, Future Scientists of America, German Club, Home Economics Club, Industrial Arts Club, Latin Club, Junior Classical League, Junior Academy of Science, Math Club, Music Club, Nature Study Club, Poetry Club, Spanish Club, Speech Club, and Commercial Club. Others found in a survey by Robbins and Williams include the Swimming Officials Club, Debate Club, Madrigals, Forensics, Skiing Club, and the Agriculture Club.

These are indicative of the types of subject matter related clubs that will be with us, at least for the next few years.

Robbins, in his study of trends in student activities in Arkansas, found that

> About one eighth of the sample secondary schools added the Spanish club as a student activity; one tenth added the mathematics club as a student activity; and about one twelfth added the science club or Future Scientists of America as a student activity during the period 1956-1957 to 1964-1965.

> Moderate or small decreases in frequency were found for the following student activities for the period 1956-1957 to 1964-1965: Future Farmers of America, New Farmers of America, or agriculture

---

[10]Harry C. McKown, *Extra-Curricular Activities* (Rev. ed. New York: The Macmillan Co., 1949), p. 191.

club; interscholastic agriculture-organization-related contests; and the distributive education club, diversified occupations club, business club, or Future Business Leaders of America.[11]

SPECIAL INTEREST CLUBS

Frederick defines the special interest club as "a small company of students who meet together informally to share a common interest."[12] The distinguishing features of the special interest club are that it (1) is local in nature; (2) is a low-pressure organization; (3) may have a long or short life-span; (4) has a simple organizational structure; (5) makes no major campaigns for new members; (6) has a high degree of flexibility; and (7) need not be large to be successful.

The seedbeds of major curriculum changes often lie in the special interest group. Many of the now major student activities began as special interest groups. Some progressive high schools are now using individual study and projects to accomplish the objectives formerly handled by special interest clubs. These clubs are still valuable for they permit small groups of students to work together on projects of mutual interest. The special interest club has been described as "the growing edge" of the educational program.

It is important that the special interest club be indiginous to a particular school, and not merely copied from somewhere else. To use extreme examples, a surfing club in Kansas would be as out of place as a mountain-climbing club in Florida. Names are not important, and similar activities in different schools may have widely different names.

Sports and Games

Many of the special interest groups are concerned with sports and games, and as such, might grow out of a physical education class. Among those sometimes found are: soccer, water polo, volleyball, table tennis, badminton, wrestling, boxing, skiing, gymnastics, archery, checkers, chess, horseshoes, fencing, bowling, rodeo events,

---

[11]Jerry H. Robbins, "Trends in Student Activity Offerings in the Public Secondary Schools of Arkansas" (Unpublished doctoral dissertation, University of Arkansas, Fayetteville, 1966), pp. 58-59.

[12]Robert W. Frederick, *The Third Curriculum* (New York: Appleton-Century-Crofts, 1959), p. 406.

sports cars, surfing, riflery, handball, sky diving, skin diving, ice skating, hiking, horseback riding, and curling. See Chapter 7 for a discussion of these recreational interest groups.

Others

Among the multitude of other special interest clubs — some of which have only the remotest connection with the usual school subjects — are these: Braille, modern dancing, poetry, painting, naturalists, stamp collectors, Young Republicans, Young Democrats, forestry, aviation, press, radio, geology, electronics, secretaries, music, creative writing, jazz, Pan-American, biology, Italian, photography, archeology, journalism, life science, forensics, drafting, philosophy, cosmetology, and art.

Vocational Interest. In many schools, students with similar vocational interests organize to study the profession or occupation they plan to enter. Some of these, such as the Future Teachers of America — perhaps the largest of these organizations — are affiliated with an adult professional group. Others sometimes found include the previously mentioned Future Scientists of America and Future Business Leaders of America; Vocational Industrial Clubs of America; the future engineers; the future nurses; and the premedical or predental club.

One novel approach of handling special interests, though not through special interest clubs, is that of the Idea Forum (IF) of Cubberley High School in Palo Alto, California. On certain days, classes were dismissed, and students were free to choose from among sessions on a great many topics — or to do nothing. Activities were selected by a student-faculty committee, with few restrictions other than that they be legal, socially acceptable, educational, and interesting to high school students. Each suggestion made by a student was required to have a faculty sponsor who agreed to provide necessary supervision.

The following were the objectives of the IF program: to involve students in the process of their own education; to allow students and teachers to join together in areas of common interest; by removing grades, to allow students to explore in areas they may have been fearful of; to use community resources more effectively; to bridge the generation gap and improve communication at the person-to-person level; to become more aware of others in the Cubberley community as thinking and feeling human beings; to provide a chance for interdisciplinary cooperation; to generate or discover new ideas for courses, either in content or methods; to provide Cubberley faculty with a clearer understanding of student interests; to provide students with a chance to grow by giving them experience in self-direction in an atmosphere characterized by a wide variety of choice; and to change the pace and routine in order to avoid end-of-the year slump, to pep up the school, and to avoid the effects of pent-up tension.

Among the 80 activities offered in the IF were horseback riding; sailing; group counseling; a symposium on drugs; boxing; co-ed archery; judo; discussion of conscientious objections, the city of 2000 A.D., Summerhill, and racial problems; tap dancing; bowling; investing; reducing; folk-singing; pen-and-ink sketching; Evtushenko; photography; the Wff'n Proof game of logic; Renaissance madrigals; chess; computer programming; key punching, Zen; matrices; shells; and camouflage.[13]

Trends. In the Arkansas study, mentioned previously, Robbins found that:

> about one-twelfth of the sample secondary schools [recently] added the photography club . . . . Moderate increases in frequency were found for the following student activities . . . the radio club, the art or art appreciation club, and the religion or chapel club or the devotional group.
>
> A moderate decrease in frequency was found for the reading, literature, or poetry club.[14]

In addition to these Robbins also found such special interest groups as the Junior Deputy Sheriffs, Lunchroom Student Hostesses, Square Dance Club, Talent Club, Coin Club, Chess Club, Great Decisions Groups, and the Driving Club.

It appears likely that we will continue to have such organizations in quantity — and this is highly desirable, as long as they make a legitimate contribution to our general objectives of education.

---

[13]Peter Paiches, "Idea Forum: An Experiment in Nonstructure," *NASSP Bulletin*, 51:12-21, December, 1967.

[14]Robbins, *op. cit.*, p. 63.

REFERENCES

Frederick, Robert W. *The Third Curriculum*. New York: Appleton-Century-Crofts, 1959.

"Future Homemakers of America," *American Education,* 3:13, May, 1967.

Gruber, Frederick C., and Beatty, Thomas Bayard. *Secondary School Activities*. New York: McGraw-Hill Book Co., 1954, p. 140.

Johnston, Edgar G., and Faunce, Roland C. *Student Activities in Secondary Schools*. New York: The Ronald Press Co., 1952, pp. 111-138.

Jordan, J. W. "Non-Athletic Activities Program," *NASSP Bulletin,* 47:20-22, October, 1963.

Kilzer, Louis R., *et al. Allied Activities in the Secondary School*. New York: Harper and Brothers, 1956, pp. 64-89.

McKown, Harry C. *Extra-Curricular Activities.* Rev. ed. New York: The Macmillan Co., 1949, pp. 160-193, 230-249.

McWilliam, Aileen L. "Science Extracurricular Activities," *Pooling and Sharing,* pp. 47-52, (Nov., 1964).

Miller, Franklin A., *et al. Planning Student Activities*. Englewood Cliffs, N.J.: Prentice-Hall, Inc., 1956, pp. 270-306.

"NCTM to Cosponsor Mu Alpha Theta," *The Mathematics Teacher,* 60:528, May, 1967.

Paarlberg, Teunis J. "The Mathematics League," *The Mathematics Teacher,* 60:38-40, January, 1967.

Palches, Peter. "Idea Forum: An Experiment in Nonstructure," *NASSP Bulletin,* 51:12-21, December, 1967.

Robbins, Jerry H. "Trends in Student Activities," *Journal of Arkansas Education,* 38:22-23, December, 1965.

Robbins, Jerry H. "Trends in Student Activity Offerings in Public Secondary Schools of Arkansas." Unpublished doctoral dissertation, University of Arkansas, Fayetteville, 1966.

Strang, Ruth. *Group Work in Education*. New York: Harper and Brothers, 1958, pp. 160-181.

Twining, Charles W. "Relationship of Extracurricular Activity to School Marks," *School Activities,* 28:181-184, February, 1957.

Wood, Donald I. "Archaic Student Clubs; Those Entrenched by Tradition May Be At Odds With Enlightened Student Activities," *Clearing House,* 31:91-93, October, 1964.

Chapter 10

SERVICE AND
RECOGNITION GROUPS

While many student interests are met and fulfilled by special interest and subject matter clubs, there are additional student interests and needs which must be recognized and met through the student activities program, including the desire to help others and the desire to be recognized for accomplishments.

SERVICE GROUPS

Background

Student activities involving some type of altruistic effort allow students to develop their personalities while enjoying fellowship. Most student service groups orient their activities toward the school: helping in the office, library, supply store, and first-aid room; guiding visitors; supervising corridor traffic; orienting new students; and assisting with audiovisual equipment and stage productions. However, there are many examples of student groups' sponsoring service projects aimed at areas away from the school; for example, International Clubs' "adopting" a foreign student, family, or community and the resultant supplying of books, medical supplies, tools, seeds, money, and other needs. Letter-writing and gift-sending to American troops overseas are examples of school-based service projects. Work in local charities and hospitals are additional examples.

Characteristics

Regardless of the specific nature of service organizations, such student activities are undertaken with the following in mind:

1. Unskilled work, such as setting up movie screens, moving stage scenery, and passing out books can be done by students, while teachers can be freed to concentrate on teaching and other professional responsibilities.

2. Such positions as library or laboratory assistants may be a reward for high scholarship. Such designations are used to encourage scholarship or proficiency among the students.

3. Student participation in school government, as well as *esprit de corps,* is increased when students are given the responsibility of patroling themselves in the hallways and in the cafeteria.

4. Community and international understanding and cooperation can be enhanced through student participation in student activities designed to help others.

In the planning for and using of student service clubs, student exploitation should be avoided at an age in which they pride themselves on their industry, their stamina, and their pioneering spirits.[1]

Types of Activities

There are, of course, numerous types of service activities. Probably the most common is the usual group of "assistants" of various types who help in the offices, supply store, library, learning center, backstage, in the corridors and lunchrooms, and in the clinic. Such groups usually devote a free period to these duties for the purpose of helping the school. No officers are elected and meetings are nonexistant except for their periods of work.

Service organizations also exist for the purpose of providing information. Students who guide visitors around buildings and students who provide orientation for new students also give of their time to the school. A number of schools have arranged for tutorial service, as at St. Hubert's High School for Girls in Philadelphia. However, these and similar groups are usually composed of highly trained individuals who know their way around the physical plant, know the history and rules of the school, and have skills in relating to people and imparting information. Although a formal organization is not necessary for the effective operation of groups such as these, it is highly recommended that these students participate in special training and familiarization programs.

Supervisors of corridor traffic, lunch rooms, and the like, as well as members of stage and audiovisual service organizations, are usually highly organized and well-trained. A Head Monitor, Stage

[1]See Chapter One.

Manager, and A-V Club President are likely to exist along with various other officers. A core of trainees is necessary to add depth to organizations as well as to provide trained service club members for following years.

Forums or other opportunities for discussion of school and community problems will help keep morale high and prevent many in-school problems from becoming serious.

Other groups may undertake to enhance the very important objective of increasing person-to-person contacts by helping elementary age students of underprivileged backgrounds. While tutoring is usually a major part of such service, assisting in social and recreational opportunities and providing simple friendship are also important.

Other groups may assume responsibility for setting up and maintaining various honor systems: in the corridors, rest rooms, smoking areas, cafeteria, assembly areas, library, and parking lots. In some schools a service group will assume responsibility for opening exercises, including patriotic items such as the Pledge to the Flag and the National Anthem, inspiration or devotional material, and announcements.

A Look Ahead

As facilities in schools become more complex, it is not unlikely that groups such as Student Life Guards for school pools, Learning Center Student Technologists, etc. will become increasingly common.

Many school service clubs, such as the hall monitors and orientation committees, continue to offer opportunities for student service to the school.

The Service Club Organization of Yankton (South Dakota) High School, for example, operates the student paperback book store; provides ushers for school plays, concerts, commencement, and other public functions in the school; provides guides for visitors and new students; and holds a year-end banquet to recognize students of merit. Nevertheless, many long-standing clubs and organizations — such as the Audiovisual Club, Office Assistants, Student Librarians, and Lab Assistants Club — are destined to become victims of educational progress as schools become able to provide additional adult personnel. It is also hoped that reevaluation of student services will end such posts as Student Fire Marshals and Student Bus Driver Evaluators.[2]

As traditional altruistic activities have become less frequent, school-based service activities have arisen. High school organizations provide teenage volunteers to serve — and learn — in hospitals, crippled children's institutions, orphanages, penitentiaries, jails, and the like. Groups make regular planned visits to hospitals and nursing homes to entertain and to help with letter-writing and other tasks.

For example, Ascension Academy in Alexandria, Virginia, has inaugurated a hospital services program which includes, for younger students, a "Visit-Vision" program in which the students are connected with patients by telephone and television. Older boys assist with the admission program by escorting patients to their rooms and helping with the office work in the hospital.

In other schools, service groups assist with charitable drives, including not only cash, but the collection of canned goods, clothing, etc., for the needy. In other instances, school groups have been instrumental in helping pass bond issue elections for new schools, hospitals, sewage systems, etc. As opportunities for student service *to* the school decrease, opportunities for students to serve *outside* the school must be found — and they are not difficult to locate.

For instance, many community civic clubs sponsor organizations that provide opportunities for altruistic efforts by students. Organizations such as Junior Red Cross, YMCA-YWCA activities, and other similar programs provide, through the schools, opportunities for student fellowship and cooperative effort of a service nature.

The Civil Air Patrol, the American Automobile Association-sponsored School Safety Patrols, and other groups provide opportunities for valuable community service by students, while in turn providing worthwhile training, pleasant fellowship, and some degree of recognition for those selected for membership.

Almost every national civic club — Rotary, Kiwanis, Optimist, for example — sponsors high school service organizations. These clubs not only provide opportunities for service by students, but also give opportunities for fellowship. Also, most of these school clubs require students selected for membership to possess outstanding qualities of

---

[2]These and other similar student positions actually exist in some states as required by state law or regulation of the state department of education.

leadership and perhaps to excell in other areas of endeavor, as well. Thus, these organizations provide recognition for their members.

Many other national and international organizations exist which provide opportunities for student groups to assist those less fortunate than they. Among these are the Keep America Beautiful, Inc. programs, People to People Program, Radio Free Europe, CARE, Foster Parents Plan, Save the Children Federation, American Field Service, the Civil Defense, and the School Partnership Program.[3] Most of these organizations regularly send materials to schools showing ways that students may be of assistance.

There is much that a school can do on its own, however, to enhance international understanding. In the "Horizons Unlimited" program of McKinley High School in Honolulu, Hawaii, many school groups assist with making the arrangements for various students, student groups, and faculty to travel to such places as Washington, D.C., Japan, and Mexico in the interest of international understanding.

RECOGNITION GROUPS

In addition to the service clubs which recognize student accomplishments, many high schools offer special organizations which exist solely or primarily to recognize outstanding student achievement. Among these groups on the high school level are academic recognition groups, Quill and Scroll,[4] athletic lettermen's clubs,[5] and the National Thespian Society.[6]

Academic Recognition Groups

The most common academic recognition groups on the high school level are the National Honor Society, sponsored by the National Association of Secondary School Principals, and the National Beta Club. Membership in the National Honor Society is granted, with faculty approval, to students in over 13,000 senior high

---

[3] As an example of the work of these organizations, see the description of the School Partnership Program in the January, 1967, issue of *Student Life Highlights*.
[4] See Chapter 8.
[5] See Chapter 7
[6] See Chapter 11.

schools. Students outstanding in leadership, scholarship, character, and service are selected for membership. Members may participate in the NHS Scholarship Program, which in 1968 provided 225 scholarships valued at $160,500.[7]

Academic recognition groups usually provide services to the school in helping with their overall purposes. Direction of honor systems, maintenance of a college catalog library, distribution of "Honor Roll" ribbons, and providing scholarship funds are common practices.

Other Academic Recognitions

For many years recognition of athletic ability has justly been recognized by award of a school letter. The awarding of *academic* letters is an innovative practice adopted by many schools recently.

The Wellesley (Massachusetts) Junior High School, for example, has an elaborate point system in which academics, athletics, and other student activities are equally valid for the accumulation of points toward a letter.

In some schools where academic letters are awarded, the actual letter presentation is contingent upon earning a specified number of points. Points are earned (similar to the practice in athletics) by various academic accomplishments. Specific points are awarded each grading period for all A's; A's and B's; consecutive periods on the honor roll, faculty list, or whatever; as well as for significant academic improvement.

Special Recognition Groups.

While academic recognition in most schools is usually carried out through a national organization, many schools have set up their own local recognition groups. Some groups, like the Honor Study Hall and the Honor Roll Club, recognize academic attainment at a level below that of the National Honor Society. Other groups, such as local leadership organizations, also exist in many forms throughout American high schools to recognize certain attainment that is considered desirable by the individual school and its students.

[7]For additional information about the National Honor Society, see the *Handbook of the National Honor Society* (National Association of Secondary School Principals, Washington, D.C., 1966).

Local communities also play an important part in giving recognition to students who have made special achievements. Community-wide academic banquets, similar to those held in Memphis, are becoming common year-end gatherings. Long-standing community recognition of the select students from various groups to compose an all-city, all-region, or all-state chorus, band, football team, or similar group, continue to influence student achievement.

Although recognition of many kinds exists, and although it is beneficial for students and schools, it must be pointed out that such recognition exists only as a *means to an end*. The attainment of outstanding scholarship, service, and leadership only to attain membership in a certain school organization, to wear special insignia, or to acquire points is not to be encouraged. Recognition groups serve to encourage special attainments, but should not be the only reason a student becomes a good citizen or an industrious student. It is to be hoped that the *ars gratia artis* concept can eventually be applied to the students' seeking for knowledge, citizenship, and leadership. Until this automatic response comes about, high schools must continue to support various recognitions.

Frederick[8] has suggested that recognition be made for students showing *improvement* in a subject field as opposed to *continued success* in the field of study. Educators must consider this concept. Certainly many school philosophies embrace such recognition experiences as Frederick suggests. Unfortunately, few schools execute this portion of their philosophy. The encouragement involved in improvement, not total mastery, in a subject field could improve student morale and study habits; for a high point of academics would not have to be reached before recognition was accorded.

GENERAL CRITERIA

The two basic needs of serving and being recognized can easily be met in the high school student activities program. Organizations, such as service and recognition groups, although undergoing changes in form, are beneficial to both the students and the school. To be fully and correctly utilized these groups should meet the following criteria:

[8]Robert W. Frederick, *The Third Curriculum* (New York: Appleton-Century-Crofts, Inc., 1959), p. 422.

Membership or Award Attainable. Honors or membership in a service group should be within the reach of a reasonable number of people. Excessive qualifications or demands upon members of, for example, the audiovisual club serve only to terminate the possibility of having sufficient members for the student activity. Likewise, extremely low qualifications for the honor society remove the "honor" from membership.

Organization Correctly Labeled. If membership in an organization is intended as an honor, it must be so labeled and considered by school authorities. For example, a group of students selected on the basis of responsibility, efficiency, and interest to *assist* in the school office should not be turned into a secretarial pool for the faculty. Purposes and duties of honor and service groups should be clear to all — faculty and students alike.

Beneficial Results. If personnel, facilities, and finances are to be provided for recognition and service organizations, the results of their activities must be *mutually* beneficial to school and students. An organization cannot be created to be totally subservient to the school, just as no group may be allowed to exist within the school that has no desire to adhere to school policy and regulations.

SUMMARY

Student interests are many and varied. They are, in fact, so varied that the other types of activities already mentioned will not fulfill their needs. The student activities program must include activities that will fulfill students' needs for recognition and service. The most common of these activities are the National Honor Society, various local school service groups (office, school store, library, etc.), and the nationally affiliated groups of service and/or recognition.

REFERENCES

Allen, Charles F., *et al. Extra-Curricular Activities in the Elementary Schools.* St. Louis, Mo.: Webster Publishing Co., 1937, pp. 554-592.

Frederick, Robert W. *The Third Curriculum.* New York: Appleton-Century-Crofts, Inc., 1959, pp. 375-382, 392-395, 417-423.

Handbook of the National Honor Society. Washington, D.C.: National Association of Secondary School Principals, 1966.

McKown, Harry C. *Extra-Curricular Activities.* Rev. Ed. New York: The Macmillan Co., 1949, pp. 502-524.

Mortensen, Lee. "The Role of the School Library in Extracurricular Activities," *School Activities,* 30:269-273, May, 1959.

Strang, Ruth. *Group Work in Education.* New York: Harper and Brothers, 1958, pp. 198-211.

Wyland, R. O. *Scouting in the Schools.* New York: Teachers College, Columbia University, 1934.

Chapter 11

FINE ARTS ACTIVITIES

The fine arts are, in general, the neglected areas of American secondary education. Relatively few fine arts courses are found in the curriculum of our secondary schools, although in recent years the situation has shown some improvement. Many of the fine arts courses which we *do* have in our secondary schools came in "by the back door"; that is, they were first added to the curriculum through the student activities program. The four major types of fine arts activities which are found today in American secondary schools are the forensic and dramatic activities, music activities, the dance, and the visual arts activities.

FORENSIC AND DRAMATIC ACTIVITIES

The forensic and dramatic activities are among the oldest types of student activities to be found in our schools. In fact, dramatics and public speaking antedate formal education as we now think of it. They were, and are, emphasized by most early societies. Later, the Greeks put heavy emphasis on dramatics, as did the Church and its schools during the Middle Ages, while public speaking, especially oratory, reached an apex under the Romans.

It is the rare school of any size that does not have one or more student activities that could be classified as dramatic or forensic. Robbins in a survey of student activities in Arkansas found that the senior play was the only student activity found in *all* the schools.

Drama is a part of both formal courses and of the student activities program. Plays and play production are studied in literature and speech classes, and occasional references to drama are made in other areas of study as well. Declamation, class reports, oral reading, assembly programs, and others are found in connection with many courses and student activities.

Galen Jones, in his famous 1935 study of student activities, pointed out that only one-sixth of the schools offering speech had started it as a class; the remainder, presumably, started speech as some sort of student activity.[1] In 1935, 45% of the schools administered dramatics as a regular subject; however, at that time, most principals felt that dramatics should be both a "curricular" and an "extracurricular" offering. Jones also found that about 44% of the schools which he studied offered classes in debating. While comparable information is not available for a recent year, it is likely that these figures have changed considerably.

The forensic and dramatic activities have a wide appeal — both immediate and long-range — to participants and audience. For example, the following story is told:

> A visitor to a large city apartment building recently was pleased to meet by chance the building superintendent, a man whom he had known years before in his high school. After the exchange of pleasantries, and inquiries after common acquaintances, the superintendent said, "You know what I remember best about Hoover High School? It was the senior play, and I was the butler." He said nothing about his French and algebra classes, about dressing for P.E., reading Silas Marner *[sic]*, or classifying verbs as intransitive copulative or intransitive complete. He remembered most vividly his walk-on role in a dramatic production. And the halo from this one experience apparently illumined his attitude toward his own and all schools, for he remarked with some gravity that he always voted yes on school-bond issues.[2]

There are many different types of dramatic and forensic activities. Among these are pantomine, proscenium theater, theater in-the-round, pageants and circuses, role playing and socio-drama, puppets and marionettes, skits, tableaux, radio and television broadcasting, choral reading and speaking, debate, public speaking, and creative writing for the voice and acting media.

Of these various types, play production is certainly one of the most common, if not the most common. Play production, of course, involves much more than acting; for it provides opportunities for

---

[1] Galen Jones, *Extra-Curricular Activities in Relation to the Curriculum* (New York: Bureau of Publications, Teachers College, Columbia University, 1935).

[2] Louis R. Kilzer *et al., Allied Activities in the Secondary School* (New York: Harper and Brothers, 1956), p. 196.

experiences in selection of plays, casting, costuming, stage design, stagecraft, props, makeup, directing, prompting, reviewing, business management, program design and production, audience management, ushering, promotion and publicity, lighting, writing and editing, crowd and safety control, and intelligent viewing and criticizing. Far too often, students have limited, if any, opportunities to participate in all these facets of play production. The dramatics coach or teacher-sponsor often chooses the play; casts it; handles most of the costuming, the stage design, and the stagecraft; personally gathers the props and applies the makeup; does all the directing (and perhaps even the prompting); closely supervises all the publicity and business affairs of the production; and sometimes even reviews the play. This is excellent experience for the teacher, but where does it leave the students? To be sure, the students do need guidance, direction, and assistance, but it is a shame that school plays are usually so production-centered, with such a great emphasis on a quality performance. In these cases, the students do not have opportunities, except by observation of the teacher, to learn how to plan and carry through the many different aspects of play production.

Williams found a most rewarding experience when he and the two other teachers forming the Senior Play Committee first gathered students interested in the business and technical facets of drama, selected a Business Manager, Stage Manager, and Student Director. Various tasks were volunteered for, and, among other things, a Cast Selection Committee was organized. The play was read and parts discussed before the Cast Selection Committee held tryouts and made their recommendations to the faculty who were, correctly, only supervising.

Many different skills are involved in play production, and many different talents may be brought to bear on the finished performance. Frederick has said:

> Theater provides an outlet for and a direct use of knowledges and skills acquired in almost every subject in the curriculum from typing class to the electrical shop. Music, dance, literature, history, bookkeeping, and public speaking are all used. Drama is an important — if not in fact the most important — activity in providing an immediate use for learning acquired in the credit curriculum.[3]

[3]Robert W. Frederick, *Student Activities in American Education* (New York: Center for Applied Research in Education, 1965), p. 39.

Forensic activities in the schools often include radio and television broadcasting, public speaking, debating, storytelling, interpretive reading, and choral speaking. Public speaking may consist of some type of public speaking club, or it may consist of some arrangement for presenting prepared speeches, extemporaneous addresses, impromptu speeches, and campaign speeches. Regional speech contests are found in many states.

Debating still remains popular in many schools, and it seems to be experiencing something of a revival. The National Forensic League, which emphasizes debating, has chapters in many schools over the country. Many schools have been changing their emphasis in debating from a matter of weeks or months of preparation (in which case it tends to become a matter of memorized speeches) to restricting preparation to a matter of hours to maintain spontaneity. The student forum or some variation of the panel discussion is increasingly found in place of, or in addition to, the debate. The forum or panel has the advantages of greater informality, audience participation, and greater interest in the topic under consideration.

Many schools have only a few dramatic events per year, because teachers, sponsors, and administrators tend to think in terms of major productions. Dramatics need not be elaborate. A stage or elevated platform, a neutral background, such as a gray cyclorama, a few spotlights and floodlights, and a switchboard with dimmers are all that is needed for many excellent productions. With the addition of some costuming, hand props, and makeup, most productions can be effectively presented with simple staging in even next-to-impossible locations such as cafeterias and gymnasiums.

Schools should investigate the possibility of doing productions "in-the-round." In general, sets and the playing area need not be as elaborate as for proscenium productions, although a more sophisticated, different type of acting is called for. It is possible that in-the-round productions could be very effectively staged on the floor of a gymnasium or another large room when adequate stage facilities are not available. Additional ingenuity in acting and with lighting is required in in-the-round productions, although the intimacy of this type of performance is rewarding to both actors and audience. If a school is fortunate enough to have a large stage, an effective in-the-round production may be staged by arranging temporary seating on the sides and the back of the stage, as well as using the first few rows of the regular auditorium seating. This permits the use of the lighting that is permanently installed on the stage.

Dramatics clubs — and there are several national groups as well as many local organizations — are found in most large high schools. In a large dramatics club the sponsor can use experienced student players to coach new members and less experienced players. In such an organization all members besides acting can participate in make-up, prompting, stage crew, wardrobe, the business aspects of the play production, and so on. Many of the active dramatics clubs present an annual series of full-length plays. Often one-act plays are presented in which students have had complete responsibility for all aspects of the production.

The Radio-Television Broadcasting Club is catching on rapidly in some quarters, and it deserves the attention of sponsors and administrators. Over 60 radio and 1000 television installations are being operated by school systems or by individual schools; and broadcasting club members have access to many real-life situations, both by observation of productions or by actual participation in productions.

In general, broadcasting clubs do not stress vocational skills. Americans spend a great deal of time listening to radio and watching television. Participation in broadcasting will lead to "information, perceptual skills, and reasoned intelligence by which they [the students] may separate the trite from the meaningful, the authentic from the exaggerated, the morally and socially viable from the debasing and dead."[4]

Even though many broadcasting clubs have access to educational and/or commercial broadcasting facilities, it is possible to have an excellent series of club activities using only an audio-tape recorder, a video-tape recorder, a public address system, or the school's inter-communication system.

The broadcast club is a logical follow-up to, and would work in close cooperation with, any ham radio club that may exist in the school.

In addition to the many valuable learning experiences that are available in the field of the dramatic and forensic arts, there are

---

[4]Richard Averson, quoted in "The Radio-TV Club," *NASSP Bulletin,* 50:76, October, 1966.

many practical merits as well. One of the most common of these is fund-raising. In many schools, especially the smaller ones, raising money is the primary purpose of the senior and/or junior play and other dramatic productions. Another, and closely related value, is that of advertising or promoting the school. The public relations value of these dramatic and forensic activities is not to be slighted. While attendance at a play or at a debate will seldom be as large as the attendance at an athletic contest or even a music concert, a play or debate tends to attract a different type of school patron. Often the people who attend the fine arts productions of the schools are of higher social classes, and in positions of leadership and influence in the community. In addition to these values, the dramatic and forensic arts may provide vehicles for those who are interested in careers in acting, radio, television, the movies, teaching, and even in such less closely related areas as law, politics, and business.

MUSIC ACTIVITIES

As has been noted in Chapter 1, music activities have had a long association with formal education. Music and literature were closely related in early cultures and in the Greek schools. Music was one of the elements of the *quadrivium*, a curriculum organization that influenced formal education for centuries. Little music was found in Colonial American schools, but course offerings and music activities increased a great deal during the nineteenth century. During the twentieth century there has been a great growth in the development of instrumental music in the public schools. Now it is highly unusual to find a school of any size at all without one or more bands, various wind instrumental ensembles, and an orchestra. In recent years, vocal and choral music in the public schools have also had a great revival, if not in the quantity of persons involved, certainly in the quality of the instruction and in the literature performed.

Music in the public secondary schools is found both as credit and noncredit experiences. Galen Jones reported in 1935 that two-fifths of the schools placed glee clubs, the band, and the orchestra on a "regular curricular basis" at the time of organization.[5] At that time slightly more than one-half of the schools studied

[5]Jones, *op. cit.*

accorded chorus a "curricular" status at
Jones also found that about four-fifths c
brought these music activities into "the r
pals of the schools which were studied ;
trend to continue until at least nine-tenth
band, chorus, orchestra, and glee clubs cur

Although statistics are not readily av
say that, at the present time, at least part
large-scale music groups such as band, c
some schools, credit is given for various s
the stage band, boys chorus, and the string
small choral and instrumental ensemble
activities program.

Not only should schools be teaching
but, through listening and appreciation g
methods, schools should be teaching how
nate among various styles and types of c
cans are now subjected to more music —
quality — in a few days than people of a
exposed to in a lifetime. Much of the ti
distance of a radio or television set;
conducted to the strains of piped-in music.
available; live music in churches, at concer
for dining has never been available to so
stated:

> Listeners are made in transistorized A
> tion is easier than production. Listening is
> active in special ways. The sale of record
> phenomenal. What its long-range effects o
> tastes will be is debatable. It is a fact that th
> increased each year, and that more symphor
> than ever before.[7]

In addition to teaching how to prod
music, music activities (1) supplement and

---

[6]In a survey of activities in Arkansas, Robbins fou
mixed chorus, or orchestra as student activities, accord
book, although it was common knowledge that these or
schools studied.

[7]Frederick, *op. cit.*, p. 40.

curriculum of the school, (2) furnish opportunities for the students to express their artistic and creative abilities to appreciative audiences, (3) afford valued public recognition for effort and achievement, (4) promote good will within the community toward the school and its people, (5) stimulate and encourage student enthusiasm in music toward sustained adult enjoyment and appreciation, and (6) serve as a means of wholesome social activity.

Opportunities for "creativity" in music are much greater for the arranger or orchestrator, and to an even greater extent, the composer than for the performer; but we seldom give much encouragement to or provide many opportunities for this type of activity. The popular music of the mid-1960's has given a certain impetus to the creativity of teenagers. Many teenagers, although seldom under school auspices, have composed and performed their own "folk songs." Many of the bands that play for dances have "written" their own music, although little of this has ever been committed to paper.[8]

A large musical production, like an operetta or a variety show, can utilize the interests and talents of all the musical groups in the school and serve as an incentive for integrating the work of many departments. This is especially true when the production is an original one. When *Bessie Green* was produced at Cleveland Junior High School in Newark, N.J., for example, original scripts were written by students in the English and music departments; dances were created and rehearsed in physical education classes; scenery was planned in the art room and built in the shop; costumes were designed by art classes and made in sewing classes; lighting facilities and acoustical properties of the auditorium were studied by science students and the production was planned in relation to them; tickets and programs were printed in the print shop; and finances were handled by commercial students and their teachers.

The Folk Festival of Fenger High School in Chicago is another excellent example of the integration of the arts. The theme of a recent program was the history of folk music in America. A special dialogue was written, sets were designed and constructed by the shop classes, and many school organizations participated in providing the music for some segment of the program.

---

[8]In many instances it is doubtful whether the "composer" has the ability to commit his music to paper.

A very rapidly growing type of musical organization is the madrigal singers. This usually consists of about 12 persons, boys and girls, who are able to sing independently and without accompaniment. Often these groups sing their madrigals dressed in costumes of several centuries ago, seated around a dinner table, and with candle light for illumination.

All-boy or all-girl ensembles have a great deal of audience appeal, and often it is easier to work with sexually segregated groups. A good barbershop quartet or boys chorus always receives many invitations to represent the school. Girls trios, quartets, and sextets, if good, receive much favorable attention. In many schools that have a select girls ensemble of twelve to sixteen voices, membership is considered a high honor. More and more girls drill teams, modeled on the famous Kilgore (Texas) Rangerettes, are being found in high schools. Close cooperation with the band is required in working with these drill teams. Baton- and flag-twirling ensembles, though technically not musical groups, are frequent crowd pleasers, especially at athletic events.

A few schools that are unable to have a marching band have a drum and bugle corps. In other schools, the drum and bugle corps is an elite group, selected from the brass and percussion sections of the marching band. Precision drill by a drum and bugle corps can be a striking performance involving only limited resources.

Informal opportunities for listening are found in some schools. Sometimes piped-in music is available in the cafeteria, in the library, and in the corridors between classes.

Music appreciation and listening clubs are fairly frequently found. Often these groups bring in student or outside soloists for performances, especially in connection with the study of a particular instrument, composition, composer, style, type of music, or period of music. Often recorded concerts are used, complete with printed programs, intermission, and applause to teach concert hall etiquette. Access to an adequate record library is imperative for this type of organization.

Among the music clubs in New Jersey high schools, one of the best known is the Musical Monday Club at Bloomfield High School. The purpose of this club is threefold: (1) to give musically gifted pupils an opportunity to enjoy one another's playing and singing, and to profit by friendly criticism; (2) to broaden the members' musical knowledge and appreciation by encouraging group attendance at concerts in Bloomfield and in nearby communities; and (3) to contribute, when possible, to the greater appreciation of good music on the part of other high school students and townspeople. At regular monthly meetings a special form of music or a particular theme is studied, and members perform on their respective instruments or sing a composition illustrating the form of music under consideration. An annual open meeting, at which all members perform, either as soloists or in ensemble, is attended by teachers, parents, and other guests.

Stage bands, ranging from combos of five or six, to swing bands of fifteen or sixteen performers, are found in many schools. A few dollars invested in "combo books" and almost any combination of instruments will get a combo going, although a good swing band will want to acquire a library of several hundred arrangements, have special music stands, lights, and other apparatus, not to mention a "uniform" for the players.

Many schools have had a tradition of an all-school operetta, although the operetta is, in general, being supplanted by the musical comedy. Obviously, much work and close cooperation among the music department, speech department, and others involved in the production are needed. Kilzer, Stephenson, and Nordberg have said:

> Music educators today seriously support operetta production only when it is possible to select and stage a better-quality work, when stage and acoustical facilities are adequate, and when pupil talents and audience reception warrant the lavish expenditure of time and effort necessary for success.[9]

The same authors go on to say

> Less elaborate musical activities, however, should not be discouraged simply because the production may not be finished in every detail. The good of the pupils participating is the criterion; professional performances or staging, however desirable or admired, should not be expected.[10]

The variety show is often an effective compromise. Because of its very nature, it can be rehearsed in smaller segments, and sets, costumes, lighting, etc. may be as simple or as elaborate as is desired.

[9]Kilzer, *et al., op. cit.,* p. 198.
[10]*Ibid.,* p. 199.

In fact, the variety show provides for the maximum amount of participation, not only in the performance, but in the technical end as well. If, for example, one or two people have the responsibility for the makeup of the participants in one act or one section of the show, and others are making up other participants, then more students have an opportunity to work with makeup than would be possible in the conventional play, operetta, or musical comedy.

Schools with exceptionally talented individuals should consider doing scenes from operas, or perhaps even occasional one-act operas. These operatic performances could range from an aria sung in costume on a bare stage with piano accompaniment, to an extended scene with several principals, a set, complete costumes, a chorus, and full orchestra accompaniment. This type of musical production should be reserved for enrichment for the highly gifted vocalists, with much more emphasis on quality than is necessary (or desirable) in other types of performances.

In many parts of the country, music contests, festivals, and clinics are part of the activities program, even when the ensemble from which the students come may not be an activity, but a course.[11] Opinions about the value of these interscholastic experiences differ greatly. The National Association of Secondary School Principals does not include any music contests in the 1967-1968 approved list of contests.[12] Many state activities associations have severely limited the distance a musical group may travel; the amount of money that may be spent for adjudicators; the nature of prizes and medals awarded, if any; the number of entries a school may have; and so on. In addition, many local boards of education and local administrators have policies that are far more stringent than the state association rules. This "tightening up" resulted in a reduction of the amount of time spent in preparing for, traveling to and from, and participating in various sorts of interschool music experiences.

On the other hand, some administrators and music teachers, especially those whose students do well in these interschool music experiences, make a fairly good case for the contests, clinics, and festivals. They point out that the contest with its rankings and awards serves as a motivating device for individuals and ensembles,

---

[11]Technically, there are differences among contests, festivals, and clinics. In practice, however, they are often euphemistically used for various types of competitions.

[12]Although computer programming and arc welding are included.

prompting the students to prepare works that probably would not be done otherwise. The clinic is supposed to provide enrichment opportunities for students who cannot be effectively challenged on the local level. The festival is an evaluative device to publicly demonstrate and to receive expert criticism of what the students have learned. All of these interschool events are purported to have great public relations potential.

At least as the contests have been administered in the past, music contests, festivals, and clinics have many shortcomings. How do you explain to a student that he cannot expect to receive a high rating from a certain judge because the student does not study privately with the judge? How do you explain to a student that he was not named to a select interschool ensemble because of personality conflicts between his music teacher and those making the selection of students? How do you justify to parents, the other teachers, the administration, and the board of education the school time missed and the cost involved in sending students to these affairs, in terms of the benefits to be gained? These and similar questions are difficult to answer.

If we need motivating devices, if we need enrichment, if we need evaluation or public relations in our school music programs, then let us handle this on the local level. A good teacher will usually be able to find motivating devices, hopefully of an intrinsic nature. The good teacher will be able to find many ways of challenging the gifted musician or of providing enrichment without having to send the student out of town. If it is valuable to engage a clinician, then let him come to the local school, just as teachers in the "academic" areas arrange for resource people. Also, a good school public relations program involves far more than a list of "blue ribbon" winners and the adjudicator's compliments (often taken out of context) on a given performance.

Avoid large-scale interscholastic competition in music. As Frederick has said, "The desire to do better, to get more enjoyment, and to give more pleasure is a higher motive than the wish to beat somebody else."[13]

---

[13]Frederick, *op. cit.*, p. 43.

DANCE ACTIVITIES

The dance is a very old educational activity. It occupies perhaps even a greater place in early cultures than does music. The Greeks were fond of the dance, and various forms of rhythmical movement have been a part of Western culture since that time. Dancing was recognized by the English writers on education several centuries ago; it was even recognized by the early colonists in this country. Every "gentleman" in England and even in America learned to dance.

The elementary schools in this country have done some work with folk and Indian dance; rhythmical movement is closely associated with physical education in primary grade programs. The upper elementary grades have sometimes been involved in Maypole and other such dances, and sometimes with square and country dancing. However, the secondary schools have, in general, ignored the serious study of the dance. Ballet and some of the other performing arts have enjoyed a revival in recent years; there is, however, a cultural lag in getting these performing arts into the schools.

Perhaps one reason why the dance is in no better graces in the public schools than it is, is because of a widespread misunderstanding of and lack of information about the various forms of dance. Social dancing is about all that some people are familiar with; it is not ordinarily considered an art form, and it is considered under "Social Activities" (Chapter 12). The dance as a form of physical exercise or physical development is something else again, and may or may not be considered an art form. There are types of dancing, such as tap and acrobatic. that may or may not be art forms depending on ones definition of the term. Without exception though, ballet and modern interpretive dance are considered art forms. Those who are knowledgeable about the latter feel that it should be an exposition of an emotion, an idea, or an experience; that there should be a feeling of unity of purpose among the members of the group; that group dancing should be an expression of group experience; that dancing should be a means of self-expression rather than the execution of set patterns imposed by the instructor and carried out mechanically; and that movement in the dance should be rhythmical rather than metrical.

A few schools have ballet clubs; a few have folk dance clubs.[14] The few modern dance clubs that exist derive their content from the dancer's experience, feeling, or belief; the members feel that form has its beginning in natural movement, and dancing is usually done with bare feet. Some experimentation is being done in these groups in the reunion of poetry and dancing.

As dancing becomes one of the fine arts supported by the public schools, it should not be allowed to become a predominantly girls activity. Some college and professional athletes quietly study dance to improve their body control. In primitive societies, the dance was and is strictly a man's art. In classic Greece, dance was a basic element of the education of boys and men. Many European folk dances were traditionally danced only by boys and men. Sailor's hornpipes, sword dances, and many of the Slavic dances are dances for men only. In the elementary grades, there is usually little or no reticence on the part of the boys to dance, and in Cub and Boy Scouts (and even in Explorer units) Indian dances are often used.

THE VISUAL ARTS

Increasingly, we find a course in "art" offered in American public junior and senior high schools. Every school has students who are interested in drawing, painting, sculpture, ceramics, etc.; and often these interests cannot be fully met, even if one or more courses in "art" are offered. Art clubs are frequently formed to meet these needs; and sometimes in the larger schools we find separate clubs for those interested in the various branches of art. Sometimes these art clubs, as a school service, and in addition to individuals' interests, assume responsibility for preparing and maintaining bulletin boards, arranging display cases, and preparing posters advertising school events.

In addition, crafts clubs are sometimes found to meet the needs of students who are interested in such areas as ceramics, leather-work, woodworking, metal work, and working in such media as cloth and paper.

---

[14]There is opportunity for creativity here. As Gruber and Beatty have said, "One of the chief delights of American country dancing is the infinite opportunity for improvisation." (*Secondary School Activities,* p. 120).

Photography, when approached artistically rather than technically, is a worthy member of the visual arts. The photography club is one of the most popular clubs in this group, and is by no means a new type of organization. As students continue to have access to better equipment, cameras, light meters, films, etc., the activities of photography clubs have changed from science club activities (with emphasis on optics, chemicals, etc.) to art club activities (with emphasis on selection of subject, composition of the picture, use of shadow and color, background and foreground, etc.). Technical information is by no means neglected, but tends to concern itself largely with artificial lighting, lenses, filters, developing, enlarging, etc. Most serious members of the photography club like to do their own developing and enlarging, in order to have full control of the entire artistic process. Most new secondary school buildings have a darkroom, often near the science suite, where it can double as an optics lab. Often the photography club is closely related to the school newspaper and the school yearbook, and often members of the photography club are asked to work closely with the public relations officer of the school. Under such cooperative arrangements, it is possible to have jointly controlled cameras, peripheral equipment, and darkroom equipment.

SUMMARY

The term *fine arts* embraces many activities — from debating to photography. As a part of the student activities program, fine arts activities have a background that reaches far back into antiquity. Ranging from the ancient appreciation of forensic and dramatic activities to the modern variations of modern dance and broadcasting, fine arts activities provide rewarding experiences for students and faculty. Fine arts activities not only provide interest for the members but also are activities in which the entire study body may find pleasure. It was pointed out that elaborate facilities are useful, but not essential to the success of the program.

REFERENCES

Averson, Richard. Quoted in Ventura, Lawrence. "The Radio-TV Club," *NASSP Bulletin,* 50:76-80, October, 1966.

Frederick, Robert W. *Student Activities in American Education.* New York: Center for Applied Research in Education, 1965.

Gruber, Frederick C., and Beatty, Thomas Bayard. *Secondary School Activities.* New York: McGraw-Hill Book Co., 1954, pp. 108-138.

Johnston, Edgar G., and Faunce, Roland C. *Student Activities in Secondary Schools.* New York: The Ronald Press Co., 1952, pp. 223-267.

Jones, Galen. *Extra-Curricular Activities in Relation to the Curriculum.* New York: Bureau of Publications, Teachers College, Columbia University, 1935.

Kilzer, Louis R., *et al. Allied Activities in the Secondary School.* New York: Harper and Brothers, 1956, pp. 196-216.

McKown, Harry C. *Extra-Curricular Activities.* Rev. ed. New York: The Macmillan Company, 1949, pp. 194-229.

Miller, Franklin A., *et al. Planning Student Activities.* Englewood Cliffs, N.J.: Prentice-Hall, Inc., 1956, pp. 378-419.

Chapter 12

SOCIAL ACTIVITIES

There is probably no more controversial area in the total life of the school than that vague domain called *social*. All children and their parents are concerned, either because they are wholesomely involved or because they are dangerously involved, or because they are not involved at all. All teachers are concerned, because in one way or another, they will be called upon to participate by chaperoning, by attending or by involving themselves in planning social affairs. Parents are completely baffled by the changed patterns of the social life of the young.[1]

THE PROBLEM

The social life of a secondary school that is geared to adult interests or even to adult perceptions of student interests is not likely to be highly successful. In few areas is the inherent conflict of the generations more evident than in the social affairs of youth.

The secondary school years fall in the period of the greatest social development in the lives of most individuals. The adolescent, as every teacher knows, exhibits the behavior of both the child and the adult, sometimes alternating rapidly between the two. In addition to being in a period of extensive physical, intellectual, and emotional changes, the secondary school student suffers from inner conflicts and tensions and is often undergoing personality changes.

The extensive need for peer approval at this age often brings the adolescent into conflict with the adults in his environment. The major social institutions in the adolescent's world — the home, the school, and the church — should seek ways to alleviate the problems of youth, rather than aggravate them, as is often the case. It is

[1]Robert W. Frederick, *Student Activities in American Education* (New York: Center for Applied Research in Education, 1965), p. 48.

difficult to find *the* answer, for each year brings a group of students whose individual problems and whose collective situation differ from those who preceded them.

SOME ANSWERS

Evaluation and innovation in social affairs should be a matter of great concern to the school if its intentions are more than intellectual. The physical hardships of growing up may be largely a thing of the past, but the psychological hardships of maturation are at least as severe now as they have ever been. With renewed emphasis on the academic program, with the development of larger attendance units, and with the racial desegregation of the public schools, the secondary schools in many instances are neglecting the social development of the students.

In some communities, recreation and social opportunities outside the school are readily available. Often movies, bowling, skating, slot car racing, pool halls, and other commercial enterprises are available. Libraries, swimming pools, athletic fields, parks, and the like may be provided by governmental units. Scouting, YMCA-YWCA, and other nonschool agencies may provide recreational opportunities, including dances, sports, camps, and hobby classes. Many churches, through their youth programs, provide additional opportunities. In many rural communities, however, these opportunities for out-of-school social opportunities may be totally lacking.

Usually, juvenile problems are reduced when a highly successful social program is available. The school cannot assume total responsibility for the social development of youth, but it can easily coordinate the total activities of the community. A well-planned social program will ease the transition from childhood to adulthood. And an adequately furnished school building for community use after hours may be a good starting place.

The social acceptance of minority groups is a problem that has recently become of much greater magnitude. Formerly, this was a small problem; for in the relatively infrequent instances in which there were students of minority groups in a school, any awkward situation could be handled on an individual basis. A few years ago an administrator or sponsor could handle social situations involving minority groups in one of the following ways: (1) The minority group could be deliberately excluded, assuming that they would not be interested in the activities of the majority group. (2) "Separate but equal" provisions could be made, providing special opportunities for the minority groups. (3) The nature of the social program could be changed to exclude dancing and any other activities which would involve having the students touch each other, handle the same objects, or remain in proximity to each other for any length of time — especially any activities that would involve pairing, for example, a white girl with a nonwhite boy. (4) All pupils could be treated alike, making no recognition of individual or group differences.

Although most schools and school systems in the country are, at least theoretically, desegregated, the number of students attending classes with those of a different race is still somewhat small in many areas. In a school with only a few members of a minority group, assimilation can, under favorable conditions, take place easily. In a school in which there is about the same number of each race, wholesale discrimination is unlikely. It is the situation in the middle, where there is a small but distinct minority group, that usually presents the most awkward situation. Generally applicable solutions to the problems produced in this situation have not yet been found. As Wey has put the problem,

> Student activities and social affairs are a vital part of the total school program. In the desegregated schools in the border states, white students and Negro students are on the same teams and in the same music groups; they take gym classes together, eat in the same lunchrooms, and attend the same dances. They are generally polite and considerate. They speak to each other in the halls and accept each other as classmates. Their relationship, however, ends at this point. They do not accept each other socially and there are very few cases where white and Negro students become close friends. The regulations of the USOE do not refer to informal social relationships, and this is understandable. The implication is clear, however, that much more information is needed if integration is to be achieved.[2]

More Than Parties

The social activities of a school, in a larger sense, and by some definitions, include far more than parties and dances. A complete

[2]Herbert W. Wey, "Desegregation and Integration," *Phi Delta Kappan,* 47:513-514, May, 1966.

listing would be virtually endless, and it would be difficult to separate the "curricular" from the "extracurricular." There are social grace clubs, friendship clubs, dance clubs, and clubs for those interested in clothes and grooming. Homeroom discussions often concern themselves with etiquette and boy-girl relations. Social dancing is sometimes taught in physical education classes, and English classes often have units on thank you notes, telephone manners, and introductions. Sportsmanship is taught on the athletic field. Home economics classes study meal time and home graces, appropriate dress, and party manners. Parliamentary procedure, verbal acknowledgments, and introduction of speakers are taught in speech classes.

Maine Township High School, East, in Illinois, publishes *Party Line*, a complete school directory and calendar. Pattison High School, an extremely small junior-senior high school in Texas, has remodeled unused rooms in an old building into a recreation room. North Division High School in Milwaukee has a Courtesy Campaign, consisting of both an advertising campaign and such features as movies, talks, a style show and Courtesy Week.

Almont (Michigan) Community High School, for a small fee, makes dancing lessons available from professional instructors. Langley Junior-Senior High School in Pittsburg makes dancing lessons available to holders of activities tickets.

The students of the New Brunswick (New Jersey) High School have provided an outdoor patio at the school to encourage social contacts.

Many schools have developed a "Courtesy Code," hold a "Courtesy Week," or sponsor a "Dress-Up Day," all of which are likely to increase school morale, improve discipline, and teach important social principles.

Problems of the "New Morality"

Recently, Robbins was conducting an evaluation of a small secondary school in the "Bible Belt." Upon inquiry, it was discovered that the school sponsored no social activities — no dances, no banquets, no parties. The community just did not permit such activities by the school. Other than an occasional church picnic, the very little entertaining that was done was done in the home, and at basketball and baseball games. There were no recreational or social outlets for the youth of the community.

Contrast this with the situation in some of the suburban high schools in which community and school social opportunities are available and abundant, where transportation and spending money is no problem, and where parental-imposed restrictions are few and liberal. In many such communities and schools, smoking is a social necessity, drug use is spreading, and the use of alcohol (even at school affairs) is winked at. A few school social events, especially parties after graduation, have achieved infamy as virtual orgies of alcohol, sex, and manslaughter.

In many instances some attempts — most noticeably some failing attempts — have been made to provide a type of adult entertainment after graduation. Normally, parents join in chaperoning what many students feel are unpleasing gatherings. What had been forbidden or severely limited for most of the evening for these students necessarily remains to be "done" in a short while after the gathering. The infamy of nonorganized gatherings remains.

What is the cause of failure of such generally well-intentioned events? Poor planning. Students could hardly be pleased at an adult-planned party. However, many schools, most notably the William H. Hall High School in West Hartford, Connecticut, have invited students, parents, and staff to join in planning.

The Hall High School Post-Senior Reception Party, staged in a nearby community center, offers something for all — including peace of mind for parents. Following a formal dance, the students are given an opportunity to change into informal attire and enjoy volleyball, basketball, swimming, conversation, games, movies, informal dancing, and a buffet. The Parent-Teacher Organization, the faculty, and the seniors have just cause to be proud of such a social gathering.

Extremes, in both directions, are wrong. Yet, values change, and differ among localities. What may be considered improper behavior in one situation may be acceptable in another. For example, in many communities, a student who appeared at a school dance with the faintest smell of alcohol on his breath would be immediately suspended from school. In other communities such a student might be asked to leave the dance if he became boisterous, but no other action would be taken.

What has caused the demise of the square dance, the pie supper, the picnic, and the box supper as sources of "good clean fun"? Which of the currently popular dances may the students do? Who makes the decisions about what is proper or improper dancing and behavior?

How much lighting must be used at school dances? What rules are necessary about students who came late to or leave early from school parties? What kind and how much supervision is needed for parking lots, rest rooms, and dark corridors at school parties and dances? Is holding hands permissible during the school day? Under what circumstances may married students attend school parties and dances?

The answer to questions such as these, involving matters of taste and morals, are not easy to obtain; nor will they be the same for all communities. Students' answers to such questions will differ from those of younger teachers, older teachers, administrators, the community-at-large, and the school board, in approximately that order. To satisfy students wants and needs without outraging the community is a difficult task that administrators and sponsors often face.

Frederick has suggested the following as guidelines:

1. Trust human intelligence — even the intelligence of the young.
2. Have confidence in the inherent tendency of humans to seek the good, the better . . . .
3. Be willing to accept the fact that the different is not automatically or necessarily bad.
4. Counter misinformation with scientific facts.
5. Start free communication between parent and child very early with the very young in the home.
6. Build systematized and sequential programs of instruction.
7. Never judge a person's value by a few actions; never label acts "wrong" or "stupid" without a thorough knowledge of circumstantial factors.[3]

THE SOCIAL CALENDAR

The social calendar should be well articulated with the calendar of other school events, including athletic contests, examination schedules, testing programs, and holidays. Ideally, the social calendar would be developed in the spring, or at the latest, during the summer

[3]*Ibid.*, pp. 62-63.

preceding the school year. Among the advantages of a long-range social calendar are that it encourages development of a variety of social activities and that it permits all concerned (sponsors, parents, community) to be notified well ahead of time.

The use of the long-range social calendar should not exclude the late-developing and more spontaneous type of social function, for these are often among the most successful events. These events, however, should be of a minor nature and should be considered supplements to, rather than part of, a well-rounded basic plan of social activities.

Table I outlines the basic social calendar for several schools.

THE ACTIVITIES

As has been previously pointed out, several groups, including students, teachers, the administration, parents, and the community, have important roles to play in the development of a good school social activities program. Several of these roles are discussed in general and at length elsewhere in this book, but a brief discussion of the features unique to the social program are given here.

Students

The students should, of course, carry the major part of the burden of school social activities from planning through cleanup and evaluation. The machinery by which this is done will vary among schools, among the types of social activities held, among the number of students involved, and so on. For all-school affairs, it is recommended that a social committee be used. The members should be appointed by the president of the student council, and the chairman should be appointed from among the membership of the student council. Other student council members may be members of the committee, but at least half the membership of the social committee should be non-student council members. The committee should be relatively large, and should be broadly representative of the entire student body, although members should *not* be appointed to represent some particular group.

Subcommittees should be extensively used, and may well include persons not on the social committee. One plan is for the chairman of the social committee to appoint a chairman and a set of subcommittees for each of the major all-school social events of the year. Another plan is to have a subcommittee that performs its functions for all the major events; that is, one committee handles the decorations for all events, another handles the refreshments for all events, and another handles the cleanup for all events. In general, the first plan is preferred.

Social functions provide a learning experience for the students: they learn to develop adequate and complete plans and to anticipate potential awkward or trouble spots. For example, most problems of student behavior can be averted by careful planning. It has been said that rowdyism is more a symptom than a disease. Rowdyism, especially among junior high school age boys, is often a reaction to an unusual, uncomfortable, frustrating experience. Planning and providing a variety of appropriate activities, such as games and entertainment, in any single social function will eliminate many difficulties — but leadership, both overt, on the part of students (not necessarily by elected leaders), and covert, by teachers and other adults, is required on a systematic basis.

Teachers

The faculty sponsors of social functions are the keys to successful functions. However, the bulk of the work done by the faculty sponsors should be done *before* the event takes place, and at almost all times, behind the scenes. Because of their immaturity and lack of experience, students are not always able to plan adequately or completely, and this is where the faculty sponsor has his most important duties. However, sponsors should be involved at all stages from the initial planning through cleanup and other follow-up functions — they should keep students within prescribed bounds, remind them of their responsibilities, help take care of loose ends, and exercise general supervision. Faculty members should not have to assume responsibilities for such things as taking tickets, guarding doors, or cleanup.

Faculty members other than official sponsors should expect to assist with large social events, under the direction of the sponsors. It is no more acceptable for official sponsors of a school-wide party to be expected to conduct the affair alone than it is for the coaching staff to personally handle all the details of a large interscholastic athletic contest. Nevertheless, faculty members assisting with a large

TABLE I[a]

SAMPLE SCHOOL SOCIAL PROGRAMS

Month	Beverly Hills H.S. (Beverly Hills, Calif. Community: City Grades 9-12 School Pop.: 1,806)	Cheltenham H.S. (Wyncote, Pa. Community: Suburban Grades 10-12 School Pop.: 1,800)	Vacaville Union H.S. (Vacaville, Calif. Community: Rural, suburban, small town Grades 9-12 School Pop.: 1,450)
Sept.	"Mum" Day and non-date Dance or Hootenanny Pigskin Prom (boy-ask-girl dance)	No major social event	After-Football-Game Dance
Oct.	Folk Singing Festival, G.A.A. sponsored "Spinster Hop" (girl-ask-boy informal dance)	"Get Acquainted" Party	Homecoming Program: Dance, Major Football Game, Queen Contest
Nov.	Sports Night (non-date, informal), Fall Play	School Play, Football Dance	Harvest Dance, Sadie Hawkins Day, Girls' League and Drill Team Dance
Dec.	Athletic Awards Banquet, Christmas Concert	Holiday Music Program, Holiday Dance	Christmas Ball, Formal
Jan.	Sophomore Dance, Donkey Basketball Game, and Sports Night	Talent Show, Review	Junior Class Dance, French Club, One-Act Play
Feb.	Knights Formal "Orchid Prom" (boy-ask-girl)	Mid-Winter Formal	California Education Club and California Scholarship Federation after-game Dance
Mar.	Formal Dance (girl-ask-boy)	March Musicale, Junior-Senior Reception	Sophomore Hop, Formal
Apr.	Bowling Tournament Spring Musicale	Musical Production	Junior Prom, Formal, Choral and Band Spring Concert
May	Musical Comedy, Class Picnics, Forty or more clubs have installation dinners, awards, luncheons, teas, etc.	Senior Work Day, and Hootenanny, Spring Musicale and Art Show	Spring Jamboree Invitational Track Meet, Carnival and Dance
June	Senior Prom, Senior Breakfast	Commencement Dance and Senior Breakfast	Senior Supper and Ball, Formal

TABLE I (Continued)

Month	Loveland H.S. (Loveland, Colo. Community: City Grades 9-12 School Pop.:1,188)	Los Alamos H.S. (Los Alamos, N. Mex. Community: Small Town Grades 10-12 School Pop.: 900)	Pawnee Rock Public School (Pawnee Rock, Kans. Community: Small town, rural Grades K-12 School Pop.: 300)
Sept.	Back-to-school Dance	Homecoming Parade and Dance	Freshman Reception and all-school dance
Oct.	F.F.A. Hay Ride, Homecoming, Powder Puff Football Dance	Musical Recital, Fall Chorus and Orchestra Concert	Homecoming and Football Queen Dance
Nov.	Junior Class Play	Drama Club Production	Class Parties, Junior Play
Dec.	Calendar Queen Party, Choir Concert Reception for Graduates	Holiday Music Program, Christmas Dance	All-school Christmas Program
Jan.	No major social events	Snowball Dance Music Recital Topper Revue	No major events
Feb.	Musicale, "L" Club Vaudeville	Sweetheart Dance Musical Recital	League Band Festival
Mar.	Fine Arts Festival	Band Concert, Honor Society Banquet	League Speech Festival, Class Parties
Apr.	Hootenanny Slave Auction	Home Economics Style Show, Spring Dramatic Production	Beatnik Day Twirp Dance
May	Senior Party, Junior-Senior Reception	Senior Trip, Junior-Senior Prom, Spring Concert	Junior-Senior Banquet and Prom, Spring Play, Spring Music Program
June	Commencement Dance		

[a] From Edwin B. Keim and Morris C. Jones, Jr., *A Guide to Social Activities* (Washington, D.C.: The National Association of Secondary School Principals, 1965), pp. 28-29.

social event have a right to have their duties and authority well-defined and announced in advance.

For a large event, it is useful to have a faculty member work with each of the major committees — decorations, refreshments, cleanup, etc. However, provision should be made for these persons to be excused when not needed. For example, when the decorations are completed, the faculty sponsor of that committee should be excused. Likewise, there is no need for the faculty member supervising the cleanup to be present during the early hours of the event.

Parents

Social climbing being what it is, there is a tendency for some groups of parents to become more and more permissive with the use of cars, about the hours their children may keep, the age at which dating may begin, and other areas of social involvement. In some communities groups of parents, often with PTA leadership, have cooperatively devised a suggested code of behavior for students of different ages, covering hours, dating, use of cars, and so on. Certainly the school should encourage the adoption of such codes and should cooperate with them. If, for example, the parents have agreed that high school students should not be out past 11:30 on Friday nights, the school should not have events that last later than 11:00 P.M. on Fridays.

Under specified and well-publicized conditions (for example, parents should not dance at student dances, or unless prior arrangements are made, uninvited parents should not plan to eat at banquets), parents should be welcome at school social affairs. Every social affair, regardless of its size, should have at least one parent couple present, in addition to one or more faculty members. For large events, several parents, preferably couples, should receive special invitations and should be present. These parents should be welcomed, given special seating, perhaps given identifying badges or ribbons, and extended other courtesies.

The faculty member in charge of a school social event should personally contact these invited guests and give information about appropriate dress ("formal" may mean a tux to a father, a suit to a student), time, place, and general duties. Parents should be requested to arrive early, at which time the faculty sponsor should go over specific duties of the parents, if any.

Community

In many localities, there are limitations placed on school social activities by community mores. An accident or licentious sexual behavior on a hayride fifteen years earlier may make such an activity taboo in some communities. Such unofficial but very real limitations on school social affairs may be very difficult to work with for teachers relatively new to a community. In any questionable circumstance, the prior approval of the administrator and the Board of Education is essential.

The social program of the school should complement the social resources of the community — the churches, commercial facilities, youth agencies, etc. Although it is seldom ever this way, the extent of involvement of the school in providing social opportunities should be roughly inversely proportional to the community resources.

In some communities a community youth advisory council is used to good advantage. Such a council should have a membership representing all community groups interested in youth activities — parents, school personnel, students, businessmen, church representatives, youth agency representatives, governmental leaders, and so on. Such a council will prevent unnecessary overlapping of social and recreational opportunities and more important, will serve as a sounding board as to what social activities the school may or may not engage in. If such a council does not exist, school personnel should provide leadership in organizing one.

Social fraternities and sororities have largely ceased to exist as official school organizations. This is not to say, however, that they have ceased to exist, either without adult leadership, or with leadership from their alumni, parents, or nonschool-related adults. The very fact that students continue to belong to such groups, sometimes in spite of laws to the contrary,[4] indicates that the school and/or community social facilities are inadequate. Schools over the country have found that the best way to combat the evil aspects of social fraternities and sororities is to undertake, with community cooperation, a long-range program of improvement of more legitimate social functions. As school and community social opportunities become mory nearly adequate, fraternities and sororities will probably die a natural death.

[4]See Chapter 17.

THE MECHANICS OF SOCIAL FUNCTIONS

Attention to the details of time, place, and internal activities of social functions is a major step toward insurance of a successful social program.

Time

One of the major advantages of long-range planning and the use of a social calendar is to insure a good and fairly even distribution of social activities during each school year. To have most social events near the end of the year, with a few near the beginning, and a few or none during the winter months is inadequate.

Social affairs for junior high schools should start early and end early. Older students may well have social affairs with later hours. Social affairs taking place during the week, if any, must end early.

The specific hours of events (start and end) should be well known to students, parents, and chaperones alike. Social events should not just gradually start and then taper off. Students should be encouraged to arrive at the beginning and stay until the end. In fact, many schools do not permit students to leave early, unless prior arrangements have been made, and some do not permit entrance of those who arrive later than some specified time. Special entertainment features or other devices can be used to encourage prompt arrival, to discourage leaving at intermission, or to discourage early leaving without resorting to formal regulations on this matter. In many schools a letter from the principal to the parents outlines times, place, regulations, and chaperones of major school social activities.

Place

As nearly as possible, all school social events should be held at the school. Problems of student control, party crashers and legal responsibilities are greatly reduced if all social events are held on the school premises.

School buildings should be designed to accommodate social affairs. Provisions for good acoustics, easy removal or rearrangement of furniture, toilet facilities, lighting, electrical outlets, stages or platforms, entrance and exit control, parking, wraps, decorations, a public address system, and a telephone should be incorporated into new construction or remodeling, especially if gymnasiums, cafeterias, multipurpose rooms, and other facilities where social events are likely to be held are being constructed.

If it is not possible to have all aspects of a given social event all in the same room, it is sometimes possible to divide the group and use several adjacent or nearby rooms.

Care should be taken to avoid any damage to the facilities. Adhesives are often damaging to painted surfaces. Leather soles, high heels, dance-surface compounds and spilled liquids are potential sources of danger to floors. Gates or other barriers should be used to prevent students from entering unused parts of the building.

Control of entrances and exits is needed, yet there must be ample provision to clear the room or building in the event of an emergency. The use of special lighting, decorations, public address systems, electronic musical instruments, and appliances necessitates extraordinary fire safety precautions.

Controversies often arise over the proper use of service systems — heating, ventilating, and especially the amount of lighting — at school social functions. Details of these things should be worked out during planning sessions and sufficient security should be provided to insure that some practical joker cannot turn off the lights during a dance.

Where proper or adequate facilities do not exist at school, local armories, community centers, and similar facilities may be used. The rental of a night club or similar facility is generally wisely forbidden by most school officials.

Food Service

Almost every social event should include refreshments. Punch and cookies are often served, although it is likely that a lot more punch gets spiked than sponsors care to acknowledge or are aware of, and many cleanup crews wish that there were not so many paper cups (or broken glass), cookie crumbs, and paper containers strewn about. Adequate waste receptacles are essential. Provision must be made for immediate removal of any spilled liquids. If soft drinks are used, bottle or cup control is necessary. It is often useful to locate the refreshment table away from the main scene of activity.

Provision for the preparation and serving of meals varies greatly among schools and among the types of activities at which food is being served. In general, it is best to leave food preparation and service to the school lunch staff. Certainly they should be involved in the planning of any function at which food will be served or prepared.

Student Control

Various policies exist about what functions are open to the public, to alumni of the school, to nonmembers of the group holding the affair, and to invited guests. The important thing is to have a reasonable, well-defined policy consistently administered and known to all in advance. In some communities it may be desirable to have security personnel of some type present either in the building or on the parking lot or both.

There should always be someone present with sufficient authority to take care of any potential trouble before it develops into real trouble. Well-trained student leaders can often nip trouble in the bud; but even with the best laid plans, behavior difficulties do sometimes arise. However, a large number of rules should be avoided, for a social event may be killed by too many regulations.

Finance

As will be discussed in Chapter 16, it is highly desirable that the general school budget include funds for student activities in general, including funds for social events. Even if this is not possible, a budget for each event should be prepared and adhered to, and funds should be accounted for. Handling the financial planning and accounting can easily be one of the major learning outcomes of social events.

Subactivities

Several hours of the same activity, even if one that the students enjoy very much, is too much of a good thing. A variety of activities is essential. Food and entertainment may be useful in dividing up an evening otherwise devoted to dancing.

Not all students care to dance; and even at a "dance," a separate room or rooms should be made available for party games, table games, square dancing, and so on.

Poor music will kill a dance quickly, and so will only partial participation. Devices for involving "wallflowers," such as an "icebreaker" or a "Paul Jones" should be used if participation lags, or if the members of the group do not know each other very well. Demonstrations of new dances by competent instructors may serve to increase participation.

Students should be given an opportunity to stand or move about during the course of a long banquet. Robbins vividly remembers a junior-senior banquet at which the students had no opportunity to stand for some three hours — a bit much for active teenagers.

Cleanup

The most disagreeable part of any social activity is the cleanup. Major responsibility for cleanup should fall on the students, although care should be taken to insure that no one student or group of students does a disproportionate share. If an event is held on Friday night, necessities — closing up, turning off electrical appliances, removing spilled liquids — should be taken care of then, but the bulk of the cleanup can be left until Saturday morning. Otherwise, cleanup should immediately follow the event, allowing for a short recess for boys to take their dates home and change into suitable clothing.

The custodian and any other concerned personnel (especially food service personnel) should be actively involved in cleanup plans.

NEW IDEAS

Originality and creativity in planning for social events should be strongly encouraged.

The types of social events held will reflect the philosophy and objectives of the school as well as the previous experiences of the students. As Keim and Jones stated,

> New ideas for wholesome social activity will emerge when students are encouraged to be creative in planning, rather than relying exclusively on what has happened in previous years. It must be remembered that the social program is for the enjoyment of students. Social activities planned by adults may fail to reflect the changes in youth's social behavior.[5]

[5]Keim and Jones, *op. cit.*, pp. 28-29.

The school should set limits, but within those limits innovation should be encouraged.

Interschool parties, especially following athletic games, are becoming popular. A "Hootenanny" is easily executed, and may be used if planning time is short. Record hops, which some schools hold as often as weekly, are also easily executed. Theater parties, covered dish suppers, carnivals, and barbecues may be new to some schools.

The popularity of the highly formal affair, with engraved invitations, corsages, tuxedos, dance programs, and receiving lines, is declining, and other worthwhile activities need to be devised to take its place. It is questionable whether the large expenditure necessary for such an affair is the best way to use the allocated money.

The following list, taken from *The Student Council in the Secondary School,* may suggest ideas for new social affairs:

Tea for home-room mothers and/or teachers
Season's party (Valentine, St. Patrick's Day, May Day, etc.)
Skating party (roller and ice)
Yearbook signing party
All homecoming activities
Dress-up Day breakfast
Valentine post office
Teachers coffee party
Farewell party for graduates
Senior (Junior) Prom
All-girls party
All-boys party
All-school picnic
All-school banquet
Progressive dinner
Community sing
Get-acquainted mixer
Senior breakfast
New Year's party
Pot-luck supper
Pizza party
Bowling party
Box supper
Coronation ball
Square dances
Chili supper
Hayride

Bob-sled ride
Penny party
Hike
Mid-winter ball
Game party
Dancing classes
Teen canteen
Stunt night
Hawaiian Luau
Buffet supper[6]

Other ideas are summarized in Table II.

EVALUATION

The evaluation of school social affairs should be of two types. First, each function should be evaluated. This may be done by a questionnaire given to each student in the school, not just to those who attended. Finding out why some students did not attend may be one of the most important outcomes of the evaluation. The planning committee for the social function should also evaluate the function in terms of the objectives of the social functions.

Second, the entire year's calendar of activities should be evaluated by a student body questionnaire, by the school's social committee, by the student council, and by the faculty and administration.

This many people devoting this much thought to the social affairs of the school should be able, over a period of a few years, to develop an excellent, well-rounded, satisfying, and educationally sound social program for a school.

SUMMARY

A well-planned program of social activities can ease the frustrations of the adolescent years. A number of agencies have legitimate roles in providing social experiences for young people, and the school has a major role in coordinating and supplementing these

---

[6]National Association of Student Councils, *The Student Council in the Secondary School,* (Washington, D.C.: NASSP, 1962) p. 86.

TABLE II

Ideas for New Social Affairs

School	Location	School Size	Innovative Social Activity
Alice Vaile Junior High School	Tucson, Arizona	Large	Government banquet honoring student leaders
Hunterdon Central High School	Flemington, New Jersey	Large	Dammed-up stream used as ice skating rink
Northfield Junior-Senior High School	Northfield, Minnesota	Medium	Hi-Bye Party to welcome freshmen and honor graduating seniors
Lower Merion Senior High School	Ardmore, Pennsylvania	Large	Spring carnival to raise money for foreign exchange program
Wachusett Regional High School	Holden, Massachusetts	Large	Exchange student banquet provided for students in area
Bloomington Junior-Senior High School	Bloomington, Indiana	Large	Winter Carnival, starting at 4:30 P.M. and using entire school plant
Hand High School	Madison, Connecticut	Medium	Youth Center held in American Legion Hall on Fridays and after home football games; chaperoned by adults, not parents or teachers.
High School of Science	New York, New York	Large	Student Canteen, open after school twice a week for one hour; dancing, games, entertainment
New Brunswick High School	New Brunswick, New Jersey	Large	Winter and Spring Sports Banquet

TABLE II (continued)

School	Location	School Size	Innovative Social Activity
Webster Springs High School	Webster Springs, West Virginia	Medium	Noon-hour recreation — dancing, games, intramural basketball
Julius T. Wright School for Girls	Mobile, Alabama	Small	Father-Daughter Banquet
Warren G. Harding High School	Warren, Ohio	Large	Luncheon for graduating seniors and their parents
Harborcreek High School	Harborcreek, Pennsylvania	Medium	Skating Party
Hayward High School	Hayward, California	Large	Noon-program — student disc-jockey of the week — has a guest, usually a local disc jockey or recording star
Gulfport High School	Gulfport, Mississippi	Medium	Banquet for homeroom chairmen, hall receptionists, guidance office receptionists, drink box crew, stage crew, cafeteria helpers, student librarians, cheerleaders, study hall monitors, projection crews, and student council members.

experiences. Social experiences provided by the school should be much more than just parties, and pains must be taken to involve *all* students. A social calendar, planned months in advance, is useful in providing a broad and sound program.

Planning the total social program should involve not only students and faculty, but parents and the community-at-large as well. Social affairs should be well-spaced through the year, held at the school, and be of interest to most students. Within well-defined limits, creativity in planning social events should be encouraged. Evaluation, not only of each event, but of the total program is necessary.

REFERENCES

Allen, Charles F., *et al. Extra-Curricular Activities in the Elementary Schools.* St. Louis, Mo.: Webster Publishing Co., 1937, pp. 554-592.

Frederick, Robert W. *Student Activities in American Schools.* New York: Center for Applied Research in Education, 1965.

Gruber, Frederick C., and Beatty, Thomas Bayard. *Secondary School Activities.* New York: McGraw-Hill Book Co., Inc., 1954, pp. 217-236.

Johnston, Edgar G., and Faunce, Roland C. *Student Activities in Secondary Schools.* New York: Ronald Press Co., 1952, pp. 139-170.

Keim, Edwin B., and Jones, Morris C., Jr. *A Guide to Social Activities.* Washington, D.C.: National Association of Secondary School Principals, 1965.

Kilzer, Louis R., *et al. Allied Activities in the Secondary School.* New York: Harper and Brothers, 1956, pp. 90-118, 298-318.

McKown, Harry C. *Extra-Curricular Activities.* Rev. ed. New York: Macmillan Co., 1949, pp. 250-264, 333-349.

National Association of Student Councils. *The Student Council in the Secondary School.* Washington, D.C.: NASSP, 1962.

Strang, Ruth. *Group Work in Education.* New York: Harper and Brothers, 1958, pp. 212-229.

Wey, Herbert W. "Desegregation and Integration," *Phi Delta Kappan,* 47:508-515, May, 1966.

Part IV
ORGANIZATION AND ADMINISTRATION OF THE PROGRAM

The student activities program has become a highly significant part of the American educational system. From the national level downward, there are numerous student activity organizations. The first two chapters of Part IV are devoted to the organization and administration of student activities on the multischool level and on the building level.

Part IV concludes with three chapters devoted to discussions of important concepts pertaining to the student activities program: allocation of resources, financing, and legal concepts.

Chapter 13

MULTISCHOOL ORGANIZATION OF STUDENT ACTIVITIES

The school activities program has long since outgrown the organizational confines of the individual school. Among the first groups to expand beyond the local school were athletics. The formal organizations which we recognize today are the outgrowths of the need to work and to compete with others. However, athletics are by no means the only organizations within the student activities program that transcend the boundaries of the local school.

In large school systems, individual school student activity programs are usually coordinated in the central administrative office. Within each state, organizations exist to exercise some administrative control over student activities such as athletics, forensics, instrumental and choral music, and others. Many commonly accepted student activities are administered on a nationwide basis and are often organized, within the national framework, into various regional and state subdivisions.

For a better and more complete understanding of the organization and administration of activities beyond the individual school, the administrator should be familiar with the structure and control of such activities.

NATIONAL LEVEL

On the national level, student activities are administered by three types of organizations: governmental agencies, educational organizations, and noneducational organizations. In some instances, the administration by national organizations leads to a chain-of-command type of organization ending at the individual school; in other instances the national organizations develop guidelines, charter local groups, and then leave the individual clubs in the schools virtually autonomous.

Governmental Agencies

Naturally, the Department of Health, Education, and Welfare, through the United States Office of Education, plays a small but important role in providing information and services regarding student activities to state and local educational units. In addition the USOE coordinates several national organizations such as the Future Farmers of America and the Future Homemakers of America. Elsewhere, there are others, such as the association between the Department of Agriculture and 4-H Clubs, and the Department of Defense and the Civil Air Patrol.[1] Administration by these governmental agencies has led to a highly organized system of national, regional, state, and local organizational bodies. In dealing with these organizations in the school, the administrator, although ordinarily he will have contact with only the lower echelons of authority, must be aware that these groups in his school do not exist as separate entities; but as parts of a nationwide organization.

Educational Organizations

Many of the subdivisions of the National Education Association sponsor student activities programs on the national level.[2] The National Association of Secondary School Principals of the NEA sponsors two major student activities programs: The National Association of Student Councils and The National Honor Society-National Junior Honor Society. In addition, such organizations as the Future Business Leaders of America, Future Scientists of America, and Future Teachers of America have some association with the NEA. In many instances, these organizations charter local groups and maintain contact through regional meetings, various publications, and reports to the national office.

In addition to the NEA-supported activities, many other student activities, such as the National Association of Science Clubs, National Cheerleader Association, National Audubon Society and its Audubon Junior Club, Science Clubs of America and its National Science Fair, National Scholastic Press Association, Quill and Scroll

---

[1]While ROTC programs exist in many secondary schools, all "extracurricular" activities related to the ROTC Units (Officers Clubs, Sponsors Clubs, Drill Teams, etc.) are creations of the local school, and, as such, are not coordinated by the Department of Defense.

[2]See "NEA Sponsored Student Organizations," *NEA Journal,* 47:337, May, 1958.

Society, and National Thespian Society have some affiliations with a large parent organization. These organizations, generally, do not maintain elaborate regional or state organizations. Workshops, conventions, and other gatherings, as well as publications, provide contact by the national office with the individual schools.

Noneducational Organizations

Numerous student activities are sponsored by organizations which exist for reasons other than to support the school systems of the nation. Many such organizations exist; some have an intermediate organizational framework between the national headquarters and the local school; others do not. Various religious and cultural groups provide national coordinating action for their affiliates, as do the national civic clubs (Rotary, Kiwanis, Optimist, etc.) that sponsor high school organizations. Among the other national groups engaged in sponsoring student activities are the YMCA (Hi-Y, Tri-Hi-Y), the American Red Cross, and American Automobile Association (School Safety Patrols).

Contests

Every year principals are beseiged with letters and personal visits from organizations sponsoring "national" essays, speeches, and other type contests. On the local level, the contest may be represented by a respected club member who knows little, if anything, about the national administration of the contest and who knows little about evaluating themes, speeches, or other required student work. To free school administrators from the burden of investigating every national contest and to relieve the faculty, particularly English teachers, of a flood of contest information, the National Association of Secondary School Principals of the NEA publishes yearly in its *Bulletin* a list of all contests approved by the National Committee on Contests and Activities. (See Appendix C.) This thorough investigation of contests and activities assures the administrator of the value of his students' participation.

REGIONAL LEVEL

As indicated previously, most student activities, even those with some national level administrative organization, have only state or local control below the national level. In the chasm between the national level and the state level, a few groups, such as the FFA, FHA, and the Civil Air Patrol (with its military-like administration) have regional organizational structures. In a few areas the need for additional athletic teams for competition, particularly in state-line areas, has led to informal or formal multistate athletic cooperatives to provide general supervisory guidelines. Otherwise, the regional or multistate level is generally overlooked in student activities organization and administration.

STATE LEVEL

The organization of activities on the state level is carried out by many organizations. The state department of education or professional organizations may directly or indirectly, through "activities associations," control or coordinate many activities. Within the state there are often regional organizations or contests that are set up on geographic, school size, or other bases. The state department of education has general responsibility for overseeing vocational agriculture and homemaking programs supported by federal legislation. Within the appropriate division of the state department of education is usually found one or more persons with the responsibilities of coordinating FFA, FHA, and other similar activities.

In most states, the forerunner of the state's activities association was the state's athletic association. With the proliferation of school-related activities and with the general organizational success of the athletic associations, it was only natural to expand the function of the existing organization to include all student activities.[3] In general, membership in such associations is voluntary and extralegal. These organizations exist to provide uniform organization and administration of various statewide activities and contests and to provide uniform standards for the various participants. The number of

---

[3]This added function may be seen in such elongated titles as the "Arkansas Athletic Association and the Arkansas Inter-School Contest Association."

activities with which these associations deal annually is legion; and weighty — and important — publications are regularly published which set forth rules, regulations, dates, deadlines, and other important information for the local directors of student activities and local administrators. The work done by these "voluntary" organizations is most valuable. However, considerable improvement in the organization of student activities on a statewide basis will come when state departments of education begin to work more closely with activities associations (such as placing a state Director of Student Activities within the department to coordinate activities and to help small schools in setting up programs), and when membership in a state-affiliated activities association becomes mandatory for all schools.

Contests

The number of statewide contests varies with the states. Generally, state professional groups, the state department of education, and the activities association direct music and sports contests (usually with preliminary substate level contests), and miscellaneous essay, speech, safe driving, and other contests. The calendar of events published by the activities association for its member schools will be a valuable reference tool for the local director of student activities.

SYSTEM-WIDE LEVEL

In a small, local school operation, the level of student activities organization immediately below the state level would be at the individual school. This type of organization is discussed in Chapter 14. However, for the larger school system there is a need for activities *coordination* at a level between the state and individual school. Therefore, we will discuss this system-wide level organization.

Within the Instruction-Curriculum Division of the local school system the post of Coordinator of Activities should be found. The Coordinator should be able to recommend to the appropriate persons actions necessary to establish the proper relationship between the academic portion and the student activities portion of the curriculum. He should be responsible for scheduling all system-wide contests and should administer the system-wide considerations about eligibility requirements and other needed regulations. Unfortunately, few systems have yet realized the need for this post.

To assist the Coordinator of Activities, an expert on athletic programs should be employed.[4] The Director of Athletics could be responsible for all athletics activities considerations, including scheduling, tournament invitations, arranging for officials for games, and other similar activities. As needed, the Director of Athletics could be responsible for the management of the high school stadium system, since, in effect, the responsibility for their use rests with him. Unfortunately, the obsession with sports on the secondary school level has led many school systems to create a post similar to Director of Athletics without coordinating this necessary post with the equally necessary system-wide administration of other student activities.

An Activities Council, composed of principals, teachers, and student leaders, should be appointed by the Superintendent to advise and assist the Coordinator of Activities. In addition, the size of the activities program of the system being administered may suggest additional staff members. Figure 1 shows one proposed type of organization within the Division of Curriculum and Instruction of a large multischool system. From the office of the Coordinator of Student Activities, the director of student activities in each school could receive valuable information and much needed coordination.[5]

The need for interschool cooperation and rivalry has always been recognized by persons working with high school athletics, thus the early establishment of coordinating organizations came about. With the establishment of large student activities programs in innovative high schools, the need for interschool cooperation and the growth of interschool rivalry continues, and no doubt becomes greater. No longer is a school judged only by the record of its football team, but by its record in such diverse areas as music, forensics, special prevocational training, and artistic and literary skills.

---

[4]It should be pointed out here that many colleges and universities offer courses in the administration, organization, theory, and philosophy of student activities. Such courses, when coupled with a personal belief in the value of the activities program and with administrative experience, should provide suitable training for the persons needed to administer effectively the local system-wide activities program.

[5]See Chapter 14.

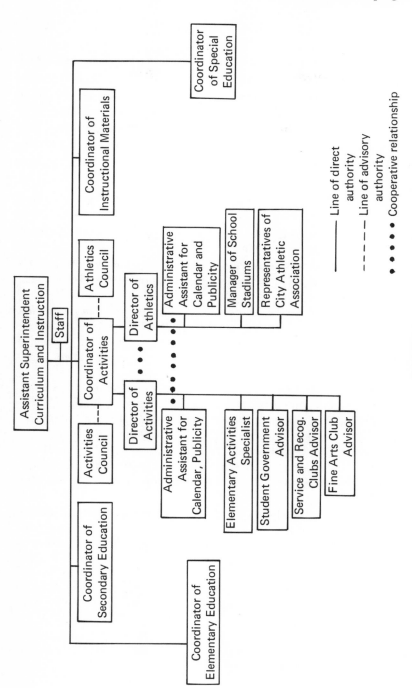

FIGURE 1
Activities Organization within the Curriculum-Instruction Division of a Multischool System.

SUMMARY

From the need for interschool cooperation has arisen a series of organizations joining school activity programs: citywide, statewide, regional, and national. Concepts and problems relating to such organizations were pointed out. The organizations of certain programs on the national level were also pointed out. Emphasis was placed upon a system-wide organizational pattern of all activities, and a proposed organizational scheme was given.

REFERENCES

Athern, Claire. "Extracurricular Activities and School-Community Relationships," *School Activities,* 34:236-237, April, 1963.

Bedicher, Roy. *Educational Competition: The Study of the University Interscholastic League of Texas.* Austin, Texas: University of Texas Press, 1956.

Gruber, Frederick C., and Beatty, Thomas Bayard. *Secondary School Activities.* New York: McGraw-Hill Book Co., 1954, pp. 258-276.

Jacobson, Paul B., Reavis, William C., and Logsdon, James D. "Managing Extracurricular Activities." *The Effective School Principal.* 2nd ed. Englewood Cliffs, N.J.: Prentice-Hall, 1963.

McKean, Robert C. "Extra-Class Activities." *Principles and Methods in Secondary Education.* Columbus, Ohio: Charles E. Merrill Books, 1962.

Miller, Franklin A., *et al. Planning Student Activities.* Englewood Cliffs, N.J.: Prentice-Hall, Inc., 1956, pp. 553-591.

"NEA-Sponsored Student Organizations," *NEA Journal,* 47:337, May, 1958.

Reeder, Ward G. "Administration of Extra-Curricular Activities." *The Fundamentals of Public School Administration.* 4th ed. New York: The Macmillan Co., 1958.

Sternes, William S. "The Director of Activities, An Emerging Position?" *School Activities,* 29:235-238, April, 1958.

Trump, J. Lloyd. *High School Extra-Curricular Activities: Their Management in the Public Schools of the North Central Association.* Chicago: University of Chicago Press, 1944.

Williams, Stanley W. "Student Activities." *Educational Administration in Secondary Schools.* New York: Holt, Rinehart and Winston, 1964.

Chapter 14

ORGANIZATION AT
THE BUILDING LEVEL

To carry out the policies and regulations of the citywide, countywide, or statewide student activities organization, each school within a system needs an overall coordinating and administrative organization. Such an organization may be useful at the building level, even if there are no additional administrative units in higher echelons. Figure 1 suggests how the activities program may be organized on the building level.

ADMINISTRATION

The organization of the activities program at each school involves many people both directly and indirectly. While only a few faculty members and a few students may be directly concerned with determining policy for the administration of the activities program, the entire student body and the faculty will be involved in carrying out the policies established to administer the program.

Principal

The principal, as the head of the school, carries out the duties assigned to him by the board of education through the superintendent. He is responsible for all facets of his school — from curriculum to plant management. In some matters the principal assumes direct control; in others, he delegates his authority to persons skilled in particular fields. Such should be the case in the student activities program where special training and competencies are demanded.

Director of Student Activities

Every large school should have a full-time person at the vice-principal level designated as the Director of Student Activities. The Director of Student Activities should be a specially trained staff

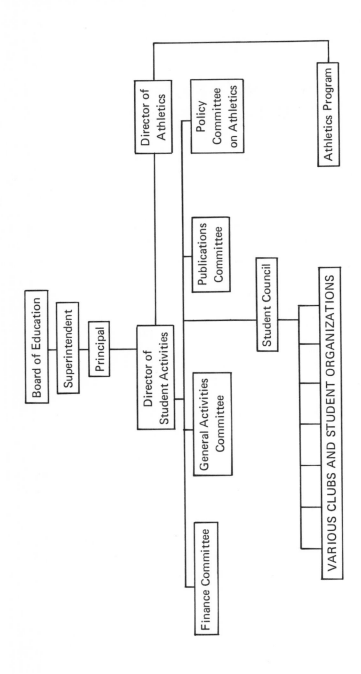

FIGURE 1

Relationships of Activities in a High School Program.

member who administers the program of student activities for the principal. The Director, with the assistance of various committees, should coordinate the student activities program. The policies which such a Director recommends to the principal are extremely important; for, among other effects, they will encourage or discourage participation by the students.[1] Among other duties, the Director should recommend to the principal the names of persons to be appointed as student activity sponsors and supervise the maintenance of records pertaining to student activities.[2]

The Director of Student Activities should be assisted by several committees. Robbins and Williams propose four committees, which, with their membership and functions, are as follows:

Finance Committee. A seven-member committee with a faculty member as chairman should receive budget requests from the individual clubs and other student activities. This committee would then recommend to the administration the appropriation of funds to individual student activities from a common student activity fund. The student council should appoint four members and the Director of Activities should appoint two faculty members, with the approval of the principal, along with himself.

General Activities Committee. This committee should be composed of a student representative from each student activity chartered by the student council, the president of the student council, five faculty members of which three are sponsors, the athletic director, and the activities director (as chairman). This committee would coordinate the calendar of student activities, recommend meeting time and place for each student activity, plan orientation programs to provide information about the student activities program, and carry out any other general responsibilities which may be peculiar to the particular school.

Publications Committee. Composed of sponsors, editors-in-chief, and business managers of each publication, this proposed committee was discussed in detail in Chapter 8.

[1]Especially in today's schools when many social changes are being attempted, the Director of Student Activities has many responsibilities in encouraging student participation. The acceptance, by peers, of underprivileged children and racial minorities in student activities may be encouraged by the activities director. This is discussed in more detail in Henry T. Hillson, "The Adviser of Student Activities," *NASSP Bulletin*, 48:85-86, October, 1964.

[2]See Robert R. Halley, "An Activities Permanent Record Card," *School Activities*, 27:193, February, 1956.

Policy Committee on Athletics. It is not uncommon for athletics programs to become involved in questions of individual eligibility, personal conduct, and other matters about which some policy must be determined. It is in these areas that this committee would function. This committee should be composed of four faculty members appointed by the principal and of the Director of Student Activities, with one of the appointees of the principal serving as chairman.

Director of Athletics

Since the athletics program is a large part of the student activities program, the Director of Student Activities will need an assistant to serve as Director of Athletics. Agreements and schedule dates with other teams are the athletic director's responsibility; however, schedule dates must be placed on the activities calendar so that tournament dates do not conflict with, for example, six-weeks examinations periods.

Student Council

One of the main functions of the student council is the chartering of student activities. Once a group has petitioned the student council to set up an organization, the council will be concerned with student interest, additional financial burden, effect on other clubs, and other similar considerations.[3]

As the organization representing the entire student body and as the group chartering all organizations, the student council must also have the power to abolish student activities under certain conditions specified in the constitution of the council and, perhaps, in the charters of the organizations. The following reasons are recommended as sufficient cause for withdrawal of a charter:

1. Lack of student interest
2. Failure to carry out school rules or council policy
3. Request by the organization to terminate activities

---

[3]For further information about the relation of the student council to other clubs and for a sample of an activity petition, see *The Student Council in the Secondary School* (Washington, D.C.: The National Association of Secondary-School Principals, 1962), pp. 343-347.

Student council constitutions or bylaws normally carry provisions about eligibility and point systems. Normally, all students are eligible to belong to any club or organization; however, the charters of some organizations may set academic requirements or course prerequisites that limit membership. Student council constitutions in many schools set specific eligibility requirements for officers of all organizations that are somethat higher than the general membership requirements. Specifically, these requirements pertain to the following:

1. Previous academic achievement
2. Current academic progress
3. Prior membership in the organization
4. "Citizenship" and conduct ratings

In many schools the only limits placed on the number of organizations to which one may belong or the number of offices which one may hold are those set by ones desires and physical capacities. However, Shepherd has pointed out the following:

> Seventy-three percent of the teenagers join high-school extra-curricular activities. They do so, they say, because colleges push activities as one of the criteria for admission.[4]

In many large schools elaborate point systems are used to encourage more generalized participation by all students. Memberships are weighted and no student is allowed to have more than a specified number of activity points. In some other schools, leadership positions are weighted and no student is allowed to exceed a specified number of leadership points. In all cases, these maximum point totals should be contained in the student council constitution and bylaws. For example, the student handbook of East High School in Memphis quotes Article VII, Section 1, of the Student Council Constitution as follows:

> A point system regulating the eligibility of a student to hold office shall be set up under the following plan:
> a. Presidents of Student Council and Senior Class, student commanding officer in ROTC, editor of the [newspaper] and [yearbook] shall be considered 4-point offices.

[4]Jack Shepherd, " 'Are You a Teenager?' 'Yeah, I'm Afraid So,' " *Look,* 30:46, September 20, 1966.

     b. Presidents of the Junior and Sophomore classes, student council officers other than president, business managers of publications shall be considered 3-point offices.

     c. Presidents of Clubs, captain of the cheerleaders, class officers, and department heads of publications shall be considered 2-point offices.

     d. Football captains, cheerleaders, members of the staffs of the publications, ROTC officers and sponsors, and homeroom presidents and club officers other than president shall be considered 1-point offices.

     e. A total of 7 points in one year shall make a student ineligible for any other office during that year. . . .

However, it is interesting to note that one leading school, Abington (Pennsylvania) Senior High School, has abandoned a point system in recent years in favor of merely recording teachers' perceptions of the degree of participation by individual students.

Sponsor

The sponsor is the representative of the school administration. The sponsor is more than that, however. According to Delaney, the "key [to the success of any school student activity] is the faculty adviser."[5] While this person's importance is recognized in all student activities — even to the extent that a sponsor is required for all student activities — not all administrators exercise much care in selecting sponsors.

Appointment. Several types of selection and appointment are used throughout the varied student activities programs in the country. Among the methods are the following:

1. *Faculty selection.* Under this plan faculty members volunteer, usually on a checklist, to sponsor certain student activities. From the choices made by the teachers, the administrator then assigns the sponsors to student activities.

While this does allow for teachers to select activities which they *want* to sponsor, it does not provide for the discovery of the student activities which the teachers are *qualified* to sponsor. Except in rare instances the administrator will arbitrarily have to assign teachers to sponsor those student activities for which no one has requested assignment.

---

[5] Arthur A. Delaney, "In Selecting a Faculty Adviser," *School Activities,* 32:12, September, 1960.

2. *Student selection.* Organization members assemble to vote on one or more faculty members whom they would like to sponsor their student activity. In systems where this practice is used, after the principal receives the results of the ballot he assigns the teacher requested, if possible.

This system of selection and appointment provides for excellent cooperation between students and teacher-sponsor, but the system easily becomes a popularity contest and does not consider a teacher's qualifications. It could also lead to awkward situations in which, for example, someone other than a home economics teacher would be chosen as FHA sponsor.

3. *Administration selection.* The most widely used of all means of appointment, administration selection, allows equalization of teaching load and emphasis on teacher qualifications. While arbitrary selection by the principal is not satisfactory, a study by the director of student activities of the teachers' records and resulting assignment of activities *is* good.

Perhaps the best method of administrative assignment takes into consideration work load, willingness to serve, experience in sponsorship, and special problems (beginning teacher, teacher with several preparations, etc.). Such considerations are best worked out at the time of employment.[6]

Qualifications. The qualifications deemed necessary for assignment to a post as sponsor of an activity vary greatly. There are two general areas of qualifications that should be considered:

1. Requirements of the activity, such as some necessary special skill.
2. Traits of the person, such as a special interest in the activity.

Certain student activities demand very special training for their sponsors (Computer Programming Club), while others require only general academic interest and ability (Spanish Club). The school's or the activity's definition of the duties of a sponsor also set requirements which determine the eligibility or suitability of a teacher as sponsor. The requirements for a sponsor whose duties are primarily to count money or record attendance at meetings is radically different from those for a sponsor who is to function as a resource person or as the initiator of projects.

[6]Robert W. Frederick, *The Third Curriculum* (New York: Appleton-Century-Crofts, Inc., 1959), pp. 225-226.

Personal traits are also important considerations, although a divergence of opinion exists on the degree of importance. School policies that require *all* teachers to be the adviser to an organization are not good. Hillson writes that the "principal should choose an adviser on the basis of personal qualities, not formal courses or experience. . . ."[7] While for many years there were few courses available for the person desiring to become competent in the administration and organization of student activity programs, a recently published partial listing shows that at least 52 institutions in 27 states offer courses in student activities.[8] Thus, formal training is not difficult to secure, and principals can often choose advisers who have both training and the requisite personal skills.

Distribution of Work Load. In considering the assignment of faculty members to posts as sponsors, administrators are faced with the recurring concept of "work load." Little has been done to measure work load with regard to student activities sponsorship. The problem of equalizing work load remains anathema to many administrators, and the administrators continue assigning "the roles of faculty adviser in a manner that defies description."[9]

In considering work load, the administrator should study the following:

1. Number of classes taught.
2. Number of preparations.
3. Number of class periods per week.
4. Number of pupils.
5. Amount of outside work required (special allowance for English teachers' grading of themes, and for other faculty members whose teaching duties require excessive outside work).
6. Special duties (department chairman, assistant principal, etc.).[10]

[7]Henry T. Hillson, "The Adviser of Student Activities," *NASSP Bulletin,* 48:82, October, 1964.

[8]"Summer Institutes for Advisers of Student Activities," *School Activities,* 37:18, May, 1966. This 1966 listing shows an increase over a 1963 listing in William S. Sterner, *The Student Council Adviser* (Washington, D.C.: The National Association of Secondary-School Principals, 1963), pp. 21-22.

[9]Delaney, *loc. cit.*

[10]The Douglas Teaching Load Formula is one mathematical attempt to determine teaching load. The reader might want to study this concept with relation to student activity sponsorship.

At the Oak Park and River Forest High School (Illinois) an attempt was made to measure effectively the work load of teachers. The teachers who sponsored or had sponsored activities were asked to weigh the added duties required by activities. The weights were based on 100 points equaling a teaching load of a 5-period-per-week class for one year. Some of the median weights are as follows:

Departmental Club Sponsorship = 26 points
Dramatics Club Sponsorship = 20 points
Interest Club Sponsorship = 20 points
Service Club Sponsorship = 22 points[11]

With increased emphasis on work load and with recognition of the necessity of equating work loads for teachers, it is likely that additional objective measures of work load will soon be forthcoming. Such devices will be particularly valuable to administrators in making assignments for the sponsorship of the organizations in the activities program. On the other hand, it may well be wise to fully recognize individual differences among teachers, give unequal work loads where necessary, and compensate the teacher-sponsor accordingly, either in terms of released time during the school day or additional salary.

Individual Activities

The need for a sponsor for each activity is easily recognized. In addition to providing some administrative control and a link with the remainder of the organization of the school, the sponsor has certain other duties. Bennett has listed these duties as follows:

1. To attend all meetings of the club or student organization of which he is adviser.

2. To confer with student officers and committees, advising them — but encouraging student initiative and planning.

3. To attend all meetings of the club's Council, and also to insure the attendance of the student president of the organization.

4. To consult with the director of student activities as to the progress of the club, and of any special events that may be scheduled.[12]

[11]Louis H. Fritzemeier, "A Fair Way to Measure Extra Work for Teachers," *Educational Executives' Overview,* 4:26, August, 1963. A copy of the questionnaire form used in the survey is printed on page 27 of the issue.
[12]Fred A. Bennett, "A Letter to New Faculty Advisers," *School Activities,* 26:13, September, 1954.

In addition to the need for a sponsor, each organization needs other leaders. These leaders should be chosen from the student members. In some instances, as in the student council, the officers are elected by the entire student body; usually, however, they are elected by the individual organizations. Officers with specific responsibilities should be mentioned in the constitution and charter of each student organization.

The number of officers needed should vary with the size of the group. Many small interest clubs will need only a chairman and a secretary-treasurer. The student council or other large organizations may need a series of vice-presidents and secretaries to relieve one student of many demands.

To provide continuity of organization and function, even when officers, members, and sponsors change, all organizations need a constitution and/or a set of written bylaws. In some schools the charter granted by the Student Council provides all information normally included in bylaws, while providing similarity in form for all organizations. If such provisions are not made, the sponsor should see that a constitution and/or bylaws are written and adopted soon after an activity is instituted.

The allocations of finances, time, and facilities are also important considerations of administering student activities on the building level. This information is provided in Chapters 15 and 16.

SUMMARY

Within each school building, an organizational structure should exist to coordinate and support the student activities program. Authority rests in the principal, but every large school needs a full-time person to serve as director of student activities. Faculty-student committees to recommend policies and actions are valuable, and four committees were recommended: Finance Committee, General Activities Committee, Publications Committee, and Policy Committees on Athletics. The responsibilities of the director of athletics, the student council, and the sponsors were discussed.

REFERENCES

Alexander, William M., and Saylor, J. Galen. "Guiding Extra-class Learning Experiences." *Modern Secondary Education.* New York: Rinehart and Co., 1959.

Allen, Charles F., *et al. Extra-Curricular Activities in the Elementary Schools.* St. Louis, Mo.: Webster Publishing Co., 1937, pp. 49-67.

Bennett, Fred A. "A Letter to New Faculty Advisers," *School Activities,* 26:13, September, 1954.

Bloland, P.A. "Role of the Student Organization Adviser," *Personnel and Guidance Journal,* 41:44-49, September, 1962.

Burrup, Percy E. "Management of Student Activities." *Modern High School Administration.* New York: Harper and Brothers, 1962.

Chamberlain, Leo M., and Kindred, Leslie W. "Directing Extra-curricular Activities." *The Teacher and School Organization.* 3rd ed. Englewood Cliffs, N.J.: Prentice-Hall, 1958.

Crum, Lewis R. "Organization and Control of An Activity Program," *School Activities,* 28:43-46, 84-87, October-November, 1956.

Delaney, Arthur A. "In Selecting A Faculty Adviser," *School Activities,* 32:12-13, September, 1960.

Douglass, Harl R. *Modern Administration of Secondary Schools.* 2nd ed. Boston: Ginn and Co., 1963. Chapts. 10 and 11.

Edmonson, J. B., Roemer, Joseph, and Bacon, Francis L. *The Administration of the Modern Secondary School.* 4th ed. New York: The Macmillan Co., 1953. Chapts. 14 and 15.

Elicker, Paul E. "The Student Activity Program: Organization." *Administration of Junior and Senior High Schools.* Englewood Cliffs, N.J.: Prentice-Hall, 1964.

Frederick, Robert W. *The Third Curriculum.* New York: Appleton-Century-Crofts, Inc., 1959.

Fritzemeier, Louis H. "A Fair Way to Measure Extra Work for Teachers," *Educational Executives' Overview,* 4:25-27, August, 1963.

Grinnell, Jolin E. "Cocurricular Activities as Public Relations." *School and the Community.* New York: Ronald Press Co., 1955.

Gruber, Frederick C., and Beatty, Thomas Bayard. *Secondary School Activities.* New York: McGraw-Hill Book Co., Inc., 1954, pp. 30-47.

Halley, Robert R. "An Activities Permanent Record Card," *School Activities,* 27:193, February, 1956.

Hearn, Arthur C. "Consider the Position of the Activity Sponsor," *Clearing House,* 31:241-243, December, 1956.

Hillson, Henry T. "The Adviser of Student Activities," *NASSP Bulletin,* 48:85-86, October, 1964.

Johnston, Edgar G., and Faunce, Roland C. *Student Activities in Secondary Schools.* New York: The Ronald Press Co., 1952, pp. 313-338.

Lawson, John D. "Evaluating Personnel in the Co-Curriculum," *Personnel and Guidance Journal,* 37:513-515, March, 1959.

McEnnerry, Vince. "The Principal's Part in Extracurricular Activities," *School Activities,* 33:137-139, January, 1962.

McKown, Harry C. *Extra-Curricular Activities.* Rev. ed. New York: The Macmillan Co., 1949, pp. 676ff.

Miller, Franklin A., *et al. Planning Student Activities.* Englewood Cliffs, N.J.: Prentice-Hall, Inc., 1956, pp. 79-115.

National Association of Secondary School Principals. *The Student Council in the Secondary School.* Washington, D.C.: NASSP, 1962, pp. 343-347.

Schorling, Raleigh, and Batchelder, Howard T. "Extraclassroom Duties of a Teacher." *Student Teaching in Secondary Schools.* 3rd ed. New York: McGraw-Hill Book Co., 1956.

Shepherd, Jack. " 'Are You a Teenager?' 'Yeah, I'm Afraid So,' " *Look,* 30:46, September 20, 1966.

Sterner, William S. "The Director of Activities, An Emerging Position?" *School Activities,* 29:235-238, April, 1958.

The Student Council Adviser. Washington, D.C.: National Association of Secondary School Principals, 1963, pp. 21-22.

Strang, Ruth. *Group Work in Education.* New York: Harper and Brothers, 1958, pp. 40-71.

Stroup, H. *Toward A Philosophy of Organized Student Activities.* Minneapolis: University of Minnesota Press, 1964.

"Summer Institutes for Advisers of Student Activities," *School Activities,* 37:18, May, 1966.

Tompkins, Ellsworth E. "Desirable and Undesirable Policies for Extra-Class Activities," *School Activities,* 26:179-181, February, 1955.

Chapter 15

ALLOCATION OF RESOURCES

Student activities programs often grow faster than the resources available for adequate support. Thus, the allocation of the limited resources available is a major consideration in the plans of the student activities program. While the financial aspects of supporting the student activities program have received major attention from many sources, and while this is quite important, it should be obvious that many additional resources must be considered. While it is, unfortunately, all too possible to cripple a student activities program by having it inadequately financed, it is impossible to have an adequate program, regardless of how well financed, without appropriate considerations for such other resources as space, time, and personnel.

ALLOCATION OF SPACE

With the evolution of the one-room school into a sprawling, multistory structure, the ever-growing curriculum has increased the need for special facilities. No modern secondary school plant is complete without an auditorium, a gymnasium, playing fields, swimming pool, language and science laboratories, cafeterias, suites of offices for administrative and guidance personnel, and a library, in addition to the ever-present general classrooms. Yet, few schools provide adequate and specially designed office and working space for the student council, the newspaper, the yearbook, or for any club or organization. The instances of organizations operating out of a teacher's bottom desk drawer or from cardboard boxes in storage rooms are all too frequent. During each school year many millions of dollars are spent on student activities in the nation's schools, but few of these student activities have an adequate place in which to file records, store materials, and plan meetings. Although more and more schools are wisely requiring detailed financial, membership, and project accounting of these organizations, few provide the necessary facilities to allow orderly processing of these records.

In any design of a new building, consideration should be given to providing office space for at least major school organizations. The prestige of the student council or other school groups is raised when adequate facilities are provided. Facilities need not be elaborate: a desk, typewriter, several file cabinets, some storage cabinets, book-shelves, a bulletin board, and a table and chairs for committee meetings will suffice for many student groups. A telephone may be advisable in some circumstances. Many groups, such as those working on publications, will need special equipment and additional storage space. In some instances it will be advisable to combine an office and the work space for the organization. In other instances, it will be advisable to separate the two, but they should still be near to each. In still other instances, the sharing of space can be arranged in an equitable manner. Providing a Club Room, for example, with storage and committee meeting space for a number of organizations may alleviate a number of problems.

In an existing building, it is sometimes possible to find usable space for these purposes by converting a storage space, by partition-ing off part of a classroom or study hall, by planning a space in an addition to a building, or by the minor remodeling of some area. Provision of adequate office and work space for student organiza-tions is likely to increase the effectiveness of the organizations.

Student activities must have space in which to meet. Appro-priate scheduling arrangements will provide each student activity with the type of physical facilities needed. The Physics Club must have its laboratory; the Music Club, an acoustically treated room. But must the Literary Club or the Distributive Education Club meet just *anywhere*?

Not all general purpose classrooms are suited by their non-specialized nature to double as club meeting rooms. A 50-seat lecture room, complete with lectern and sound equipment, will not enhance rapport and interest of the 10-member Sky Diving Club. The 30-seat classroom where the club sponsor teaches class is not necessarily the best location for a club meeting; for the club meeting should be an enrichment of classroom experiences, not a continuation. Nor should it be expected that an organization will always meet in the same place; for with a variety of projects, an organization may need a variety of places in which to work.

A sufficient number of portable lecterns and sound equipment should be provided by the school, so that any of several spaces might be adapted for meeting places of large groups. However, it is also important that there be a number of small meeting rooms (or large rooms that may be divided in some way) for smaller groups, especially the special interest groups that flourish for short periods of time. Adequate meeting space is available in just enough schools to indicate that such provisions are quite possible, if building planners consider student activity needs while designing conference rooms, seminar rooms, and small-group instructional areas. However, as Boles points out:

> Special space provisions for "activities". . . are by no means common. Rarely are any activities other than athletics and those closely related to music instruction given overt recognition in the planning of new, revised, or enlarged facilities. . . . [T]hose [activities] with peculiar needs are rarely considered and, if specialized facilities are provided, someone is often called upon to justify the facilities. . . . Perhaps this is indicative that those in education have done a poor job of educating lay people to the fact that not all learning is a result of classroom instruction.[1]

Fortunately, the prospects of improved facilities for student activities are brightening. Along with trends of greater financial support, more appropriate scheduling, and more and better qualified personnel to work with student activities, school administrators and sponsors are, in some schools, developing specifications for student activity spaces along with specifications for general instructional areas.

ALLOCATION OF TIME

Time is rapidly becoming the preeminent resource. With the explosion of knowledge and the many legitimate demands on students' and teachers' time for home, church, and community affairs, there has recently been a very significant concern about the extent to which the school has a claim on the time of students and staff or has an obligation to provide experiences for students outside the usual school day.

[1]Harold W. Boles, *Step By Step to Better School Facilities* (New York: Holt, Rinehart and Winston, 1965), p. 81.

The 14-hour work day is not uncommon to many administrators. Many teachers devote 50 to 60 hours per week to professional activities. The "school day" (thought of by the general public), occupying the late morning and early afternoon hours, has little meaning to the student who leaves home at 7:00 A.M. and returns at 5:00 P.M. with two hours of homework yet to be done. The school day is long for the student who remains until 6:00 P.M. for athletic practice, or who returns in the evening for an athletic event, a concert, a play, or the like. As the work-week for most wage-earners becomes shorter and shorter, the "work-week" for students becomes longer and longer, producing, quite logically, a major problem in some localities.

Some schools have bravely included all student activities (and even "home" work) into a school day roughly corresponding to business hours. In these schools, all students and staff go home in the afternoon with no school duties until the next morning. Other schools have done quite the opposite, in which *all* student activities take place after 3:30 P.M. and on Saturday. Most schools, however, have difficulty justifying either of these positions and end up doing both — holding some student activities during the school day and some at other times. It is difficult to determine the criteria by which schools decide which student activities may use "school time" and which may not. It would seem that tradition, pressure groups, inertia, and other such nonobjective factors influence scheduling decisions for student activities more than educational soundness, morale, convenience, and other such important factors.

Although appearing relatively simple in principle, the allocation of time for student activities involves many decisions for the administrator. Transported pupils, conflicting needs for limited facilities, community use of facilities, teacher involvement, and other similar considerations deserve great attention. As an overall basis for scheduling student activities, Frederick suggests the following:

1. No pupil should be excluded from an activity because of schedule difficulty.
2. No pupil should be denied the chance to participate in an activity because of the accident of residence or family circumstances.
3. Employment and transportation necessities should not limit participation.

4. The convenience of the staff must be considered.

5. A variety of scheduling schemes or plans must be used.[2]

In our opinion, to a very large degree the concept of a school day — a period of time during which the building is open and all students and teachers are present, after which the building is locked and all go elsewhere — no longer exists. Thus, it would be a good idea to officially recognize the ideas of staggared schedules and around the clock and calendar use of facilities and to capitalize on this vastly increased flexibility.

Such a concept may well call for some teachers to work a 3:00 P.M. to 11:00 P.M. schedule of athletics, recreation, and the like; for some teachers to work from 7:30 A.M. to 11:30 A.M. and from 3:30 P.M. to 6:00 P.M.; and for some students to be scheduled at the school from 8:00 A.M. to 11:00 A.M., from 2:00 P.M. to 5:00 P.M., and from 7:30 P.M. to 9:30 P.M. If such an arrangement will result in increased educational effectiveness, increased use of facilities, and greater service to students and community, then we feel that educators have no choice but to adopt these scheduling arrangements.

The implications for the scheduling of student activities should be obvious. If student activities are valuable enough to be sponsored by the school, if they are legitimate means of accomplishing the objectives of the school, student activities can, and should, be scheduled for students and teachers just as the more formal curricular experiences.

For schools that are not yet ready to make this drastic a change in scheduling, some of the following ideas may be helpful.

To keep from unduly burdening a certain period of time, the activity period may be scheduled on a rotating basis for a different class period each week, as in the following chart:

[2]Robert W. Frederick, *The Third Curriculum* (New York: Appleton-Century-Crofts, 1959), p. 241.

Class Period	Six-Week Grading Periods					
	1	2	3	4	5	6
1	Activity Period					
2		Activity Period				
3			Activity Period			
4				Activity Period		
5					Activity Period	
6						Activity Period

Not all activities would meet every week. If one group of activities met one week and another group met another week, a student could belong to two groups that met at nonconflicting activity periods. By increasing the number of groups of student activities and by decreasing the frequency of meetings for each group, a student could belong to more student activities.

Under a special schedule plan, a set period of time is allotted on certain days for activities. No class is missed, but all are slightly shortened. Such a schedule may be used as often per week or per month as is needed. For best use, clubs should be organized in set groups so that the least possible number of conflicts might arise. An example of this follows:

Regular Bell Schedule		Special Bell Schedule
Homeroom	8:30 - 8:45	8:30 - 8:42
1st Period	8:48 - 9:45	8:45 - 9:35
Activity Period		9:38 - 10:20
2nd Period	9:48 - 10:45	10:23 - 11:07
3rd Period	10:48 - 11:45	11:10 - 12:00
4th Period		
(Lunch)	11:45 - 1:15	12:00 - 1:20
5th Period	1:18 - 2:15	1:23 - 2:20
6th Period	2:18 - 3:15	2:23 - 3:15

Another alternative is to hold an activity day once a month or so. The activity day lasts all day and may include one or more assemblies, as well as all club meetings. When not in meetings, students may arrange to visit teachers for individual help in subjects they are taking.

In a few schools, students register for six subjects, but there are only five long periods per day. Each subject meets four times a week, which leaves one period per week to be used as an activity period.

More and more innovative high schools are turning to types of scheduling that are not as rigid as mosaic schedules. Under these more desirable schedules for large student bodies, some arrangement of time must be found for student activities.

Under a core curriculum concept, where students are assigned to one teacher or to a team of teachers for a large segment of time, it is possible to develop and carry out students' special subject interests during the time period allotted for class. This eliminates the necessity of much of the special student activities scheduling.

With modular scheduling, particularly when combined with ability grouping, the need for a special activity time for history clubs, science activities, and the like may be precluded. The enrichment-of-curriculum aspect of student activities may be effectively carried out with the top-level students working together or individually during the various class meetings. Other levels of students may also work on their own degree of enrichment on class-time when modular scheduling and grouping are combined. In modular scheduling, several modules per day or week can be made available for publications, athletics, clubs, and other student activities which cannot be carried out in the classroom as enrichment activities.

As exemplary arrangement of student activities was recently undertaken by Highland Park (New Jersey) High School. Abandoning the rigid activity or study hall choice which made unenthusiastic club members out of many students, the school set up three activity periods during the week. Students could be members of as many as three organizations or could leave school. While some clubs dropped in membership, all student activities were assured of enthusiastic members. Also, an opportunity is now available for very active clubs to meet as often as three times per week.

Use of data processing procedures in student activity scheduling is found in schools such as Ed W. Clark High School in Las Vegas.

Thus, student activity scheduling and accounting of all students is possible.

Size of the student body, extra-length special classes, limited facilities, and other difficulties may lead school administrators toward other plans of scheduling — and various other plans exist — than the traditional within-school-hours plan. The scheduling predicament that Williams observed can be avoided with a more elaborate scheduling plan; in that case, one frustrated senior boy was scheduled to be in a Saber Club, Key Club, DECA, and Senior Class meeting all at one time.

Some administrators faced with cramped facilities and increased student interest have opened buildings for student activities at night and on Saturday. This "added-on" approach to scheduling often allows greater development of student interests and more extensive use of facilities. Questions frequently arise under these various out-of-session plans about extra pay for teachers and the cost of additional building care. Frederick cites Thompkins and Story in evaluating this scheduling concept:

> The advantages of an out-of-session activities program are:
> 1. It extends the school day only for those participating.
> 2. It requires no elaborate machinery or extra personnel to manage.
> 3. It permits larger sections of activities.
> 4. It permits the individual pupil to engage in a greater number of activities.
> 5. It does not complicate the daily time schedule.
> 6. It permits meetings to end as desired, without prescribed limits.
> 7. It is more easily adapted to the larger school or the school on double session.
> 8. Teachers who desire to sponsor activities make the best sponsors.
>
> The disadvantages of an out-of-session activities program are:
> 1. A selective rather than an extensive pupil participation frequently occurs.
> 2. Only a segment of the teaching staff is usually concerned.
> 3. There is likely to be an overdemand for certain staff members as sponsors.
> 4. It appears to place activities in a role subsidiary to the curriculum.
> 5. It forces pupils to choose between extra class and personal non-school activities.

6. It tends to exclude other pupils who may have other duties before and after school.[3]
7. It tends to operate against pupils of lower scholastic achievement.
8. It results often in an uncoordinated activity program.
9. It is likely to result in a lack of coordination of homeroom activities with other activities.[4]
10. It makes for a relative difficulty in collecting data, statistics, and establishing trends.[5]

The most significant statement that may be made about the scheduling of student activities is that scheduling should be an individual concern for each school. A plan of time allotment used by one school is not necessarily the best for another school. Likewise, the enrollment, the number of student activities, the type of class schedule, and other related matters can be sufficient to change a schedule considerably from year to year. The decisions made in setting up a schedule of student activities should be cooperatively made by the principal and his staff. All persons concerned — students, teachers, parents, custodial crews, and others — should be taken into consideration as the schedule is developed.

ALLOCATION OF PERSONNEL

The administration of individual activities, including emphasis on faculty sponsors, was discussed in Chapter 14. In that chapter reference was made to the various methods of assigning teachers to activities, which may include assignment by formulae, point values, and volunteering. Such procedures, however objective they may be,

---

[3]It should be pointed out that this item is of increasing importance to education. Since 1951 when Messrs. Thompkins and Story composed this list, many American high schools have increased the number of vocational subjects which extend beyond the usual school day. Cooperative vocational programs such as Distributive Education and Diversified Occupations release students from as much as one half of the school day, which denies them participation in a nonschool-hours student activities program. Other vocational courses — printing, auto mechanics, electronics, and the like — prepare students to take their places in industry; this often includes placing them in jobs during part of the school day. In addition, the policy of practicing athletics, plays, etc., immediately after school will deny other student activities participation to these students.

[4]See Chapter 3 of this book for a definition of *student activities* in the high school, as opposed to this concept of "homeroom activities."

[5]Ellsworth Thompkins and Robert C. Story, *The Activity Period Bulletin* (1951) No. 19, pp. 6-7, as quoted in Frederick, *op. cit.,* pp. 243-244.

have evolved in an erratic way and the methods used to obtain sponsors still leave much to be desired in many schools. That the faculty sponsors are essential personnel in the student activities program is not to be denied. However, they are not the only personnel to be considered.

As the school plant is used for student activities, the allocation of custodial personnel is not to be overlooked. Provision must be made to have available (and paid) the number of custodians necessary to supply certain needs of the student activity and to clean the building following the activity. Particularly if an activity, such as a party, is held after school hours, it may be necessary to move furniture, clean floors, and disconnect equipment in preparation for the next day's classes. It is a wise policy to require a custodian to be in the building for out-of-school-hours student activities. This policy, however, will require coordination and scheduling of custodial personnel and may involve overtime pay.

Large-scale functions such as athletic contests, concerts, and plays require a number of personnel. Outside agencies are involved in the selection of some of these persons such as the game officials, who are certified by athletics associations for their member schools. Local assignment to specific games should be carried out at a central location, such as the office of the Coordinator of Athletics or in the office of the Director of Student Activities. However, a number of scorekeepers, clock operators, ticket sellers, door watchers, and other faculty or staff members are also required. An equitable distribution of assignments should be made, or some financial compensation should be given to the personnel working at these large events. The coordination and equitable assignment of these duties must also be considered in allocating human resources.

In addition to the personnel mentioned above there are others that are only indirectly associated with student activities, but whose presence is essential to the success of the program. A bookkeeper to work with financial records of the various activities, a secretary to assist the Director of Student Activities with routine paper work, other school secretaries, teacher aides, and community resource people[6] are among the additional human resources which can contribute to the success of a student activities program.

[6]See Kenneth R. Bender, "Better Use of Community Resource People in the Classroom," *Kappa Delta Pi Record,* 4:89, February, 1968.

SUMMARY

The proper allocation of resources — finances, space, time, and personnel — is essential to the success of a student activities program. Space for storage, files, and committee work of student organizations is desirable, and space of the appropriate size and with appropriate equipment is necessary for meetings of the various organizations. Various methods of scheduling student activities were discussed, both in terms of within the conventional school day and in terms of extended school days. While good sponsors are essential to student activities, many other school personnel are indirectly involved with the student activities program and proper coordination of their work can greatly enhance the success of the student activities program.

REFERENCES

Bender, Kenneth R. "Better Use of Community Resource People in the Classroom," *Kappa Delta Pi Record,* 4:89, February, 1968.

Boles, Harold W. *Step by Step to Better School Facilities.* New York: Holt, Rinehart and Winston, 1965, p. 81.

Frederick, Robert W. *The Third Curriculum.* New York: Appleton-Century-Crofts, 1959.

Johnston, Edgar G., and Faunce, Roland C. *Student Activities in Secondary Schools.* New York: The Ronald Press Co., 1952, pp. 339-354.

Kilzer, Louis R., *et al. Allied Activities in the Secondary School.* New York: Harper and Brothers, 1956, pp. 20-33.

McKown, Harry C. *Extra-Curricular Activities.* Rev. ed. New York: Macmillan Co., 1949, pp. 650-675.

Morgan, Paul C. "Scheduling Student Activities in Secondary Schools," *School Activities,* 28:241-244, April, 1957.

Rodgers, J. "Characteristics of an Adequate Student Activities Program," *NASSP Bulletin,* 42:169-175, November, 1958.

Chapter 16

FINANCING THE STUDENT ACTIVITIES PROGRAM

INTRODUCTION

The rapid growth of student activities within the last few decades has brought about many problems. Perhaps no particular problem has been emphasized as much as the financial management of the student activities program. The reasons for the problems of financial management are closely related to the development of the student activities program in the schools.

As has already been stated, during the early stages of the movement, student activities were largely ignored by school officials. Nevertheless, the student activities program has grown in importance until it has become an integral part of the schools of today. Unfortunately, however, the weak financial systems that were developed to support the earlier student activities were often merely expanded to support the wider system of student activities.

Some years ago McKown made the following statement which is still true today:

> With but few exceptions the extra-curricular activities just "grew up" undirected and unsupported by school authorities. Even today in many schools they still just "exist." And this is certainly as true of their financial administration as it is of the activities themselves.[1]

The rapid growth of the student activities movement in recent years has further strained the archaic financial systems with which student activity programs have been burdened.

[1]Harry C. McKown, *Extra-Curricular Activities* (rev. ed., New York: The Macmillan Company, 1949), p. 631.

Definition

According to Knezevich and Fowlkes, *student activity funds* may be defined as follows:

> [receipts] obtained from or for functions sponsored in the name of or controlled essentially by the pupils of a school and whose expenditures are for student sponsored or controlled events.[2]

Activity Funds

The size of these student activity funds has greatly increased within a few decades. In 1926 McKown's study of 268 schools found activity fund budgets ranging from $300.00 to $125,000.00 per school per year. By 1957-1958, Davis estimated that the student activity budget for the Los Angeles public schools alone would reach $7 million at that time.[3] "Over two and one-half million dollars was expended for extracurricular activities in only the predominantly white schools in about one-third of the school districts of [Mississippi] in 1964-1965."[4] However, it must be emphasized again that in too few instances are sound business and educational practices being used in the financial administration of these funds.[5]

Students and the Funds

Student activity funds must be considered not only from the point of financial management, but also from the standpoint of the effect on the students. It is the students who suffer from limited financial support of the program and from poor administration of the finances of the program. As Johnston and Faunce have pointed out, one research study found that the more wealthy students "outparticipated the lower-income group on a ratio ranging from 1.4

---

[2]Stephen J. Knezevich and John Guy Fowlkes, *Business Management of Local School Systems* (New York: Harper and Brothers, Publishers, 1960), p. 188.

[3]Quoted in Knezevich and Fowlkes, *op. cit.*, p. 189.

[4]Joe William Dollar, "An Analysis of the Activity Funds in the Predominantly White Schools of the Municipal Separate School Districts of Mississippi in the Fiscal Year 1964-1965," (unpublished doctoral dissertation, The University of Mississippi, University, 1967), p. 80. As a further indication of the magnitude of these funds, it must be remembered that per-pupil expenditures for education in Mississippi are the lowest in the nation.

[5]Edgar G. Johnston and Roland C. Faunce, *Student Activities in Secondary Schools* (New York: The Ronald Press Company, 1952), p. 326.

to 1 to 6.5 to 1." It was also reported that the costs of participation in student activities included the following: participation in athletics, up to $100.00; class dues, up to $5.00; and the median cost of school clubs, $19.30.[6]

At times, large numbers of students may be denied participation in student activities because they cannot afford the sometimes large amounts of money needed to support the program. Thus, administrators need to devise some method to prevent the cost of student activities from inhibiting participation. Frederick has recommended the following:

> *The expenses involved in participating in any student activity and in the total program for a school year should be set at a figure which will permit 90 per cent of the students to participate without financial strain* [emphasis in original].[7]

While Frederick has suggested that provision be made for the participation of 90% of the student body without financial burden, it would seem desirable to propose that arrangements be made for low-expense or expense-free participation by the entire student body.

SOURCES OF INCOME

Money for the student activity fund has traditionally come from an assortment of fees, dues, tickets, contributions, profits, and, in some instances, school subsidy. The primary sources of income today are the following: dues and fees, fund-raising campaigns, activity tickets, profits from various businesslike enterprises, admissions, and school district subsidy.

Dues and Fees

The payment of dues or fees has long been an established practice in the student activities program. Student body organizations, various types of clubs, and other student activities supported their undertakings either wholly or in part by these assessments. A

---

[6]*Ibid.,* pp. 326-327. These costs would probably be somewhat higher now.

[7]Robert W. Frederick, *The Third Curriculum* (New York: Appleton-Century-Crofts, Inc., 1959), p. 161.

few schools have levied a "tax" on all students in the school for general support of the student activities program.

By the time of Hand's survey (1949), the decline of dues as a means of financial support of student activities could be seen. Among his findings were the following:

1. A large majority of schools no longer made assessments for student body memberships.
2. Approximately one-half of the schools charged class dues.
3. About one-fourth of the schools had eliminated all costs for major athletics.
4. Only service clubs traditionally charged no dues.[8]

Certainly today the number of student activities charging dues is declining. Unfortunately, some student activities with few other means of financial support still make some sort of assessments on their members to carry out their projects. In addition to the financial burden on some students and their families, the amount of work involved in collecting a small sum of money from a number of students over a long period of time has justly caused many persons to question the value of dues. Particularly when proper accounting procedures are considered — and the interminable number of entries necessary to record some small sum — no reasonable argument may be made for the support of student activities through student dues or other assessments.

Fund-Raising

Quite often the financial support of some particular student activity or of all student activities is boosted by an extensive effort of fund-raising. While fund-raising knows no season, two major times of fund-raising are in September — as financial support for the year is sought — and in December — as plans for Christmas service or social projects are planned. With sufficient advertising and the cooperation of members, parents, the administrators, and businessmen, many a car wash, candy sale, or similar activity has been successful. However, many projects have failed because of the lack of public interest in bake sales, Christmas card sales, and similar projects sponsored by some school group.

[8]Harold C. Hand, "Hidden Tuition Charges in Extra-Class Activities," *The Educational Forum*, 14:95-96, 99, November, 1949.

While there are no estimates on the yearly revenue obtained for student activities from fund-raising campaigns, they are generally highly successful if the following standards are adhered to:

1. The drive should be *consistent with school board policies.* The principal, the Director of Student Activities, and sponsors should have a voice in the formulation of these policies, should be aware of the policies, and should carefully enforce them.

2. The fund-raising drive must be *dignified.* It should in no way reflect unfavorably upon the school or the student activity. For example, raffles, games-of-chance, public dances, etc. are not condoned in many communities as appropriate projects for school groups.

3. The project must be *controlled* by the representatives of the student organization as well as by the school administration. School regulations should be made clear to all participants when the project is being considered and again prior to undertaking the project. For example, door-to-door sales of food, magazines, and Christmas cards are not permitted in many schools.

4. *Organization* is a primary factor. Hardly anything is more detrimental to schools and their student organizations than to have a disorganized campaign that contacts some people more than once and others not at all.

5. ". . . not be in conflict with the American ideal of a free education for everybody regardless of his individual economic status."[9]   No financially well-to-do child should be given more tickets, candy, etc., to sell than any other student only because his father's friends can buy more. Neither should a less well-to-do student have to sell more of an item or work longer because he could not contribute in a lump sum to the organization's treasury.

Activity Tickets

A fairly common means of raising money for the student activities program is by selling student activity tickets. The activity ticket allows distribution of monies for the activity program in a manner that is predictable, as well as equitable to all of the individual student activities which participate in the program. The tickets are

[9]Louis R. Kilzer, Harold H. Stephenson, and H. Orvill Nordberg, *Allied Activities in the Secondary School* (New York: Harper and Brothers, Publishers, 1956), p. 253.

usually sold at the beginning of the year for a certain sum of money which may be paid out in regular installments.

Two types of activity tickets may be available. The *regular* activity ticket admits students to all plays, clubs, concerts, carnivals, contests, and games, and allows the student to receive the newspaper and the yearbook. The *economy* activity ticket admits a student to a limited number of activities for a reduction in costs.

A finance committee with student and faculty membership is essential for successful administration of activity ticket financing.[10] This committee, with administrative approval, allocates a portion of the combined revenue to each organization involved. Individual student activities should present to the finance committee a budget outlining their program and financial needs for the coming year. The committee is then charged with the responsibility of determining an equitable distribution of the funds.

In addition to the educational values which may result from the sale of activity tickets, the following additional values have been found by Johnston and Faunce:

1. It reduces total costs to the individual, thus encouraging participation.
2. It reduces the need for numerous, competing drives for funds by all-school organizations.
3. It enables revenue-producing activities to help carry non-revenue activities which have educative value.
4. It provides a business-like basis for compiling an activities budget.[11]

While it would appear that activity tickets are a productive means for financing student activities, the administrator should consider the following:

1. Time is still required for the sale of the activity tickets; and, when the tickets are sold on an installment plan, time, personnel, and supplies must be expended in accounting for the funds.

2. A campaign must be conducted to sell the tickets, and campaigns may easily put pressure on the student body.

3. Activity tickets are like fees and dues in that they require the students to assume all or a large part of the financial burden of

[10]See Chapter 14.
[11]Johnston and Faunce, *op. cit.*, p. 328.

supporting the student activity program. As such, they are not ideal, although some savings to the individual may be had in purchasing an activity ticket.

4. Activity tickets require students to pay for "packaged" activities. Usually no opportunity is available for students who wish to participate in only one or two student activities. Even in economy activity tickets, a number of student activities are contained. Working or part-time students who want only a subscription to the yearbook cannot obtain their limited desires with most activity ticket arrangements.

Business Profits and Admissions

Certain school activities are inherently revenue-producing. Athletic contests, musical performances, and dramatic productions attract many nonstudents who pay admission. Such income may be used in supporting the individual activities, groups of student activities, or may, in some instances, be placed in a common fund to be divided among all student activities by the finance committee.

In some schools many public-use facilities may provide support for the student activities program. For example, vending machines, school supply stores, and cafeterias yield profits which can be used in support of a common student activities fund. Often, however, it is questionable whether or not the school can justify the supplying of space, employees, and facilities to maintain adequate service and inventory in these enterprises, for they are often in competition with business establishments in the community.

Student publications often supply sources of income for a part of the student activities program. Fortunately, the days are now gone in most areas of the country where students have to bear the entire cost of school publications. In the past, newspapers and yearbooks became items available only to those who could afford them, and not to all who should have received them. Such publications as handbooks and directories are now often furnished by the school to the pupils and are financed entirely by the school. The literary magazine and other similar publications often have shaky financing. In some schools, however, these may obtain the support of "patrons" whose names are usually listed in the book or by total support from the English department budget. Sales to the public often are used to gain additional income.

It is the traditional publications, the newspaper and the yearbook, that have brought about so much comment pertaining to financing. The advertising sections (often of questionable worth as advertising), particularly in yearbooks, are burdens to the business staffs of yearbooks and newspapers as well as to the beseiged businessmen who are confronted with numerous requests to "advertise with and support" a particular school or publication. As administrators have come to recognize the value of school newspapers, schools have begun to supplement the income derived from advertising contributions and sales so that the paper may be distributed free or at low cost to all students. In some schools subscriptions to newspapers are still sold to supplement the income from advertising. The trend is certainly toward complete school subsidation of the cost of student newspapers.

Yearbooks are minimizing advertising sections by selling "Compliments of a Friend" space to numerous persons and making only one such insertion. More progressive yearbooks have supplemented income from student purchases by arranging for the advertising to be placed only at the bottom of pages, such as the line "Compliments of City Laundry." Indeed, the large advertising sections are disappearing as businessmen have recognized the small advertising value of such expense. Hopefully, the sections will disappear entirely, or to such an extent that only a list of patrons will be printed. It is hoped that schools through their student activity budgets will be able to support the yearbook in such a manner that copies of this publication will be available to all students.

Subsidy by School System

It cannot be denied, even by the most ardent critic of the student activities program, that student activities have become an integral part of the American educational system. The problem of financing this integral part of the school system is analyzed by Miller, Moyer, and Patrick:

> No final, satisfactory solution to the problem of supporting activities is possible unless school officials and school boards provide financial assistance in the same manner and from the same source as that provided for other educational programs. All other methods are

at best illogical and undignified and discourage full development of the program. They are always uncertain, often unethical, and certainly unjustifiable.[12]

Indeed, after considering all possible sources of income, total subsidy by the local school board appears to be the best and most justifiable method of supporting a student activities program. This method may be found in a few instances; for example, the Board of Education of the Yazoo City (Mississippi) Municipal Separate School District financially supports all of the clubs and organizations at the high school. Financial support includes all publications except the yearbook, which is supported in the traditional manner.

For such reasons as the following, many school boards have decided to assume more support of student activities programs:

1. Financial aid from public funds provides a *certain source of income,* while other means provide an amount that can fluctuate greatly from year-to-year and which may never be received if installment payments on activity tickets or dues are not collected.

2. Support from public funds permits *all* students, of whatever economic ability, to participate equally.

3. *Instructional time is saved* when the school does not have to sacrifice instructional time to sell activity tickets, yearbook subscriptions, season tickets for sports, and the like.

4. Public financing *removes doubts about ethics.* Schools do not become competitors to local businesses, and there is no opportunity for teachers or administrators to be accused of "coercing" students into joining a club or buying a publication.

5. Supplement from general revenues is in keeping *with the dignity of the school.* Pie sales, baby-sitting, car washes, "slave days," and fund drives are no longer necessary for support of the activity program.

6. Financial support of the student activities program is a *reasonable extension of financial aid already given to the schools.* Since the more formal phases are publicly supported, it is only logical to support the entire curriculum of the school.

[12]Franklin A. Miller, James H. Moyer, and Robert B. Patrick, *Planning Student Activities* (Englewood Cliffs, N. J.: Prentice-Hall Inc., 1956), p. 149.

Federal Assistance

In addition to subsidy by the local governmental agencies, many school systems receive financial assistance which indirectly supports the student activities programs from outside agencies. For example, schools that offer certain vocational subjects and those with the Reserve Officers Training Corps (Junior Division) receive state and/or federal· financial assistance which may be used, in part, for the support of student activities related to these subjects.

CONTROL OF EXPENDITURES

Once a means of financing the student activities program has been found, an orderly procedure of expending and accounting for these funds must be used. Certainly, since the students are directly concerned with the student activities program in general and with the financial support of the program in particular, it would be unwise to remove them from the workings of the financial program. Unfortunately, many schools do exclude the students from all except the tasks of collecting the money and giving it to the school treasurer — thus a valuable learning experience is lost.

Hopefully, more schools will have their students take an active part in the business management of the student activities program and thereby gain valuable educational experiences. Such experiences may be provided through budget committees, student treasurers, and student business managers. Fretwell has suggested that the financial administration of the extracurricular activity program provides a valuable laboratory for business education students.[13]

Principles of Accounting

Regardless of who is responsible for the administration and implementation of the program of financial support for student activities, the following principles of accounting, recommended by the U.S. Office of Education, should be implemented:

1. The general administration of school activity fund accounting should be governed by rules and regulations prescribed by the board of education of the school district.

[13]Elbert K. Fretwell, *Extra-Curricular Activities in Secondary Schools* (Boston: Houghton Mifflin Company, 1931), pp. 444, 463-467.

2. The board of education should designate a person . . . to implement all policies and rules pertaining to the supervision and administration of funds in the schools under his jurisdiction.
3. One person should be designated . . . to be responsible for the funds in each individual school.
4. Expenditures for school activities should be carefully planned within the resources of the activity, which would make the use of a budget control of receipts and expenditures desirable and sometimes necessary.
5. Persons handling the school funds should be bonded through the regular school district procedures, and the bond should be in an amount sufficient for the adequate protection of the funds of the school.
6. An annual audit should be made of all school activity funds by trained and recognized auditors.
7. Regular financial reports should be made to the administrative head of the school and to the board of education.[14]

Accounting Systems

Two types of accounting systems exist for recording student activities transactions. They are as follows:

Decentralized. Under this system, each organization is responsible for its own business dealings and its own records. If the administration of the school operates on this *laissez faire* basis, no audit or an informal audit is usually performed on these records.

Centralized. Forms and procedures of a standard nature are used throughout a school or a school system. One bank account is used by the school treasurer who keeps records for all accounts. The school treasurer is responsible for the following: (a) keeping the cash book or journal; (b) keeping individual account ledgers; (c) receiving all monies; (d) drawing checks for all disbursements; (e) conducting all transactions with the commercial bank, and keeping all bank records; (f) taking care of and providing all necessary financial supplies and forms; (g) rendering periodic statements of each student activity account; (h) instructing sponsors and student treasurers in their duties; (i) checking individual organization accounts and receipt books at periodic intervals; and (j) checking for compliance with the accounting system.

[14]Everett V. Samuelson, George G. Tankard, Jr., and Hoyt W. Pope, *Financial Accounting for School Activities* (Washington, D.C.: Government Printing Office, 1959), pp. 51-52.

Student treasurers handle all transactions with the school treasurer, but it is the school treasurer, not the organizational treasurer, who makes the actual disbursements from the various accounts.

The centralized accounting system is recognized as a more sound business practice because of the following:

1. A single entity is provided through which all transactions may be made.
2. Expenditures can be controlled.
3. Budgeting is more easily executed.
4. Funds which are non-revenue producing may be supported through the general funds.
5. Subsidies from local board funds may be more easily distributed.[15]

Snyder found that 98.3% of the senior high schools in Oregon used central accounting funds for student activities in 1959. It was also reported that 78% of the respondents in his study used written procedures in obligating funds; 100% of the large schools in Oregon indicated this policy.[16]

Forms

The use of written procedures for depositing and withdrawing funds is a necessary and complimentary action of a formalized system of income. Regardless of how affluent the student activities program is, the use of proper procedures for withdrawing funds is necessary for sound financial management.

The system may be adequately administered with only the following forms:

Deposit Form. This form, made out in duplicate by an organizational treasurer, provides a receipt for deposit of funds (when properly stamped or signed by the school treasurer) as well as a record for the school treasurer to use in bookkeeping procedures. These forms should be numbered serially for reference. The form should include spaces for date, account number or name of account to be credited, and source of revenue, as well as other information needed.

[15] Ralph I. Snyder, *The Management of Student Body Finances in Oregon Senior High Schools.* Oregon School Study Council Bulletin (Eugene, Oregon: University of Oregon, School of Education, 1960), p. 4.
[16] *Ibid.*

Withdrawal Form. This form, when made out in duplicate by the treasurer or business manager of an activity and when signed by both the treasurer and the sponsor of the student activity, authorizes the school treasurer to issue a check to the person or firm indicated. The form, essentially a purchase order, provides both the organizational and the school treasurers with records of the transaction. Space should be provided for signatures of the persons authorizing the payment, the account used for the expenditure, the date, name and address of the person or firm to receive the payment, reason for the expenditure, and a space for the check number used in payment, as well as other information as needed. These forms should be numbered serially for reference.

Ledger Sheet. The ledger sheet is maintained by the school treasurer or bookkeeper. Simple ruled sheets can be inserted in a loose-leaf notebook. Columns should be marked for deposits and expenditures, with a space provided for date, amount, and deposit/ withdrawal form number under each of the headings. The name of the organization, its sponsor, and treasurer should be provided at the top of each ledger sheet. A reproduction of the ledger sheet for each organization should be sent to the sponsor, the treasurer, and the school principal at the end of each month.

Each club sponsor should, along with the elected officers of the organization, establish set procedures for handling expenditures so that the operation of the organization may proceed in as efficient, yet businesslike, manner as possible. A certain time each month should be set aside for the student treasurer and the sponsor to review bills and to sign withdrawal forms on the organization's account. Copies of the official minutes, resolutions, and other statements of intent by the organization should be given to the treasurer when matters involving expenditures are concerned. *All members of the organization should be instructed that they may not purchase any item or service for the organization without at least the approval of the treasurer and the sponsor.* Detailed planning and careful orientation of the membership and officers by the sponsor and the student treasurer/business manager will keep the organization from facing debts incurred in the name of the organization by a member acting without authorization.

SUMMARY

Student activity programs have matured without a corresponding maturation of financial arrangements to support them. Activity funds have become "big business," amounting to millions of dollars per school system and state. There should be adequate financial arrangements so that students do not have to assume the support of student activities in which they wish to participate. Primary sources of income for student activities are dues, and fees, fund-raising projects, activity tickets, profits, admissions, and school subsidy.

Students should be involved in policy formulations for and the administration of the financial arrangements for student activities. Proper accounting procedures are essential, and careful attention to forms and procedure will provide valuable learning experiences, as well as fiscal soundness.

REFERENCES

Allen, James E., Jr. "Relationship of Extra-Curricular Activities to Salaries," *Harvard Educational Review,* 22:141-149, Spring, 1952.

Bernerd, Gladys. "Extra Pay *Versus* No Extra Pay," *School Activities,* 24:97-100, November, 1952.

Crenshaw, J.W. *Student Administration of Activity Funds: Study at Pratt Institute.* New York: Bureau of Publications, Teachers College, Columbia University, 1954.

Evans, J. C. "Popcorn, the No. 1 Refreshment Money Maker!" *Scholastic Coach,* 34:54, January, 1965.

Frederick, Robert W. *The Third Curriculum.* New York: Appleton-Century-Crofts, Inc., 1959.

Fretwell, Elbert K. *Extra-Curricular Activities in Secondary Schools.* Boston: Houghton Mifflin Co., 1931, pp. 444-476.

Gruber, Frederick C., and Beatty, Thomas Bayard. *Secondary School Activities.* New York: McGraw-Hill Book Co., 1954, pp. 48-66.

Hand, Harold C. "Hidden Tuition Charges in Extra-Class Activities," *The Educational Forum,* 14:95-96, 99, November, 1949.

Johnston, Edgar, and Faunce, Roland C. *Student Activities in Secondary Schools.* New York: Ronald Press Co., 1952.

Kilzer, Louis R., *et al. Allied Activities in the Secondary School.* New York: Harper and Brothers, 1956, pp. 251-271.

Knezevich, Stephen J., and Fowlkes, John Guy. *Business Management of Local School Systems.* New York: Harper and Brothers, 1960, pp. 188-189.

McKown, Harry C. *Extra-Curricular Activities*. Rev. ed. New York: Macmillan Co., 1949, pp. 631-649.

Miller, Franklin A., *et al. Planning Student Activities*. Englewood Cliffs, N.J.: Prentice-Hall, Inc., 1956, pp. 116-149.

Olsen, Ola, and Rieke, Lola. "Manual for Treasurer of Class or Club," *School Activities,* 27:154, January, 1956.

Olsen, Waldo. "Duties of the Supervisor of Student Activity Accounting" in *Association of School Business Officials of the U.S. and Canada Yearbook,* 47:371, 1961.

Samuelson, Everett V., Tankard, George G., Jr., and Pope, Hoyt W. *Financial Accounting for School Activities*. Washington, D.C.: Government Printing Office, 1959.

Snyder, Ralph I. *The Management of Student Body Finances in Oregon Senior High Schools*. Eugene, Oregon: University of Oregon, School of Education, 1960.

Vaughn, Ronald L. "The School Bank," *The Balance Sheet,* 44:15, September, 1962.

Vore, Marilyn. "The Pasadena City College Bank," *Junior College Journal,* 35:28, December, 1964.

Wootan, Jerry D., Jr. "Sources of Student Activity Funds" in *Association of School Business Officials of the U.S. and Canada Yearbook,* 43:294, 1957.

Chapter 17

LEGAL ASPECTS OF THE STUDENT ACTIVITIES PROGRAM

LEGISLATION

National Level

The United States Constitution is silent on the matter of education. Although it is sometimes argued that education falls under the "general welfare" clause, our traditional interpretation is that, by the passage of the Tenth Amendment in 1791, matters concerning education were "reserved" to the states. The Tenth Amendment reads:

> The powers not delegated to the United States by the Constitution, nor prohibited by it to the states, are reserved to the states respectively, or to the people.

Relatively little legislation has been passed by Congress which directly relates to the curriculum; although support has been given in recent years to vocational subjects, mathematics, science, foreign languages, etc. Almost no legislation has been passed that affects the student activities program. A few youth organizations, such as the Future Farmers of America and the Boy Scouts of America, have legal recognition at the national level. One of the most recent actions of Congress affecting student activities was the enactment in 1958 of P.L. 85-875 "to require the Commissioner of Education to encourage, foster, and assist in the establishment of clubs for boys and girls especially interested in science."

State Level

State constitutions seldom are specific on the matter of the curriculum of the schools, and in no case is there a state constitutional provision of direct concern to the student activities program. The state constitution may, as in Utah and Louisiana, require certain inclusions in the curriculum, or (in rare instances) there may be constitutional provision prohibiting instruction in certain areas.

In essence, the legislature of each state possesses plenary authority over all educational matters not restricted by a higher authority, such as the state or national constitution. Almost all states have legislation requiring certain subjects to be taught, and a few states have legislation directing school personnel in what *not* to teach.[1] The state has the legal right to require that designated studies be taught and that nothing be taught which is contrary to the public welfare. However, most statutes pertaining to the curriculum are general; and they delegate authority to local boards or to professional personnel to determine policies and specific aspects of the curriculum. The local school board, subject to state law, has a great deal of latitude in the development of the curriculum, including the student activities program.

The legislation concerning student activities most often found among the states concerns the prohibition of fraternities, sororities, and secret societies. The first legislation of this type was adopted by Indiana, Kansas, and Minnesota in 1907; and 23 other states now have some statute on the books prohibiting secret societies. This legislation falls into two categories: the first, and most prevalent, is that prohibiting fraternities, sororities, and secret societies. The other category, of which there are only a few instances, gives the local school board discretionary authority to prohibit such organizations. The usual penalty provided under such legislation is suspension or expulsion from school, although other disciplinary measures found include denial of credits, denial of graduation privileges, or denial of participation in various school honors.

States with antifraternity statutes are Arkansas, California, Colorado, Florida, Idaho, Illinois, Indiana, Iowa, Kansas, Louisiana, Maine, Michigan, Minnesota, Mississippi, Missouri, Montana, Nebraska, New Jersey, Ohio, Oklahoma, Oregon, Pennsylvania, Rhode Island, Texas, Vermont, and Washington.[2]

The most recent piece of legislation in this category was passed in Missouri in 1963 — it is typical of the laws of many of the other states:

[1]For example, Arkansas and Mississippi have antievolution statutes on the law books which restrict science teachers in theory, if not in practice. The U. S. Supreme Court, in November, 1968, struck down the Arkansas statute, and the ruling may apply to Mississippi as well.

[2]Massachusetts has a statute which has been interpreted to exclude fraternities and sororities from the public schools.

1. As used in this section, a school fraternity or sorority is any organization composed wholly or in part of public school pupils, which seeks to perpetuate itself by taking in additional members from the pupils enrolled in public high schools, junior high schools or elementary schools on the basis of the decision of its membership rather than upon the free choice of any pupil in the school who is qualified by the rules of the board to fill the aims of the organization.

2. The school board of any school district, by rule, may prohibit membership of pupils in school fraternities or sororities composed of pupils in any high school, junior high school or elementary school in the district, when it deems that membership in the fraternities or sororities detrimentally affects the conduct and discipline of the schools in the district. Any rule adopted under this subsection shall prescribe the aim of school organizations which may be formed and the qualifications of pupils eligible for membership therein. The board may adopt other rules that are necessary to carry out the purposes of this section.

3. Upon the adoption of the rule authorized by subsection 2, the school board may suspend, discipline and expel from the school under its control, any pupil who remains a member of, who joins or promises to join, or who becomes pledged to become a member, or who solicits any other person to join, promise to join or be pledged or to become a member of a school fraternity or sorority. Upon direction of the board, by rule or otherwise, the superintendent of schools may suspend and discipline any person who violates the rule authorized by subsection 2 until the time that the matter is considered by the board.[3]

When the law is silent, the local board has the power to make and enforce reasonable regulations concerning the management and discipline of the school, as well as all aspects of the curriculum.

Specific legal provisions exist in Alaska, Arizona, California, Hawaii, New York, Tennessee, and Washington which abrogate the common law rule of tort immunity. In several states either "save harmless"[4] statutes or statutes waiving immunity, with restrictions, exist. A discussion of the implications of this legislation for the student activities program appears later in this chapter.

---

[3]Missouri School Laws, 171.141.

[4]"Save harmless" statutes permit boards of education, themselves immune from suit, to defend their teachers who are personally liable. This is of particular importance in student activities.

Local Level

One of the less-appreciated roles of the local school board is its legislative role. School districts and school boards are creations of the state legislature, and certain authority has been delegated to the local level.

Properly adopted, recorded, and publicized, school board policies and regulations have a certain legal force. Most school boards have adopted regulations for all or part of the student activities program. The courts have upheld local board policies on such matters as operating recreation and social activities, and prohibiting or regulating high school fraternities, sororities, or social clubs. However, the courts have held some policies to be unreasonable: requiring students to serve on school patrols; requiring students to participate in a flag salute ceremony contrary to their religious beliefs; prohibiting a child from attending any social party during the school term; and administering the student activities program for the benefit of various private groups.

Since the area of student activities is an area in which the law and regulations are vague or silent, it is often difficult to ascertain what would be considered legal and what would not be considered legal if a case were taken to court. Bolmeier has stated:

> Application of the following suggestions would likely add legality and propriety to the "extracurricular" program: (1) Conduct the worthwhile so-called "extracurricular" activities as a legitimate part of the total curriculum; (2) Support the activity by public funds; (3) Make the activities available to all children who could profit therefrom; (4) Do not prohibit participation discriminately as a punitive device.[5]

ADMINISTRATIVE CONTROLS

Attorney-General Rulings

In a case of questionable legality, and in the absence of a court ruling, a school board may request a ruling from the attorney-general of the state. An attorney-general's ruling has the effect of law until a

---

[5]E. C. Bolmeier, "Legal Aspects of the Curriculum and the Extra-curriculum," *NASSP Bulletin*, 49:142, March, 1965.

statute is enacted or a court rules otherwise. An example of such a ruling would be that issued by Mississippi Attorney General Joe T. Patterson to a Mississippi principal which reads in part:

> In regard to contracts signed by high school principals and superintendents for rings, annuals, diplomas, etc., I am unable to find any statutory authority on this subject. General inquiry reveals that in most instances these contracts are contracts between members of the senior class or an organization of the school rather than the school itself.
>
> Frankly, I doubt very seriously whether or not the school district is bound by any such contracts entered into by the school principal but the principal may be bound himself and in all probability is.[6]

State Department of Education Regulations

In all states there is a state department of education headed by a chief state school officer; and in most states there is a state board of education to which the legislature has granted, in most instances, considerable authority to adopt rules and regulations for the conduct of schools. These regulations are administered by the state department of education, and because of the source of authority, have the color of law.

In some states, these regulations include items applicable to the student activities program, and administrators, sponsors, and coaches should be aware of and carefully observe what is expected of them. To a very great extent, however, state departments of education have left the regulation of student activities to other agencies, particularly the voluntary athletic associations or activity associations discussed elsewhere in this chapter.

COURT CASES

As has been indicated, there are few pieces of legislation and few attorney-general's opinions affecting student activities. Most regulations concerning student activities come from action of the board of education and from the action of administrators and

---

[6]Opinion issued by Mississippi Attorney General Joe T. Patterson to Mr. Daniel Harvey, Magee, Mississippi, on August 26, 1965. No. 227, Schools, Misc.

teachers connected with the student activity program. The appeal from these regulations is generally to the courts, and there are a fair number of court cases which have involved the less formal phases of the school program.

Technically speaking, a particular court case is legally binding only on the litigants involved in the court proceeding. Ordinarily, however, all the lower courts of record within a particular judicial jurisdiction follow the rulings of the appellate court within the respective jurisdiction. Rulings of the State Supreme Court are expected to be binding on all the courts located within the particular state. Court cases, however, are very valuable, as they are commonly cited as precedents in reference to the proper disposal of a pending legal issue, whatever the jurisdiction in which the precedent may have arisen.

In general, the courts will refuse to interfere with the administrative acts of an administrative agency, including boards of education, unless they find the acts to be unlawful, or that the administrative body abused its discretion by acting arbitrarily or unlawfully, or that it exercised its discretion in a fraudulent manner. Courts are not inclined to hold legislation unconstitutional, or to hold actions of boards of education unlawful unless deemed necessary.

Although most state constitutions provide for a uniform system of public schools, it is not mandatory for every school to offer identical programs or even provide identical educational opportunities for each of its students. The welfare of the state, often considered the primary purpose of public education, requires limits to be placed on the freedom of individual pupils by imposing such rules and regulations as are required for the efficient government of the school. In the course of governing a school it is necessary to enforce regulations which control the activities of pupils. School boards have the authority to make rules and regulations which, in the interest of promoting the objectives of the school, prohibit certain pupils from participating in the total school program.

However, beyond a point school officials might be violating individual rights guaranteed by the United States Constitution. This point is determined by the courts on the basis of the reasonableness of the regulation involved in each case. For example, there has recently been much concern about the desegregation of schools and student activities within schools. One court has ruled:

No student shall be segregated or discriminated against on account of race or color in any...athletics or other extracurricular activity.... A student attending school for the first time on a desegregated basis may not be subject to any disqualification or waiting period for participating in activities and programs, including athletics, which might otherwise apply because he is a transfer or newly assigned student except that transferees shall be subject to long-standing, non-racially based rules of city, county, or state athletic associations dealing with the eligibility of transfer students for athletic contests. All school use or school-sponsored use of athletic fields, meeting rooms, and all other school related services, facilities, activities, and programs such as commencement exercises ...shall be open to all persons without regard to race or color.[7]

Facilities and Equipment. In a District of Columbia case and a Pennsylvania case the courts have held that boards of education may invoke their power of eminent domain to acquire land on which to construct athletic facilities. The Arizona Supreme Court upheld the authority of a school district to expend public funds for the construction of a stadium.

Occasionally school districts and municipalities cooperate in financing the construction of auditoriums, gymnasiums, stadiums, and swimming pools. The courts have generally upheld such cooperative arrangements. Most courts, rendering decisions in agreement with the Arizona court, have upheld the authority of school districts to expend public funds for the construction and maintenance of auditoriums, gymnasiums, and stadiums. In a 1953 Kentucky case, however, the ruling was that money from a special school building fund could not be used for such expenditures, because, in the court's opinion, a stadium was not a school building.

The courts have ruled that a school district may rent its athletic facilities to private athletic groups so long as the contract can be fulfilled without interfering with school activities. Although some taxpayers have attempted to prohibit school districts from using their buildings for certain events, the courts have held that they cannot enjoin a school board from using its buildings for athletic contests, dances, and other social activities.

---

[7]*Ura Bernard Lemon et al.* v. *The Bossier Parish School Board, et al.* Civil Action No. 10687, U.S. District Court, Western District of Louisiana, March, 1967, p. 9.

In many instances, school boards furnish supplies to be used by students participating in student activities. Several courts have declared that such expenditures were legitimate and within the power of the school board to make. However, in two decisions rendered by the Supreme Judicial Court of Massachusetts, the authority of a school district to provide apparel for basketball and football teams was stricken down.

Financial Matters. Several courts have ruled that proceeds of student activities events are public funds and must be accounted for in the same manner as other school district funds. A Kentucky court recognized the authority of a board of education to control activity funds, yet regarded its duty to do so as quasi-private; this made the school district liable for debts incurred by those in charge of the activities fund. School districts sometimes encounter the problem of becoming involved in lawsuits as a result of profit-making ventures associated with student activities, although in most cases the courts decide in favor of the school districts. But one court ruled that unless all funds received from activities were used for educational purposes, the school district would be required to pay state sales tax on the money received.

Although the consensus is not unanimous, the majority of the courts have ruled that the board of education does not operate outside its governmental capacity by supporting enterprises which produce funds for the support of the student activities program. Nevertheless, the courts have not established any sound legal principles that can be applied universally to any situation involving the distinction between governmental and proprietary functions. Consequently, it is difficult to determine into which category a given student activity will be placed until after a court has ruled. A Pennsylvania court declared that an athletic contest for which admission was charged was a proprietary activity which was outside the authority of the school district to perform. The court, therefore, rendered a decision favorable to the plaintiff who was injured while attending a football game.

Not all courts have been willing to declare that a school district can be held liable for injuries resulting from negligent acts of its employees when such acts are associated with a student activity which might be classified as proprietary. The supreme courts of Minnesota and Montana upheld the doctrine of governmental immunity by ruling that charging admission did not change a school district's activity from a governmental to a proprietary classification.

The right of boards of education to charge a radio station fees for broadcasting football games has been upheld by the courts.

It is not uncommon for school districts to expend public funds to provide transportation for student activity groups, yet few cases pertaining to the subject have reached the appellate courts. Of the cases to come before the courts, the number is too few and the opinions too varied to arrive at a definite legal principle regarding this phase of the student activity program.[8]

Secret Societies. The courts in Washington, North Carolina, Texas, Arkansas, Kansas, and Ohio have upheld the right of school boards to restrict secret society members to classroom activities. The only court to render a decision adverse to the school board in the area of secret societies was the Missouri Supreme Court prior to enactment of the state law previously quoted.

Married Students. Exclusion from some or all school student activities is the most popular restriction on married students. Three courts in Texas, Ohio, and Utah have upheld the board of education's regulations established against the participation of married students in student activities and a fourth, in Michigan, deadlocked on the issue. In each case the married students urged the Fourteenth Amendment, arguing that the exclusionary rules were arbitrary and unreasonable. The plaintiffs, in all four cases, were star athletes whose chances for college scholarships would be seriously jeopardized if they were excluded from competitive sports. As is indicated in the following quotation, one line of thinking may bring about, in some future case, a reversal of some of the courts' earlier opinions:

> In the words of a Yakima, Wash., school officer, "Married students may attend but since marriage is an adult family responsibility, participation in school activities is discouraged." In this district, activities are only discouraged. Many districts do not give the young adults the choice. The courts have given scant

___

[8]A United States district court upheld an Oklahoma school district's claim that it was not liable for injuries sustained by persons who were involved in an accident with a school bus which the board of education had provided to transport students on a senior class trip. Teachers might, however, be held personally liable for injuries to students resulting from transportation accidents if arrangements for such transportation are made without the official approval of the board of education.

consideration to this ground for exclusion. Perhaps the judges see some inconsistency between a school system calling the young marrieds "adults" and then assuming an *in loco parentis* role by telling them what is best for their marriage.

Over all, the exclusion of married students from school activities may withstand constitutional attack in the future as it has in the past. But the reason rests on the nature of the exclusions and not on whether or not they are arbitrary. More specifically, for the average married student, exclusion from gym or sports or glee club is not a great deprivation. Consequently the harm in these cases is so trivial as to render the deprivations *de minimis,* or at least, not of constitutional dimensions. For example, a school system which excludes married students from commencement exercises cannot justify the regulation on reasons of school morale, or discouragement of dropouts, because commencement terminates the school career of the single classmates of the married couple. Nevertheless, the regulation, which is pure punishment, may be constitutionally unassailable because it is such a small loss to the students.

On the other hand, a student may be able to prove severe losses if he is denied the right to compete in certain activities. Scholarships based on sports or musical ability certainly are jeopardized, if not lost, when a talented student is excluded from participation. Indeed, few other pre-college forums are available to display scholarship talents. Excluding *talented* married students from functions which may be a road to college education would appear to be unconstitutional — although the state cases which have considered this point have upheld the school authorities.[9]

Activities Association. Many states now have a state activities association, although in every state and in the District of Columbia there exists a voluntary high school association which supervises and controls interscholastic athletics. All of these state associations except that of Texas are members of the National Federation of State High School Athletic Associations (NFSHSAA). The purpose of this national organization is to promote teamwork among the state organizations to further the cause of wholesome interscholastic athletics among the secondary schools of the nation. The NFSHSAA has also devised a type of legal insurance under which all state associations support a member in a lawsuit which reaches the state

[9]Laurence W. Knowles, "What Schools Do About Student Marriages," *Nation's Schools,* 77:76, April, 1966.

supreme court. All state associations have a direct interest in lawsuits of this nature because of the persuasive influence the decision might have in future cases in which the same or similar questions might be dealt with by the courts of other states.

Voluntary associations have no legal entity apart from their members, and they must, in the absence of statutory provisions, sue and be sued in the names of their members. Before a school sues the association of which it is a member, all remedies of appeal within the association must be exhausted. Even then, the courts will not interfere in the internal affairs of a voluntary association unless law and justice so require, as in a case where property rights are violated. There are no significant cases in which a high school athletic association has received an adverse decision in the courts of record when the authority of the association to control public school student activities was challenged.

Courts in Colorado and Ohio have ruled that school boards have the authority to permit schools under their direction to join high school athletic associations. Oklahoma and Florida courts have held that, by becoming a member of a high school athletic association, a school assents to abide by the constitution and rules and regulations of the association. Athletic associations have been upheld by the courts in their regulation of contracts made by member schools, so long as provisions for such regulations were present in the constitution or bylaws of the organization.

In the absence of mistake, fraud, collusion, or arbitrariness, the courts have upheld athletic associations that awarded harsh penalties for the violation of rules and regulations, so long as these penalties were provided for in the constitution or bylaws of the association. Any violation of the constitution or rules and regulations of a high school athletic association may result in the member's suspension or expulsion from the association. The courts have not interfered with the operations of high school athletic associations so long as all internal activities are conducted according to the constitution and rules and regulations of the association, and no property rights are violated.

Sponsors. The Pennsylvania Supreme Court ruled that a board of education had the authority to assign teachers duties for which they were properly qualified and certified and that their failure to perform such duties would make them guilty of willful and persistent negligence, for which they could be dismissed. The Supreme Court of Rhode Island declared that a school committee had the authority to assign student activity duties to its teachers, so long as the rules and regulations did not violate the general statutes and teacher tenure law or were not in excess of the school committee's proper power. In a New York case the court said that a board of education could fix the hours of a teacher, even to the extent of evening hours, if the student activity assigned was related to the teacher's field of certification.

A court of common pleas in Pennsylvania declared that the assignment of a teacher to collect tickets at an athletic event was an improper assignment for a professional employee. Had this teacher been assigned to supervise pupils in the cheerleading section the court would have regarded the duty as one of educational significance within the jurisdiction of the board of education. In a more recent case the Supreme Court of Pennsylvania ruled that a teacher may be assigned extra duties only if the student activity to which he is assigned is related to the school program.

A teacher in California brought suit against the board of education for assigning him supervisory duties at athletic games for which he received no extra compensation. The court ruled in favor of the school board by stating that a teacher's duties extend beyond the classroom and that such assignments, when reasonable and distributed impartially, could be assigned by the board of education.

Boards of education have the authority, according to a Massachusetts ruling, to hire athletic coaches to conduct the athletics program. Although athletic coaches are subject to the same rules and regulations under their contracts as are other teachers, their athletic duties are not always included under the teacher tenure laws. The Illinois Supreme Court ruled that contractual continued service did not attach to "extracurricular" coaching duties when they were contracted for separately. The District Court of Appeals of Florida came to a similar conclusion by declaring that the rights of tenure applied only to the subject area in which a teacher was certified by the state.

The need for a teacher to be a reasonably careful and prudent person is illustrated by an incident in which a high school student was accidentally electrocuted at the hands of fellow students during an athletic club initiation. Although the athletic coach contended that he had no official jurisdiction or supervision over the club members during the initiation, he was held liable for the accident because he gave the students permission to use an electrical shocking appliance, tested its wires, and was in full charge of the club at the time of the accident. In a similar case in which a school district was allegedly negligent for not providing supervision of a club initiation ceremony, the court ruled in favor of the defendant board of education. The court held that there was no cause for action against the board of education for injuries suffered by a student in an automobile accident which occurred after a club initiation ceremony at 2:00 A.M. on a Sunday morning, for the events which resulted in the injuries to the plaintiff could not have been anticipated and did not arise from a breach of duty.

Liability. Although the courts of some states, including Illinois, Michigan, Wisconsin, and Minnesota, have abrogated the doctrine of governmental immunity, the majority of the school districts in the United States are immune from liability. In states where governmental immunity prevails, the courts have permitted recovery in some cases if the injuries were sustained while the school district was performing proprietary functions. Numerous plaintiffs have brought suit on the grounds that the board of education was engaged in a private or proprietary activity for which it could not claim immunity from tort liability. This legal approach is particularly common in actions to recover damages for injuries sustained in connection with "extracurricular" events, namely interscholastic athletic contests for which admission was charged.

The courts have ruled that a board of education can be held liable for negligence in relation to ministerial acts performed by the board of education or any of its agents, but that it cannot be held liable for injuries inflicted by the unlawful or willful misconduct of its students in the absence of guilt for some act of commission or omission amounting to negligence. Because of the relationship that teachers have with their students, they are under the legal duty to exercise prudent or reasonable care not to injure them, and to prevent injuries to them. The degree of care that is expected of a teacher is not only a function of the age and maturity of the student, but of the hazardousness of the conditions.

Since the rule of *respondeat superior* (the responsibility of a master for the acts of his servants) does not apply in most school tort cases, teachers can be held personally liable for their negligent acts.

In the area of student activities, the athletic coach is most vulnerable as a result of governmental immunity. Accidents occur most frequently in interscholastic athletics, and a coach who is found negligent for the injury of an athlete can be compelled to pay damages to the student. A teacher, who is a governmental employee, is not immune from personal liability for acts of negligence while performing his duties, and his failure to supervise students adequately might constitute negligence on the part of the school district. Athletic coaches have been held liable for injuries that resulted from coercing students to participate in athletic contests and not exercising reasonable care when moving an injured athlete. However, in other jurisdictions the courts have held that a coach was not negligent for permitting an allegedly "inexperienced football player" to participate in an interscholastic event, or for failing to obtain immediate medical attention for a student who was not seriously injured.

The Supreme Court of New York found two teachers, charged with the responsibility of conducting a softball game, negligent for failing to provide adequate supervision of spectators whose close proximity to the baseball diamond was responsible for an injury to a player.

Religious Exercises. Some of the recent court rulings on the exercise of religion, expecially those of the United States Supreme Court, may have some effect on various aspects of the student activities program, such as opening exercises and the assembly, and should be noted here.

> The practices of selecting and reading verses of the Bible and recitation of The Lord's Prayer by students in unison, at the opening of the day in public schools are religious in character, and the laws that required such exercises are unconstitutional under the First Amendment of the Federal Constitution as applied to the states by the Fourteenth Amendment. On the other hand, study of the Bible for its literary and historic qualities and study of religion, when presented objectively as a part of the secular program of education, are not legally improper.[10]

[10]Robert L. Drury and Kenneth D. Ray, *Principles of School Law* (New York: Appleton-Century-Crofts, 1965), p. 37.

SUMMARY

Only a small amount of legislation exists on either the state or national level directly pertaining to student activities. Twenty-seven states have statutes restricting or prohibiting fraternities and sororities. School board regulations have the force of law if they are not in conflict with some other legal provisions. Attorney-general rulings and state department of education regulations affect student activities in some states.

Courts have prohibited racial discrimination in student activities and have held that facilities and equipment for student activities are a legitimate part of the school operation. Proceeds from student activities are public funds and must be accounted for as such. Secret societies may be restricted or prohibited by school boards. Married students may be prohibited from participating in student activities. Courts seldom interfere with voluntary activities associations. Teachers may be assigned as sponsors to student activities for which they are qualified. Teachers may be personally liable for negligent acts in connection with the student activities program.

REFERENCES

Bolmeier, E. C. "Legal Aspects of the Curriculum and the Extra-curriculum," *NASSP Bulletin,* 49:128-142, March, 1965.

Davis, Lester D., and Lofton, Ray J. "Married High School Students Should Not Participate in School Activities; Debate," *School Activities,* 36:3-6, 26, October, 1964.

Drury, Robert L., and Ray, Kenneth D. *Principles of School Law.* New York: Appleton-Century-Crofts, 1965.

Knowles, Laurence W. "What Schools Do About Student Marriages," *Nation's Schools,* 77:76, April, 1966.

McKown, Harry C. *Extra-Curricular Activities.* Rev. ed. New York: Macmillan Co., 1949, pp. 250-264.

Miller, Franklin A., *et al. Planning Student Activities.* Englewood Cliffs, N.J.: Prentice-Hall, Inc., 1956, pp. 553-591.

Part V
A LOOK AHEAD

The changes in student activities in the past few decades have been dramatic; it is likely that the changes in student activities in the next few decades will be even more dramatic. While no one can say with certainty what these changes will be, or the extent of influence that the changes will have on the broader aspects of American education, there are some ways that predictions can be made.

From a study of previous changes and patterns of change; from a study of the general curriculum trends now appearing in the literature and in the papers presented at professional meetings; from the practices of forward-thinking school personnel; and, above all, from the goals and directions of American education, some indication of the type of student activities program that will be found in American schools during the last third of the century may be found.

Chapter 18 is devoted to our prediction of the future student activities program.

Chapter 18

FORECAST

Authors of many textbooks on student activities — or extra-curricular activities as they once were commonly known — written during the 1920's and 1930's often predicted the directions which they felt student activities would take in American public education in the future. From the vantage point of thirty to forty years later, it is interesting, and sometimes amusing, to see what has happened in the areas in which predictions were made.

As might be expected, many of the predictions completely missed. For instance, it is a rare school in which the activity program is as much an outgrowth of the "curriculum" as was suggested it might get to be. Other predictions of several decades have been proven correct. The diversity of student activities now available in secondary schools, the assimilation of student activities into the total school program, and a few other areas were reasonably well pre-dicted.

Prediction was an easier job in past days when education and society did not change either fast or dramatically. As education in particular and society in general change at an accelerating rate, prediction of trends over a period of years will become more and more difficult, unless new planning and management tools such as PERT, CPM, and systems analysis become generally accepted and refined. It has been said that we are now at the point of educating people in what nobody knew yesterday, and preparing in our schools for what no one knows yet, but what some people must know tomorrow.

These difficulties notwithstanding, it seems fitting for us — after a great deal of reading about student activities, visiting in schools, working with students and sponsors from over much of the country, and meditation on the matter — to comment on some directions in which we expect student activities to move. It would not, of course, be reasonable to affix dates or other specifics to these ideas; for the sections of the country move at different rates and, to a certain extent, toward different goals. Neither is it possible to separate general curriculum trends from those trends that will affect only the student activities program, for the lines dividing the various parts of the curriculum of the school will continue to fall.

The American Association of School Administrators, in a 1966 publication, identified nine imperatives in American education. These are:

1. To make urban life rewarding and satisfying.
2. To prepare people for the world of work.
3. To discover and nurture creative talent.
4. To strengthen the moral fabric of society.
5. To deal constructively with psychological tensions.
6. To keep democracy working.
7. To make intelligent use of natural resources.
8. To make the best use of leisure time.
9. To work with other peoples of the world for human betterment.[1]

While the AASA carefully states that the imperatives mentioned above are not intended to be educational goals, they cannot help but influence crucial educational problems that will arise in coming years. Let us take the AASA imperatives as our guideposts. What implications do these have for student activities and how may we expect the student activities programs of the American system of public education to change?

To Make Urban Life Rewarding and Satisfying

Life in an urban area involves a great many physical and psychological tensions. In addition to problems of smog, garbage, noise, etc., there are fewer opportunities to commune with Nature, to enjoy a moment of solitude and quiet, and "to get away from it all" than there are in a small town or rural area. Some social psychologists feel that tensions are closely related to population density in ones "life space." While it is quite possible to be lonely in a crowd, to be lonely in a city of millions, in an urban area people rarely work or play alone.

---

[1]American Association of School Administrators, *Imperatives in Education* (Washington, D.C: The Association, 1966).

More and more, people will be in groups of some sort, rather than alone. Student activities that teach people how to work together in groups, how to respect the rights of others, and how to release the power of groups of people working toward common goals will assume increasing prominence.

Many schools are now providing leadership training for student council members, club officers, and other leaders that is essentially elementary social psychology. In our opinion, such study is very likely to expand to include more students and to go into greater depth with problems of interpersonal and intrapersonal relationships. Only with such training, whether provided through leadership courses or workshops, through social studies clubs and organizations which have such goals as a purpose, or through some other arrangement not yet in general use, can tomorrow's adult be prepared to cope with the problems of group life and urban life. The problem is, however, much more than one of learning to cope with or to adjust to the difficulties of the bustle of the city; the problem is to learn how to rise above such levels and make urban life rewarding and satisfying.

Urban areas typically contain many opportunities not available in more sparsely settled parts of the country, such as museums, galleries, theaters, concerts, commercial amusement facilities, and frequent opportunities for contact with persons of widely divergent backgrounds and interests. It would seem quite likely that special interest groups of various sorts that are interested in the opportunities unique to the city would continue to expand in the schools. Art clubs, music clubs, theater groups, and the like will probably continue to expand, not only in the urban areas but in the more rural areas as well. Just as many youths of the city would not be interested in many of the meaningful projects of the FFA chapter in a small, rural school, it is likely that the city youth might be far more interested in the problems of municipal government than his country cousin. Propinquity breeds interest, and the urban school that does not take advantage of the fruits of the culture that are available in any large area is missing golden opportunities. The urban schools, despite their many problems, will rise to the challenge of making urban life rich and rewarding in a great variety of ways involving all areas of the curriculum.

To Prepare People for the World of Work

"Vocational" courses and student activities are something of a misnomer: many people who take a course in typing or who study shorthand in a special interest group never intend to work as a secretary; yet, a student activity as band might be a vocational oriented activity for the boy who is interested in becoming a band director, or the Biology Club might be a valuable prevocational experience for the prospective physician. Never has general education had the importance in preparation for the world of work as it has today. There is every likelihood that general education will continue to increase in importance.

We are faced with the paradox of unemployment on the one hand and great shortages in some occupations, especially the professions, on the other hand. Obviously all social institutions, especially the school, bear responsibility for matching men and jobs. Prevocational special interest groups, such as the Future Teachers of America, future scientists, and future nurses, may continue to grow to give students an opportunity to explore interests before becoming too involved in the preparation for some specific profession. The function of many of these groups must be changed drastically to include opportunities and projects with substance — opportunities to work with, to observe, and to do the same sorts of things that the professional does — or else prevocational special interest groups will die a natural death as students look elsewhere for the information and experience they crave.

All student activities which in any way contribute to the guidance function of the school will assume increasing importance as the options available to students increase. Guidance-oriented homerooms; work experience programs; career days; the rather routine aspects of school that teach a person dependability, accuracy, good social behavior, and good work habits; and those students activities that increase judgment will all contribute to the preparation of people for the world of work. Development of these traits is a legitimate objective of the academic part of school experience, but development of these traits has been among the traditional objectives of the student activities program as well, and much of the present student activities program is well-suited to assume such a role.

Curriculum revision, especially with respect to vocational development, will take its toll of student activities. The AASA authors recalled that W. W. Charters, a man long interested in student activities, held the following view.

> When asked for. . .clarification of [the] basic curricular offerings of the future, he [Dr. Charters] included the study of man, his personality and development; the study of society and group living; and the study of occupations and how to live a rich and satisfying life. He suggested postponement of much subject matter until a student could see purpose in his life and the direction his talents and interests would take as a result of studying himself in relationship to available opportunity.[2]

Perhaps the meaning of this statement is that part of what we now consider as student activities, on the fringe of academic respectability, may become the central focus of the school, and vice versa. We have seen something of a movement in this direction in the humanities in the past few decades. Music, for example, has moved far from the town bands, glee clubs, and Sunday School orchestras of a few decades ago into academic acceptability in most schools. Some schools are even moving in the direction of offering opportunities for composition and advanced work in music theory in the high schools, as well as extensive coordination of music with the other fine arts. Music, art, drama, and other forms of the humanities have rapidly moved into the heart of the curriculum from their former status as student activities. On the other hand, copying of drawings, study of "Old Masters," and calligraphy have moved from a central place in the art curriculum to a much more minor role.

It is likely that such trends will continue and that similar trends will develop in other areas of the curriculum as well.

To Discover and Nurture Creative Talent

Talent comes in many forms, and one of the major contributions of the student activity movement in American education lies in the fact that student activities have permitted the school to expand the areas that students may explore. This is particularly true at the junior high school level. Special interest clubs in science, for example, permit a student to explore certain aspects of science to see

[2]*Ibid.*, p. 34.

if his interest is merely a passing fancy or something deeper. If he finds that he is not interested in science, it is (or should be) a much simpler matter to drop out of the science club and pick up some other area of interest than it is to drop a science course.

Fortunately, the scope of student activities has expanded in rough proportion to the expansion of the academic portion of the curriculum, and opportunities for the development of talent are now available in such widely diverse fields as computer science, television, the laboratory sciences, shop, the theater, choreography, and creative writing.

For decades men in education have stressed the importance of individualizing instruction; yet relatively little has been done in this direction. In recent years, with the advent of flexible scheduling, team teaching, and other organizational innovations which have provided for and encourated individualized instruction, opportunities for self-expression, originality, and self-direction have become much more common.

Individualization of instruction will undoubtedly leave a strong mark on the student activities program. Since several of the traditional objectives of the student activity program are now being incorporated into the academic program of the school through more individualized instruction, the role of the student activities program has been usurped in this respect. Educators will probably see the disappearance of what is now, at best, a fine line of demarcation between student activities and the remainder of the school program. In some instances, educators will simply see certain student activities or certain types of student activities disappear as their functions are incorporated into the mainstream of the instructional program; in other instances, educators will probably see student activities become more specialized to accomodate special interests within special interests.

For example, the next few years may bring the demise of science fairs in the secondary schools, as an increasing number of secondary schools modify science programs to include field experiences and more unstructured or semistructured laboratory work.

On the other hand, it would not be at all surprising to find students who were interested in or doing research in marine biology, sailing, and hydrology organizing an Oceanography Club. It is likely that such an association would be of an impermanent, informal nature rather than the more typically formal type of school club.

Such groups of talented, creative students with overlapping or similar interests can, because of pooled abilities, perform outstanding feats of creativity and ingenuity. It is not uncommon to read of the success of high school students in developing atomic devices, space tracking stations, rockets, and sophisticated electronic equipment, often out of scraps and improvised materials. In the future, it would appear that informal special interest groups will be one of the major ways of discovering and nurturing creative talent.

To Strengthen the Moral Fabric of Society

In an age of constantly increasing facility in communication and transportation, citizens will have to learn to live with a constantly changing culture. Thus, values will continue to change, prejudices will be rearranged, and human behavior will be unlike it has ever been before.

Nevertheless, most people believe that there is a right and a wrong; that there are certain abiding truths, even if all do not agree as to what these truths are. Many people feel that a major responsibility of the schools in our society is to perpetuate those things of lasting importance, whether they be values, facts, skills, or whatever.

Certainly the school, as an agency of society, has an obligation to assist society. Lessons from history vividly point out the relationship between dying civilizations and decay of the moral fabric of these civilizations. Therefore, every aspect of the school, including student activities, has an obligation to strengthen the moral fabric of society.

Society can be strengthened in a great variety of small, subtle ways. Shallow acts of flag-waving, the recitation of prepared prayers, or the mumbling of inconsequential passages of Scripture probably do less to strengthen society than the inculcation in students of self-discipline, a sense of fair play, a recognition of the worth of *each* individual, an improved environment, or the opportunity to develop in ones best way.

Much of this personal development, whether done in the classroom or elsewhere, is *caught* rather than *taught*. However, student activities provide excellent opportunities for the development of these attitudes. Racial desegregation, for example, first gained acceptance in this country in the sports and entertainment fields, both of which are closely related to many of our prominent student activities.

Certainly the schools have no more important task than the teaching of how to get along with ones fellow man. Fortunately, the schools are assuming greater and greater responsibilities in this area. While some of the actions of the school, such as racial desegregation, have come about only under pressure, others, such as courses or student activities related to sociology, anthropology, psychology, interracial or intercultural study, and international relations have been developed by students and teachers at the local level of their own volition.

The study of the inter- and intrapersonal relationships of man will continually increase in importance in the schools and will influence both academics and student activities. More and more groups of students will have learning experiences that involve international relations, exchange students, recent history, poverty, juvenile delinquency, criminology, law enforcement, educational travel (within and without the country), pen pals, non-Romance languages and cultures, political science, leadership, human relations, group dynamics, theory of organizations, and social class structure.

As schools redirect their offerings in the social studies away from almost exclusive attention to history, civics, and political geography toward a study of all social relationships, and as student activities in the social studies expand from a History Club and an occasional exchange student to a provision of opportunities for a much broader study of man's relationship to man, dramatic progress will be made in strengthening the moral fabric of society. Without question, the schools have great responsibility for teaching the understanding of man in his social role in all phases of the school program.

To Deal Constructively with Psychological Tensions

Man has always lived with tensions, from worrying about the sabre-toothed tiger lurking outside his cave to the plethora of more sophisticated worries of the contemporary world. Nevertheless, a strong argument can be made that society has changed more rapidly in recent years than many people have been able to successfully adapt to or comprehend. Ample statistics, reflecting sharp increases in mental health problems, an increased suicide rate, and the like, indicate that this is, indeed, an age of anxiety. However, it would also appear that "the good old days" — the memory of which is characterized more by nostalgia than by accuracy — are no more, and that society (and schools) will continue to change at an increasing, rather than a decreasing, rate.

This gap — between the known and the unknown, between the familiar and the unfamiliar, between the old and the new, between the tried and the untested — causes psychological tension. Members of contemporary society must learn to live with psychological tension: indeed, we must learn to capitalize on it. Dr. Viktor Frankl, the noted psychiatrist, is a leader in a school of thought that holds that only as man copes with adversity does he (or can he) become more human, more able to handle the problems of the world.[3]

One would expect the school, of all places, to be a haven of psychological security. After all, the school includes in its objectives the maximum development of all children; and it is staffed with professional people who have carefully studied the behavioral sciences in order to set up "meaningful learning experiences." Alas, it is not always this way! Some schools are not warm and friendly to all youth: they repel those who need the school most. Some schools provide few or no problem-solving situations for youth; rather, they encourage conformity rather than creativity. Such schools teach only the noncontroversial; for they are in the grip of the past, while youth looks ahead to decades in the future. In short, some schools not only fail to solve the problem of psychological tensions, but contribute to it.

All this is a familiar indictment. Fortunately, not only theorists but those actually in a position to make changes in school programs are coming to realize the problem and to take steps to solve it. Again, the traditional objectives of the student activity program lend themselves to solutions of this problem. Student activities involving action, such as sports and social events, are useful in this respect and will undoubtedly continue in some form. Rarely in student activities is a student required to do something beyond his abilities, as is sometimes the case in academic work. Even if he should be pushed beyond his limit, he can usually back out without losing face, an accomplishment seldom possible in academic work. Since

[3]See Viktor Frankl, *Man's Search for Meaning* (New York: Washington Square Press, Inc., 1959).

participation in student activities is, by the definition used in this book, voluntary, the student only participates in that which pleases him or satisfies him. This has the effect of at least offsetting some of the tensions that may develop elsewhere in the school program. Thus, it is likely that school programs of the future will provide opportunities for optional programs of recreation and special interests to reduce psychological tensions. The student activity program will probably be the vehicle for many of these endeavors.

To a very large degree, student activities will follow a law of the survival of the fittest. Those student activities that are most rewarding to the students, that are least tension-producing, and that are most psychologically satisfying will survive; the others will wither. Literary societies expired as a student activity, because they ceased to be satisfying to very many students. High school fraternities and sororities have, to a large extent, died, because administrators substituted at least equally satisfying and more socially acceptable student activities. Many present high school clubs will and should fall by the wayside in the next few decades, because they will cease to have relevance to the students. Hopefully, new ones will emerge that will have relevance to the psychological needs of a particular time and place.

To Keep Democracy Working

History has no lessons for our country in how to make democracy work with a population the size of our nation. Our society must improvise as it goes. Obviously, not all persons will be satisfied with any given development that materializes. On any issue there is a lineup of a majority (or at least a plurality) and minorities. This interplay among majorities and minorities, this reshuffling and realigning according to the issue, is what democracy is all about. Schools have a major responsibility to teach, not only about the will of majorities, but about the protection of the minorities, the checks and the balances, and the avenues of social change and social resistance to change.

It is imperative that the schools provide opportunities for the practice of democracy. This is not to say that we let the students "run the schools" or that teachers must abdicate any of their responsibilities. Neither is it to say that all issues must be resolved by voting. (After all, especially in small groups, voting only becomes necessary when concensus is difficult to reach.)

As the AASA has said so well,

> Democracy becomes reality to students when they recognize the rights of others in daily classroom work and in the school yard; work together on classroom projects; play together in games or on teams; sing or play together in orchestras, bands, or choruses; serve on student councils and safety patrol; join with others in drawing up and complying with school regulations and codes of dress and good grooming; engage in "clean-up, fix-up, paint-up campaigns;" contribute to the March of Dimes, United Fund, UNICEF, Junior Red Cross, public school health funds, and Goodwill Industries clothing collections; participate in neighborhood improvement projects or Civil Defense; and donate their services to hospitals and welfare agencies.

> In both elementary and secondary grades children develop understanding of the meaning of democracy as they see, hear, and read about history in the making; debate, without rancor, controversial issues; and search for their roles in the world picture. Their studies are supplemented and enriched by visits to courts, municipal service agencies, centers of business and industry, museums, institutes, and exhibitions; by discussions and presentations of civic, governmental, professional, labor, business, and industrial leaders on classroom radio and television programs and in talks before classes and assemblies; by the study of election procedures and the experimental use of voting machines; and by attendance at forums and lectures.[4]

Recent years have seen great growth in citizenship opportunities among the student activities available in the secondary schools of this nation, including the student council, service organizations, the other clubs, and the teamwork of athletics. It appears likely that such opportunities to practice democracy in microcosm will continue to increase at a lively pace; indeed it is highly desirable that the school encourage the development of such opportunities. One rarely finds a former student council member or person who has had some out of the ordinary citizenship training experience among the juvenile delinquents, the beatniks, subversives, extremists (of either the left or the right), or others who have a detrimental influence on effective democracy.

[4]*Imperatives in Education,* pp. 104-105.

The student council will remain the preeminent student organization for years to come, although it is likely that the role and the composition of this organization will undergo some change. Students are maturing at earlier ages and can assume greater responsibilities than educators have been previously willing to grant them. The American adolescent of the latter part of the twentieth century should have as much responsibility for the conduct of the school and of his affairs as he is able to assume effectively — no more *and no less.*

To Make Intelligent Use of Natural Resources

"Conservation" has been a matter of concern to Americans through most of the twentieth century, but only in recent years has the magnitude of the problems of air and water pollution, erosion, the destruction of wildlife, litter and junk, shortages of water, shortages of fossil fuels, and the loss of other vital and valuable materials become evident to many Americans.

At the same time that more and more Americans have become aware of the problems associated with our natural resources, our schools have, in general, been doing less and less. Many states have legislation which requires the teaching of conservation in the schools, but such provisions are difficult to enforce; and many schools have considered their duty done by including a unit on conservation in a science course somewhere along the line. The AASA has said:

> Conservation is regarded by most people, even by many teachers, as an abstraction — as something that should be left to the government, to well intentioned people with missionary spirits, or to some mystical power that will ensure that each succeeding year will be better than the one before without any effort or concern on their part.[5]

The growing public concern for conservation will affect the schools sooner or later, but there is little way to predict just what programs will be set up by the schools to cope with the problem. The AASA has said:

> The imaginative and well-informed teacher will find a thousand ways to teach conservation. For example, in the study of a

[5]*Ibid.,* p. 112.

mineral he may help children learn its value, its use, its chemical properties, how it is mined, what substitutes can be used for it, how it was formed, how much exists, how the land is affected through the mining process, and ways to eliminate unnecessary waste.

Live, rich, and vital teaching and learning experiences are left by the wayside while children are pushed through vicarious experiences inside the classroom that many times have little or no relevance. . . .

Comprehension of the nature and amounts of commodities used by a great city may be developed by observing the flow of materials into and out of industrial plants, department stores, food stores, and fueling stations. The pupils in the large city school are in closer proximity to the causes for pollution of rivers and the atmosphere than their country cousins. With powers for observation sharpened, they can easily observe the pressures for living space; the causes for congestion; the sources of noise, dust, and smoke; and at the same time, properly guided, they can become sensitive to the measures gradually being instituted to meet and deal with these common problems of urbanization. . . .[6]

The great variety of approaches that can be taken to teach conservation makes the future effect on student activities unclear. Much of the problem associated with the conservation of natural resources involves development of proper attitudes. Since few existing student activities are set up with a primary objective of changing attitudes, it would appear that the conservation movement will have relatively little effect on the student activity program in the next few years. In the near future some effect will be felt by science clubs, organizations dealing with social problems, service groups, a few special-interest groups, the FFA, and the FHA. Perhaps student organizations more directly concerned with the development of positive attitudes will come into existence. Perhaps new student organizations related to conservation will emerge as the concern becomes greater or the problems become more severe.

To Make the Best Use of Leisure Time

Perhaps the segment of society with the least amount of leisure time these days is the students. Nevertheless, our society as a whole is blessed with more leisure time than has ever been known before.

[6]*Ibid.,* pp. 119-122.

Whether this time is wasted or used wisely depends to a large extent on what people are taught to do with their leisure time.

The worthy use of leisure time was identified as one of the objectives of education in the so-called Seven Cardinal Principles of Education formulated in the early part of this century. Schools do teach things appropriate for leisure time, although they are not always recognized as such. Reading, music, shop work, physical skills, games and sports, and art are just a few of the parts of the curriculum that have strong implications for leisure time. Yet there are so many things that schools do not teach. Many leisure hours are spent before the television set, yet few schools teach much about discriminating viewing. Many idle hours are spent in conversation, but the quality of what is said is often low. Many people who learned to play football, basketball, and the bass drum in school now wish they knew how to play tennis, golf, and the piano instead. Many people read for recreation, which is good. But far too much of this recreational reading is devoted to the pulp magazines, the tabloids, and books of questionable literary merit. Obviously public education has a long way to go to adequately cope with the problems of increased amounts of adult leisure time.

On the other hand, many of the student activities are strongly oriented to skills and attitudes necessary for meaningful adult leisure time activities. For example, all the sports and games associated with the school have carryover for adult recreation, either as a participant, or as an informed viewer. It is encouraging to see the number of schools that are offering or putting greater emphasis on gymnastics, bowling, swimming, tennis, golf, archery, camping, hiking, dancing, badminton, and other similar individual or low organized recreational opportunities. Every community has opportunities for the chorister or the competent pianist to perform in adult life, and opportunities for the wind or string instrumentalist are increasing. Those who enjoy writing have many more opportunities to publish, and those who enjoy the theater are seldom far from some community theater group that they can watch or in which they can participate. Adult life is full of service opportunities and social activities for those who have developed the necessary interest while in school.

Student activities which contribute closely to leisure time and recreational opportunities and skills will continue to thrive and grow. It is likely that greater emphasis will be put on individual sports and games in the future, just as it appears likely that greater emphasis will be put on opportunities for the individual to make something or to express himself in such areas as painting, sculpturing, woodworking, handicrafts, or even baking a cake. In the future, greater emphasis in music will be placed on duets, trios, quartets, and other small ensembles. Group activities will not be slighted, however, and there will be no decreased interest in bands, orchestras, ballet, and drama.

Community service groups will continue to have some sort of connection with secondary school activities, such as the Key Club-Kiwanis Club, and the Junior Red Cross-Red Cross. We expect to see shop work and homemaking groups modified but not diminished, with greater emphasis on handiwork.

In all likelihood, there will be more emphasis on communications as a recreation form; more discussion groups on great books or contemporary issues; and more special interest groups concerned with reading, movies, television, conversation, and listening.

Adult education, as a leisure time activity, will grow by leaps and bounds and cover every conceivable area of human interest from flower arranging to computer programming; from baking bread to reading Sanskrit; from typing to calculus. This interest will spill over into the secondary school, with the gradual provision for many small special interest groups, loosely organized, if at all.

To Work With Other Peoples of the World for Human Betterment

Isolationism is a lost cause. A person can move from any spot on this planet to any other in a matter of a few hours. Instantaneous communication is possible with most of the world, both by sound and by picture. An event of major significance, such as the assasination of a major civil rights leader, is known to most of the world's billions within minutes.

"A physical world neighborhood of men has been created, but a psychological neighborhood based on common moral principles and mutual confidence and respect is yet to be realized," says the American Association of School Administrators.[7]

The schools of this country have a major responsibility for the alleviation of this problem. There is much that can be taught, both

[7]*Ibid.*, p. 143.

through the academic program and the student activities program, to improve international understanding and to promote human betterment.

This is similar to Imperative No. 4, "To Strengthen the Moral Fabric of Society," discussed earlier in this chapter. The concern is with man's relationship to man, whether the individuals involved live on the same side of the ocean or not.

Recently a group of outstanding high school student leaders from over the country was presented with the question "What changes would you expect to find happening to student activities in general between now and the last part of this century when your children will be in high school?" Among the answers received were these: a lessened emphasis on most clubs as now organized; greater emphasis on electronics clubs, astronomy and space clubs, and astronautics clubs; use of closed circuit TV for regional and national meetings; more exchange students (perhaps even interplanetary!); a slightly lessened emphasis on team sports; greater emphasis on individual sports; more travel associated with student activities; greater emphasis on special interest groups; greater emphasis on science and technology organizations, especially oceanography; and a greater emphasis on student council and other aspects of student involvement in management of their own concerns. We certainly agree with most of these predictions.

During the 1940's and 1950's the late Paul Mort held it was not too difficult to predict what the typical school of the 1980's would be like, for many of the aspects of the school of 1980 were already in existence in leading schools of that time. Similarly, one can state that the practices of the typical school of the 1990's — including its student activities program — can be inferred from the student activities in the innovative high schools of the late 1960's.

The needs of the future are before us as goals — some have already been partially attained by some schools. New needs, new demands, presently unknown, will arise and create other imperatives for the next generation. The field of student activities, like the broader fields of curriculum and of education in general, is ever-changing. Our step as educators must be paced to meet this rapid movement and to provide satisfaction of the needs of society and of its members. To be content with the present is foolhardy. It is well to remember that the hand of the future is already shaping the needs of that time, and the achievements of today will be but history tomorrow.

REFERENCES

Braham, R. V., and Smith, C. E. "What Role for Student Activities in the New Emphasis on Quality in Secondary Education?" *NASSP Bulletin,* 44:110-113, April, 1960.

Campbell, Laurence R. "Co-Curricular Activities — Success or Failure?" *School Activities,* 33:115-118, December, 1961.

Campbell, Laurence R. "What's Wrong with Cocurricular Activities?" *School Activities,* 35:81-84, November, 1963.

Dallolio, Helen C. "Too Many Activities for Pupils," *Clearing House,* 33:152-153, November, 1958.

Eash, Maurice J. "The School Program: Nonclass Experience," *Review of Educational Research,* 30:57-66, February, 1960.

Gilchrist, Robert S., Dutton, Wilbur H., and Winkle, William L. "What Is the Role of Student Activities and Organizations in the School Program?" *Secondary Education for American Democracy.* Rev. ed. New York: Rinehart and Co., 1957.

Grinnell, John E. "Our Most Dangerous Neglect," *Phi Delta Kappan,* 41:213-216, February, 1960.

Hamilton, H. H. *The Educational Value of Pupil Activities.* Austin, Texas: Texas Study of Secondary Education, 1960.

Hare, Alexander P. "Evaluation of Extra-Curriculum Activities," *School Review,* 63:164-168, March, 1955.

Johnston, Edgar G., and Faunce, Roland C. *Student Activities in Secondary Schools.* New York: The Ronald Press Co., 1952, pp. 355-362.

Jones, Galen. *Extra-Curricular Activities in Relation to the Curriculum.* New York: Bureau of Publications, Teachers College, Columbia University, 1935, pp. 78-90.

Kaminsky, A. "Principles for a Successful Program of Student Activities," *Clearing House,* 36:41-42, September, 1961.

Karner, Erwin. "Check Points for Improving School Activity Programs," *School Activities,* 32:133-135, January, 1961.

Miller, Franklin A., *et al. Planning Student Activities.* Englewood Cliffs, N.J.: Prentice-Hall, Inc., 1956, pp. 623-632.

Robbins, Jerry H. "Trends in Student Activities," *Journal of Arkansas Education,* 38:22-23, December, 1965.

National Study of Secondary School Evaluation. "Student Activity Program." *Evaluative Criteria.* Washington, D.C.: N.S.S.S.E., 1960, pp. 241-256.

"Newspapers Grow in High Schools," *The Oxford* (Mississippi) *Eagle*, (January 5, 1967), p. 2.

Unruh, Adolph. "Improving Extra-class Activities," *School Activities,* 35:141-143, January, 1964.

Wood, D. I. "Student Activities: A Hope or a Delusion?" *NASSP Bulletin,* 46:201-205.

APPENDICES

Appendix A

INNOVATORS

The interests of the authors — no matter how great — and their professional experiences — no matter how long and/or diversified — are mere starting points for writing a textbook.

To help anyone interested in a particular field, a number of publications exist. In the field of student activities several textbooks (generally outdated) and numerous journal articles have been written. From these the best, newest, and most useful must be harvested and the rest discarded. In gathering material from publications, it is not always possible to include all material relating to the material discussed in each chapter. Information judged to be useful has been included in the reference section at the end of each chapter.

However, printed materials of this sort are available to any person interested in student activities who has the time, facilities, and patience to locate, read, and digest the journals. To make this text useful, we felt obligated to the readers to present information of an interesting or useful nature that had not yet appeared in print in the various journals of the profession.

In the summer of 1967 a request for information was sent to several hundred school administrators in the fifty states. Many of the specific examples used in this book are the results of the well-written, conscientiously undertaken replies received from very busy men during their "vacation" period.

The education profession may well be proud of people who take time from their other work to attempt to help fellow educators. We would like to thank the following school systems and the person mentioned for their valuable contributions to this work.

Abington Senior High School; Abington, Pennsylvania
Ascension Academy; 4401 West Braddock Road, Alexandria, Virginia 22304. Phillip J. Armstrong, Assistant Headmaster
Atlanta City Schools. Mr. Elton Powers, Director of Operation Upstream, 2930 Forrest Hills Drive, S.W., Atlanta, Georgia

Bloomington Junior High School; 510 East Washington Street, Bloomington, Illinois 61701. Robert N. Knight, Principal

Centennial High School; Pueblo, Colorado

Clark County School District; 2832 East Flamingo Road, Las Vegas, Nevada 89109. Willard J. Beitz, Principal

Columbus Senior High School; Columbus, Indiana. Mel Harrison, Assistant Principal

Como Park Junior High School; St. Paul, Minnesota 55117. R. O. Isacksen, Principal

Cuba Independent Schools (District 20, Sandoval County); Cuba, New Mexico 87013. Melvin Cordova, Principal

Cubberley High School; Palo Alto, California

Eastern Junior High School; Riverside, Connecticut. Donald A. Stokes, Assistant Principal

Fenger High School; 1120 South Wallace Street, Chicago, Illinois 60628. E. Robert Olson, Moderator of Student Council

Frank F. Garside Junior High School; Las Vegas, Nevada. J. Hal Fincher, Principal

Franklin High School; 31000 Joy Road, Livonia, Michigan 48150. J. Kenneth Bourgon, Director of Student Activities

General Brown High School; Brownville, New York. Dr. Merrill F. Hurd, Supervising Principal

Highland Park High School; Highland Park, New Jersey 08904. Dr. Melvin L. Michaels, Principal

Highland Park High School; 2424 California, Topeka, Kansas 66605. Erle W. Volkland, Principal

The Hill School; Pottstown, Pennsylvania 19464. Charles C. Watson, Director of Studies

John Marshall High School; 4225 Old Brook Road, Richmond, Virginia

McKinley High School; 1039 South King Street, Honolulu, Hawaii 96814

Mapleton High School; 601 East 64th Avenue, Denver, Colorado. Fred R. Petrillo, Student Council Adviser

Norwich Senior High School; Norwich, New York

Oak Park and River Forest High School; East Avenue at Ontario Street, Oak Park, Illinois 60302. Russell J. Fuog, Assistant Principal

South Side High School; 1880 Prospect Street, Memphis, Tennessee 38106. Bennett E. Hunter, III, Principal

Troy High School; 2200 East Dorothy Lane, Fullerton, California 92631. Richard Bartholome, Supervisor of Student Activities and Attendance

Tucson High School; 400 North Second Avenue, Tucson, Arizona 85705. John J. Mallamo, Assistant Principal for Student Activities

University Junior High School; Northern Illinois University, DeKalb, Illinois

Wellesley Junior High School; Wellesley, Massachusetts 02181. James M. Peebles, Principal

Wellesley Senior High School; 50 Rice Street, Wellesley Hills, Massachusetts 02181. Samuel M. Graves, Principal

William H. Hall High School; 50 South Main Street, West Hartford, Connecticut 06107. Robert E. Dunn, Principal

Yankton Senior High School; Yankton, South Dakota 57078. Gene B. Nelson, Assistant Principal

Yazoo City Municipal Separate School District; Yazoo City, Mississippi. Dr. J. Linfield Miller, Director of Curriculum

Appendix B

ADDRESSES OF NATIONAL LEVEL ACTIVITIES ORGANIZATIONS

The following names and addresses are furnished for use as potential sources of information for the local school about certain activities which have national level organizational structures.

American Industrial Arts Association, 1201 - 16th Street, N.W., Washington, D.C. 20036

Boys Nation, c/o The American Legion, Box 1055, Indianapolis, Indiana 46204

Distributive Education Clubs of America, Inc. (DECA), 1025 - 15th Street, N.W., Washington, D.C. 20005

Future Business Leaders of America (FBLA), 1201 - 16th Street, N.W., Washington, D.C. 20036

Future Farmers of America (FFA), U.S. Office of Education, Department of Health, Education, and Welfare, Washington, D.C. 20202

Future Homemakers of America (FHA), U.S. Office of Education, Department of Health, Education, and Welfare, Washington, D.C. 20202

Ford-Future Scientists of America, National Science Teachers Association, 1201 - 16th Street, Washington, D.C. 20036

Girls Nation, c/o American Legion Auxiliary, 777 North Meridian Street, Indianapolis, Indiana 46204

Junior Engineering and Technical Society (JETS), 345 East 47th Street, New York, New York 10017

Key Club International, 101 East Erie Street, Chicago, Illinois 60611

Mu Alpha Theta, Frank B. Allen, President, 567 Berkeley Avenue, Elmhurst, Illinois 60126

National Association of Student Councils, 1201 - 16th Street, N.W., Washington, D.C. 20036

National Cheerleaders Association, 6703 Winton Street, Dallas, Texas

National Forensic League, Ripon, Wisconsin 54971

National Honor Society-National Junior Honor Society, National Association of Secondary School Principals, 1201 - 16th Street, N.W., Washington, D.C. 20036

National Junior Classical League, 315 Wilson Street, Henderson, Texas 75652

National Junior Horticultural Association, Box 603, North Amherst, Massachusetts 01059

National Scholastic Press Association, 18 Journalism Building, University of Minnesota, Minneapolis, Minnesota 55455

National Student Traffic Safety Program, National Committee on Safety Education, 1201 - 16th Street, N.W., Washington, D.C. 20036

National Thespian Society, College Hill Station, Cincinnati, Ohio 45224

Quill and Scroll Society, University of Iowa, Iowa City, Iowa 52240

American National Red Cross, 17th at E. Street, N.W., Washington, D.C. 20006

Vocational Industrial Clubs of America (VICA), 1025 - 15th Street, N.W., Washington, D.C. 20005

Appendix C

NASSP APPROVED LIST OF NATIONAL CONTESTS AND ACTIVITIES 1967 - 1968[a]

Approved National Contests and Activities (Nonathletic) for 1967 - 1968

Sponsor	Title
American Association of Teachers of French, Wisconsin State University, River Falls, Wisconsin 54022	National French Contest
American Association of Teachers of German, St. Joseph's College, Philadelphia, Pennsylvania 19131	AATG German Contest
American Association of Teachers of Italian, University of California, Berkeley, California 94720	AATI Italian Examination
American Association of Teachers of Spanish and Portuguese, Wichita University, Wichita, Kansas	AATSP National Spanish Examination
American Automobile Association, 1712 G St., N.W., Washington, D.C. 20006	School Traffic Safety Poster Contest
American Legion, Box 1055, Indianapolis, Indiana 46206	Boys Nation
American Legion, Box 1055, Indianapolis, Indiana 46206	National High School Oratorical Contest
American Legion Auxiliary, 777 N. Meridian St., Indianapolis, Indiana 46204	Girls Nation
American Legion Auxiliary, 777 N. Meridian St., Indianapolis, Indiana 46204	Poppy Poster Contest
American Maritime Industry, AMMI, 11 Broadway, New York, New York 10004	Poster Contest
American National Red Cross, 17th & E Streets, N.W., Washington, D.C. 20006	National Convention
American Wool Council, 909 - 17th St., Denver, Colorado 80202	Make It Yourself with Wool

Sponsor	Title
American Veterans of World War II and Korea, 1710 Rhode Island Ave., N.W., Washington, D.C. 20036	AMVETS Memorial Scholarships
Association for Educational Data Systems, 1201 - 16th St., N.W., Washington, D.C. 20036	AEDS Computer Programming Contest
Association for Promotion of Study of Latin, Box 501, Elizabeth, New Jersey 07207	APSL Nationwide Latin Examination
Bausch & Lomb, Inc., 635 St. Paul St., Rochester, New York 14602	Honorary Science Award Program
Bausch & Lomb, Inc., 635 St. Paul St., Rochester, New York 14602	Science Scholarship Program
Chrysler Motors Corp., Chrysler-Plymouth Division, 12200 E. Jefferson Ave., Detroit, Michigan 48214	Plymouth Trouble Shooting Contest
Colonial Williamsburg, Williamsburg, Virginia 23185	Williamsburg Student Burgesses
Daughters of the American Revolution, 1776 D St., N.W., Washington, D.C. 20006	Good Citizens Award
Distributive Education Clubs of America, Inc., 1025 - 15th St., N.W., Washington, D.C. 20005	National Leadership Conference
Electric Companies Public Information Program, 230 Park Ave., New York, New York 10017	National Youth Conference on the Atom
BPO Elks, 2750 Lake View Ave., Chicago, Illinois 60614	Youth Leadership Contest
Elks National Foundation, 2750 Lake View Ave., Chicago, Illinois 60614	Most Valuable Student Awards
Employment of the Handicapped, President's Committee on, Washington, D.C. 20210	"Ability Counts" Contest
Fisher Body Division, General Motors Corp., Warren, Michigan	Craftsman's Guild Model Car Competition
Freedoms Foundation at Valley Forge, Valley Forge, Pennsylvania 19481	School Awards Program
Future Business Leaders of America, 1201 - 16th St., N.W., Washington, D.C. 20036	National Convention

Sponsor	Title
Future Farmers of America, U.S. Office of Education, Washington, D.C. 20202	National Convention; Judging Contests; Public Speaking Contests
Future Homemakers of America, U.S. Office of Education, Washington, D.C. 20202	National Meeting
General Federation of Women's Clubs, 1734 N St., N.W., Washington, D.C. 20036	Hallmark Art Talent Contest
General Mills, Inc., 9200 Wayzata Blvd., Minneapolis, Minnesota 55440	Betty Crocker Search Scholarship Award
W. R. Hearst Foundation, 1020 Hearst Building, San Francisco, California 93103	U.S. Senate Youth Program
Improved BPO Elks of the World, 526 Beale St., Memphis, Tennessee 38103	Elks Oratorical Contest
Institute of American Poultry Industries, 67 E. Madison, Chicago, Illinois 60603	Junior Fact Finding Contest
Junior Engineering Technical Society, 345 E. 47th St., New York, New York 10017	Engineering Exposition
Junior Engineering Technical Society, 345 E. 47th St., New York, New York 10017	Aptitude Search
Kemper Insurance, 4750 N. Sheridan Rd., Chicago, Illinois 60640	Traffic Safety Contest
Key Club International, 101 E. Erie St., Chicago, Illinois 60611	Key Club International Convention
Knights of Pythias, 1212 Dodds Ave., Chattanooga, Tennessee 37404	Public Speaking Contest
James F. Lincoln Arc Welding Foundation, 22801 St. Clair Ave., Cleveland, Ohio 44117	Arc Welding Award Program
Mathematical Association of America, Polytechnic Institute of Brooklyn, Brooklyn, New York 11201	High School Mathematics Examination
Music Educators National Conference, 1201 - 16th St., N.W., Washington, D.C. 20036	Division Meetings
National Association of Secondary School Principals, 1201 - 16th St., N.W., Washington, D.C. 20036	National Honor Society Scholarships

Sponsor	Title
National Association of Student Councils, 1201 - 16th St., N.W., Washington, D.C. 20036	National Conference
National Council of Teachers of English, 508 S. Sixth St., Champaign, Illinois 61820	NCTE Achievement Awards
National Forensic League, Ripon, Wisconsin 54971	National Speech Tournament and Student Congress
National Junior Classical League, 315 Wilson St., Henderson, Texas 75652	National Convention
National Junior Horticultural Association, Box 603, North Amherst, Massachusetts 01059	Projects and Convention
National Merit Scholarship Corp., 990 Grove St., Evanston, Illinois 60201	National Merit Scholarship Program
National Restaurant Association, 1530 Lake Shore Drive, Chicago, Illinois 60610	Heinz Scholarship Awards
National Scholastic Press Association, 18 Journalism Building, University of Minnesota, Minneapolis, Minnesota 55455	Conference
National Scholastic Press Association, 18 Journalism Building, University of Minnesota, Minneapolis, Minnesota 55455	Critical Services
National Science Teachers Association, 1201 - 16th St., N.W., Washington, D.C. 20036	NASA-NSTA Youth Science Congresses
National Science Teachers Association & Ford Motor Co., 1201 - 16th St., N.W., Washington, D.C. 20036	Ford-Future Scientists of America
National Thespian Society, College Hill Station, Cincinnati, Ohio 45224	National Dramatic Arts Conference
National Tuberculosis Association, 1790 Broadway, New York, New York 10019	School Press Project
NEA National Commission on Safety Education, 1201 - 16th St., N.W., Washington, D.C. 20036	National Student Traffic Safety Program
Odd Fellows and Rebekahs of America, 16 West Chase St., Baltimore, Maryland 21201	United Nations Pilgrimage for Youth

Sponsor	Title
Optimist International, 4494 Lindell Blvd., St. Louis, Missouri 63108	Boys' Oratorical Contest
Quill and Scroll Society, University of Iowa, Iowa City, Iowa 52240	Current Events Quiz
Scholastic Magazines, Inc., 50 W. 44th St., New York, New York 10036	Creative Writing, Art, and Photography Awards
Science Service — Service Clubs of America, 1719 N St., Washington, D.C. 20036 [*sic*]	International Science Fair
Science Service — Science Clubs of America, 1719 N St., Washington, D.C. 20036	Westinghouse Scholarships
Sons of the American Revolution, 2412 Massachusetts Ave., N.W., Washington, D.C. 20008	Douglass G. High Historical Oration Contest
Soroptimist Foundation, 1616 Walnut St., Philadelphia, Pennsylvania 19138	Citizenship Award
United Nations Association of the U.S.A., 345 E. 46th St., New York, New York 10017	H.S. Contest on the U.N.
Veterans of Foreign Wars of the United States, Broadway at 34th St., Kansas City, Missouri 64111	Voice of Democracy
Vocational Industrial Clubs of America, 1025 - 15th St., N.W., Washington, D.C. 20005	National VICA Leadership Conference

[a]Adapted from *Approved List of National Contests and Activities 1967-68,* Reprinted from *NASSP Bulletin,* September, 1967.

APPENDIX D

TABLE I[a]

MOTION PICTURES RELATED TO STUDENT ACTIVITIES

No.	Title	Producer	Year of Issue	Length (Minutes)	B&W or Color	Sale Price	Prime Source for:	
							Sales	Rental
1.	Citizenship in Action	U. of Indiana	1958	24	B&W	$100.00	U. of Indiana	U. of Indiana
2.	Majority Vote	NFB, Canada	1953	7	B&W	$ 50.00	McGraw-Hill	McGraw-Hill
3.	National Conference NASC	NASC	1959	20	Color (Silent)	unknown	NASC	NASC
4.	Parliamentary Procedure	NFB, Canada	1955	22	B&W	$ 90.00	NFB, Canada	Contemporary Films
5.	Parliamentary Procedure	Coronet	1952	11	B&W Color	$ 60.00 $110.00	Coronet	Film libraries
6.	Parliamentary Procedures in Action	Coronet	1941	13	B&W	$ 62.50	Coronet	Film libraries
7.	Mr. Chairman	EBF	1959	13	B&W Color	$ 75.00 $150.00	EBF	EBF
8.	Speech: Conducting a Meeting	Young America	1952	12	B&W	$ 60.00	McGraw-Hill	Film libraries
9.	Student Council 1960 Elections	Whitehall-Yearling	1960	13	B&W	unknown	Whitehall-Yearling	Whitehall-Yearling
10.	Student Government at Work	Coronet	1953	11	B&W Color	$ 60.00 $110.00	Coronet	Film libraries
11.	How to Conduct a Discussion	EBF	1952	25	B&W	$100.00	EBF	EBF
12.	Who's Running Things?	NFB, Canada	1956	6	B&W	$ 45.00	McGraw-Hill	Contemporary Films
13.	All I Need is a Conference	Henry Strauss & Co. for General Electric	1954	28	B&W	$165.00	Henry Strauss	purchase only

Table I (continued)

No.	Title	Producer	Year of Issue	Length (Minutes)	B&W or Color	Sale Price	Prime Source for:	
							Sales	Rental
14.	Are You a Good Citizen?	Coronet	1949	11	B&W Color	$ 60.00 $110.00	Coronet	Film libraries
15.	Build Your Vocabulary	Coronet	1949	10	B&W Color	$ 60.00 $110.00	Coronet	Film libraries
16.	Citizenship and You	Coronet	1959	13	B&W Color	$ 75.00 $137.50	Coronet	Film libraries
17.	Defining Democracy	EBF	1954	18	B&W	$ 90.00	EBF	EBF
18.	Developing Leadership	Coronet	1949	10	B&W Color	$ 60.00 $110.00	Coronet	Film libraries
19.	Freshman Orientation	Inglewood	1959	23	Color	unknown	unknown	Inglewood
20.	How We Elect Our Representatives	Coronet	1947	10	B&W Color	$ 60.00 $110.00	Coronet	Film libraries
21.	Make Way for Youth	Assn. Films for National Social Welfare Assembly	1947	20	B&W	$ 60.00	Assn. Films	Film libraries
22.	Make Your Own Decisions	Coronet	1951	11	B&W Color	$ 60.00 $110.00	Coronet	Film libraries
23.	Mike Makes his Mark	Agra Films, Inc. For N.E.A.	1955	30	B&W Color	$ 75.00 $170.00	N.E.A.	State education associations
24.	Our Basic Civil Rights	Coronet	1950	13	B&W Color	$ 75.00 $137.50	Coronet	Film libraries
25.	Our Constitution	Academic	1940	20	B&W	$ 90.00	Academic	Film libraries
26.	Our Living Constitution	Coronet	1949	11	B&W Color	$ 60.00 $110.00	Coronet	Film libraries
27.	Political Parties	EBF	1952	21	B&W	$ 85.00	EBF	EBF

Table I (continued)

No.	Title	Producer	Year of Issue	Length (Minutes)	B&W or Color	Sale Price	Prime Source for: Sales	Prime Source for: Rental
28.	Practicing Democracy in the Classroom	EBF	1953	22	B&W	$100.00	EBF	EBF
29.	Production 5118*	Wilding for Champion Paper Co.	1955	30	Color	Free Loan		Modern Talking
30.	Shy Guy	Coronet	1948	13	B&W Color	$ 62.50 $125.00	Coronet	Film libraries
31.	Speech: Group Discussion	Young America	1955	12	B&W	$ 60.00	McGraw-Hill	Film libraries
32.	Tuesday in November	United World	1945	22	B&W	$ 34.27	United World	Film libraries
33.	What About School Spirit	McGraw-Hill	1959	15	B&W	$ 80.00	McGraw-Hill	Film libraries

[a] Adapted from *Student Councils Investigation of Their Visual Aids and Utilization* (University, Mississippi: Department of Educational Film Production, [n.d.]), pp. 46-47.

TABLE II

FILMSTRIPS RELATED TO STUDENT ACTIVITIES[a]

No.	Title	Producer	Year of Issue	Price
1.	Parliamentary Procedure (for grades 4 to 7) Part I. The order of business Part II. Nominations, elections and committees	Educational Filmstrips	1957	$11.00 (color) sale 3.00 rental
2.	Parliamentary Procedure in Action (for junior and senior high schools) Part I. The order of business Part II. Motions, discussion, voting and reports Part III. Amendments and nominations	Educational Filmstrips	1958	$16.50 (color) sale 3.00 rental
3.	The Student Council in Action Part I. How to make the student council more effective Part II. How the student council solves a real problem Part III. Fifty prize winning ideas for the student council	Educational Filmstrips	1958	$16.50 (color) sale 3.00 rental
4.	The Club Officers in Action Part I. The President Part II. The Secretary Part III. The Treasurer Part IV. The Committee	Educational Filmstrips	1958	$16.50 (color) sale 3.00 rental
5.	Lincoln High School Organizes a Student Council	Denver Public Schools NASC	unknown	apply to NASC

[a] Adapted from *Student Councils Investigation of Their Visual Aids and Utilization* (University, Mississippi: Department of Educational Film Production, [n.d.]), p. 48.

INDEX